iRoBert1

Bringing Out
the Best
in People

Bringing Out the Best in People

How to Apply the Astonishing Power of Positive Reinforcement

New & Updated Edition

Aubrey C. Daniels

McGraw-Hill, Inc.

New York   San Francisco   Washington, D.C.   Auckland   Bogotá
Caracas   Lisbon   London   Madrid   Mexico City   Milan
Montreal   New Delhi   San Juan   Singapore
Sydney   Tokyo   Toronto

Library of Congress Cataloging-in-Publication Data

Daniels, Aubrey C.
   Bringing out the best in people : how to apply the astonishing power of positive
reinforcement / Aubrey C. Daniels.—New & updated ed.
       p.   cm.
   Includes bibliographical references and index.
   ISBN 0-07-135145-0 (alk. paper)
       1. Employee motivation.   2. Reinforcement (Psychology)   3. Affirmations.
   4. Performance.   I. Title.
   HF5549.5M63   D36   1999
   158.7—dc21
                                                                                99-054058

McGraw-Hill

A Division of The McGraw·Hill Companies

   3 4 5 6 7 8 9 0   AGM/AGM   0 9 8 7 6 5 4 3 2 1 0

ISBN 0-07-135145-0

*The sponsoring editor for this book was Betsy Brown, the editing supervisor
was Janice Race, and the production supervisor was Elizabeth J. Strange. It
was set in New Baskerville by North Market Street Graphics.*

Printed and bound by Quebecor/Martinsburg.

McGraw-Hill books are available at special quality discounts to use
as premiums and sales promotions, or for use in corporate training
programs. For more information, please write to the Director of
Special Sales, McGraw-Hill, Professional Publishing, Two Penn
Plaza, New York, NY 10121-2298. Or contact your local bookstore.

This publication is designed to provide accurate and authoritative information
in regard to the subject matter covered. It is sold with the understanding that
neither the author nor the publisher is engaged in rendering legal,
accounting, or other professional service. If legal advice or other expert
assistance is required, the services of a competent professional person should
be sought.
       *—From a Declaration of Principles jointly adopted by a Committee
       of the American Bar Association and a Committee of Publishers.*

This book is printed on recycled, acid-free paper containing a minimum of 50 percent recycled de-inked fiber.

*This book is dedicated to my mother,
Carrie Belle Daniels, who always
brings out the best in me.*

About the Author

Aubrey C. Daniels, Ph.D., is Chairman and CEO of Aubrey Daniels & Associates, Inc. His firm helps companies solve problems in cost, quality, productivity, education, and safety. One of the most sought after and effective speakers and writers in the business management arena, he has instituted his performance management, behavior-based safety and instructional design systems in hundreds of organizations in the United States, Canada, Great Britain, France, Italy, Brazil, and Mexico. He and his team of professional consultants have provided services to such organizations as BP Amoco, Goodyear, Westinghouse, Hewlett-Packard, CSX, Kroger, Dow Chemical, Allied Systems, and many others. Dr. Daniels in the founder and publisher of *Performance Management Magazine,* and is the author of the text, *Performance Management: Improving Quality Productivity Through Positive Reinforcement* and his latest book, *Other People's Habits.* The first edition of *Bringing Out the Best in People* is available in Hong Kong and Singapore in English, and has been translated into Japanese for circulation in Japan. Dr. Daniels is an associate professor and lecturer at the Kennedy School of Government of Harvard University and is a visiting Professor at Florida State University, North Texas University, and Western Michigan University. He was a founding board member of the Cambridge Center for Behavioral Studies and is active in the Association for Behavior Analysis. He currently sits on the advisory board of the Institute for Nuclear Power Organizations. He is also on the Alumni Board of Furman University, his alma mater.

Contents

Part 2. The Astonishing Power of Positive Reinforcement

Part 5. Revitalizing the Workplace

Preface to the Second Edition

I felt compelled to write a second edition of *Bringing Out the Best in People* because of the changes that I have seen since the first edition was released in 1994. These have not been changes to the science of behavior analysis, because science, unlike theory, is rooted in research and fact. Rather, this new edition is needed because of the expanded applications of behavior analysis that have taken place in business.

When we released the first edition of *Bringing Out the Best in People,* the term *behavior* was just finding its way back into the vocabulary of business. After many years of being ignored or avoided, behavior seemed to be on the verge of acceptability. At that time, I felt that this subject deserved increased visibility and a clear explanation. These objectives are well on the way to being accomplished. Not in my career have I seen so many references to behavior in business than in the past five years. Many major organizations have installed behavior-based management systems, behavior-based safety systems, and behavior-based organization change initiatives. Of course, with this increased notoriety come increased opportunities for misuse of the science and criticism from sources that had never even considered the phrase "behavior-based."

So it has become imperative that this second edition be released to accomplish two objectives different than the first edition. First, it is very important to deliver this message to the many who have come in contact with some form of behavior-based initiative delivered by those who are using the term but do not understand the science.

Second, it is important to recognize the recent research in the applications of behavior analysis that have been made to education, safety, changing worker profiles, and motivation. Because of the dual purpose of this edition, you will find many chapters virtually untouched. What was lawful in 1994 is lawful in 1999 and will continue to be lawful in the twenty-first century. However, you will also find new chapters that present new information concerning changes in the workforce, new approaches to education, and applications of behavior analysis for developing innovations in business and for expanding creativity in general.

All of us must stay in tune with behavior analysis as its applications change the world, and are, in turn, changed by the world. The use of behavior analysis must not be allowed to become a business fad, and as such, suffer the vagaries that have affected other worthy business initiatives that have come and gone. Behavior analysis is not a good idea to be tried for a while and then cast aside for some other good idea. It is a science that explains how people behave and the influences that affect that behavior. It cannot go away anymore than gravity can go away, and it cannot be ignored as long as people continue to be the most important element of every organization. In a changing world, the science of behavior must remain the bedrock, the starting place for every decision we make, every new technology we apply, and every initiative we employ in our efforts to bring out the best in people.

Aubrey C. Daniels
Aubrey Daniels & Associates, Inc.
3531 Habersham at Northlake
Tucker, Georgia 30084
(770) 493-5080
www.aubreydaniels.com

Preface to the First Edition

"... if then, the care as to the state of your inanimate machines can produce such beneficial results, what may not be expected if you devote equal attention to your employees (your living machines) which are far more wonderfully constructed? When you have a thorough understanding, you shall acquire a right knowledge of them ... you will become conscious of their real value, and you will readily be induced to turn your thoughts more frequently from your inanimate to your living machines."

These are the words of Robert Owen written in 1813. They were true in 1813 and they are true today.

The question remains, however, "Has business heeded these words?" I've heard hundreds of business leaders say things like, "Our people are our most important resource." In spite of that, reduction of the workforce—downsizing—is often the *first* recourse for controlling costs, not the last.

In addition, almost every management book written in the last 20 years has addressed the important role people have in organizational performance. Yet the advice given is usually stated in mentalistic concepts that require employees to motivate themselves. Management's role in the motivational process, according to the majority of these authors, seems to be to remind employees in a variety of ways that, "They can do it if they really want to."

If people are really the most important resource in business, why does the average executive spend more time learning to read a balance sheet than acquiring a "thorough understanding" of human behavior? And why do executives delegate the design and delivery of motivational programs to staff with little or no expertise in human behavior? There are at least three reasons.

First, psychologists—the people who supposedly know the most about people—are not usually seen as bottom-line-oriented. Their advice is often vague, and there may be as many different answers to the same question as there are psychologists. Ed Anderson, a member of the board of trustees of the Cambridge Center for Behavioral Studies, said in a speech recently, "Being a chemist by profession, I often wondered why there is only one chemistry, one biology, one physics, and there are 10,000 psychologies." He went on to say, "Of course there can be only *one* science of behavior." Business people often feel that they can't get a straight answer from psychology.

Since I was a clinical psychologist before working with business, I still had some "nondirective therapy" behaviors in my repertoire. When the first plant manager I worked with asked me what he should do about a certain problem, I responded, "Howard, what do *you* think you should do?" He replied, "Well, if I knew what to do, I wouldn't be talking to you!" With this kind of experience, it is no wonder that most managers think that their commonsense solutions are as good as any psychologist's.

A second reason is that even though practically all managers will tell you that "Correlation is not causation," their decision making belies that fact. If company X does something that was associated with improvement, that is all the data many executives need to try that same approach in their company. One of the biggest problems in industry today is "fad chasing." If company X solves a problem, and we have that same problem, then let's do what they did, with little critical analysis, especially in the realm of human behavior.

The third reason is that the subject of human performance has been trivialized by many books, the popular press, and management folklore. "Attaboys," "warm-fuzzies," and "one-minute managing" are not the kinds of concepts that would cause business leaders to take the subject seriously.

Human performance is a serious subject and one that can be explained scientifically, but the science underlying all behavior, and hence all organizational performance, is generally unknown to business. It developed from research and applications in nonbusiness settings and has been applied to business for only about 30 years.

This book is about this science of human behavior. Although the science has its roots in psychology, it is not psychology. It is *behavior analysis*. Behavior analysis is as scientific as biology, chemistry, and physics. It is my contention that only by using this systematic, data-focused approach to managing people at work will we be able to bring out the best in people and maximize the potential of the organization.

All managers will agree that the human factor is an important issue, but in most cases they feel it is only one of a number of equally important issues. They don't appreciate the degree to which human behavior affects everything that is done in an organization. Whether making a decision about a merger, increasing production on a new piece of equipment, or increasing discoveries in the laboratory, human behavior is the key to success.

The behavior of people in business is not another issue to be considered—it is at the center of every business decision.

This book is not written to be controversial and confrontational. It is an honest attempt to translate what is known about human behavior in a way that is readable and, at the same time, true to what the science has discovered about how we behave. However, I know that there will be those who will disagree and possibly be punished by what I have written. There will no doubt be statements in this book that fly in the face of common sense, your own personal experience, and your company policies and procedures.

Toward the end of the second day of one of my seminars, a man raised his hand and asked, "Are we doing anything right?" I replied that I had not said he was doing anything wrong. He responded, "Yes, but so far everything you have said to do, we're doing the opposite."

Whatever I say to do is valid only if it solves a problem permanently and solves similar problems consistently. In order to do this you must approach a problem with a precise definition of the measurable outcomes and the behaviors associated with them, a precise implementation plan, and a systematic evaluation. This needs to pervade *all* decision making in the organization.

When leaders initiate any change in the organization, they will do so in ways that will cause people to either increase or decrease their effort, their creativity, their cooperation, the quality of their work. This book will tell you precisely why and how that happens.

Aubrey C. Daniels

Acknowledgments to the Second Edition

I am deeply indebted to all those who contributed to the first edition of *Bringing Out the Best in People*—our staff and customers. They have encouraged me to share the success that they have experienced with the astonishing power of positive reinforcement in improving business results and, at the same time, the lives of people at work. Many thousands of copies later, there is a growing business community that is using the terminology often and implementing the methodology presented in the first edition in their organizations. I know many people who, after reading the book, have used the concepts to manage their business more effectively and to transform their personal lives. This has to be the ultimate positive reinforcer for a writer.

As with the first edition, John Domenick played a major role in making the second edition a reality. He has participated in every step on its development. His influence on the content and the process has been considerable. Joanne Donner was helpful in editing the book so that it made sense. She has provided me with positive reinforcement for my writing at critical times.

Without the success of the first edition, this second edition would not be possible. So I would like to thank my daughter, Laura Lee Glass, who worked tirelessly to market, deliver, and manage the entire process of distributing *Bringing Out the Best in People* through Performance Management Publications.

Of course, the behavior analysis community continues to provide me with valuable insights and research into the science. In addition to those acknowledged in the first edition, I would add my thanks to Dr. Anders

Ericsson of Florida State, Dr. Sigrid Glenn of North Texas University, and most recently, Finnur Oddsson of West Virginia University.

All of the associates at ADA have supported *Bringing Out the Best in People*, but I would like to thank some of those who were not acknowledged in the first edition. They include Phil Hurst, Judy Agnew, John O'Connell, Wes Spring, Guy Bruce, John Cole, and Darnell Lattal. Their extensive use of the first edition and their suggestions to me regarding what needed to be considered for the second have been very valuable indeed.

Finally, I would like to thank the consultants who adopted the first edition and shared it with their clients. After all, the more of us who learn how to bring out the best in people, the quicker we will be able to fulfill our corporate vision of "Changing the way the World Works."

Acknowledgments to the First Edition

Without John Domenick this book would probably never have been written. He worked with the publisher, prompted me, reinforced, wrote, edited, and reedited. Through all the problems associated with a project like this, he never lost his patience or his sense of humor. For all his help I am extremely grateful.

Special thanks to Darlene Davidson, who also worked on this project from its inception. She was responsible for the overall coordination of the project, took care of the many details of the manuscript preparation, and kept me on schedule—not an easy task.

Thanks also to Jeff Davidson, who did some of the initial manuscript preparation and research, and Gail Snyder, who provided much-needed help in structure and syntax. Tracy Keever developed the charts and graphs in record time—and with her usual good humor.

I am deeply indebted to the many researchers in the field of behavior analysis who have provided the foundation of knowledge from which I have been fortunate to be a beneficiary. B. F. Skinner, Ogden Lindsley, and Richard Herrnstein have had a profound impact on my thinking and understanding of human behavior and, more importantly, on the practice of Performance Management.

Dr. Jon Bailey, Professor of Psychology at Florida State University, Dr. Beth Sulzer-Azaroff, chairman of the board of trustees of the Cambridge Center for Behavioral Studies, Dr. Bill Hopkins, Professor of Psychology at Auburn University, and Drs. Alyce Dickenson and Bill Redmon, Professors of Psychology at Western Michigan University, have all been a constant source of reinforcement for me as I have worked to apply behavior analysis to business problems.

All of the employees of ADA have been extremely supportive. Without the work of the company's consultants, there would be limited practical application of the concepts in this book. I have drawn heavily from their experiences, especially Courtney Mills, Wilson Rourk, James Daniels, John Davis, Betty Loafman, Betty Shunk, Andy Morency, Ned Morse, and Jerry Pounds.

Aubrey C. Daniels

Bringing Out
the Best
in People

PART 1
The Perils of Traditional Management

1
Fads, Fantasies, and Fixes

What if American management, after all these years of trying, has been dead wrong about how to manage effectively? What if the latest celebrated management theory is just another quick fix, destined to reap only short-term gains and produce long-term frustration? What if the only people benefiting from this cycle of hypothetical theories are the management gurus promising "the answer" to companies so desperate for a management approach that works, they're willing to try anything?

In 1971, Professor Joe Bailey of the University of Texas said that ". . . the half-life of all panaceas in the educational and business worlds is seven years, plus or minus two." (*Training Magazine,* April 1993.) I believe that in the last half of the 1990s the time frame has shrunk to about 18 months. And with the new computer technology promising "new and better" every six months or so, the temptation to jump from one solution to the next—or many all at once—is even greater.

As the temporary impact of each fad wears off, no longer producing the kind of changes expected and promised, many executives drop the old and charge off in search of the new—and currently "hot"—management theory. As years pass, approaches such as "situational analysis," "Theory Z" cross-functional teams, and quality management fade from memory and take their places in the graveyard of departed management systems.

The cycle of temporary answers continues because most approaches to management are never rooted in anything more substantial than limited observations, in limited settings, over limited time periods. The lesson American management steadfastly refuses to learn is that managing by emotions, perceptions, or common sense is not really managing at all. Leaders also refuse to accept the fact that people—the very engine of the business machine—cannot be ignored or treated as expendable parts. Human performance is not a factor in a complicated equation for business success; it is *the answer* to the equation.

We all selectively perceive and retain experiences and information. We then evaluate and interpret them from a base of previous experiences and perceptions. With all of these individual variables, it's obvious that those who manage only from personal experience, and the thoughts and feelings that accompany that experience, are subject to unpredictable results. Today's business environment demands a much more precise approach— one that produces consistent results; one that is based on science, not opinion. My concern is that business leaders will continue to treat management as a mysterious, somewhat personal art form. Management folklore, such as "management by exception," "management by objectives," "thriving on chaos," and so on, will continue to delay the progress of American business.

One recent management book, for example, likened organizational leadership to leading a jazz band because ". . . good jazz, like good business, requires strong leaders and strong players." The leader "chooses the music, picks the players, and performs for an audience." This analogy holds true to a point, but good business is not an orchestral production or a Broadway show, well-scripted and choreographed. Rather, it is an ongoing process requiring constant vigilance and diligence to meet the demands of an ever-changing and unpredictable marketplace.

Another management philosophy stresses that "effective management results from individual initiative and savvy, not from a grand design." This sounds like "management by the seat of your pants." Simply being "savvy," a word subject to an array of definitions, and taking initiative based on it, might produce good results from time to time, but it won't consistently bring out the best in people. And taking a nonsystematic approach to managing will not allow you to profit from either your successes or your failures.

Other management fads (to name a few) that have rocked the business landscape in recent years include:

- *Quality circles.* Americans copycatted the quality circle approach from the Japanese because of their tremendous advances in manufacturing quality, but Americans made little attempt to understand why it worked in Japan. It just seemed like it would work here too. Probably less than one out of 100,000 quality circles lasted more than a few years. Even fewer produced significant business results.

- *Corporate culture.* Business professors and consultants have succeeded in making corporate culture change into a complicated and expensive process. The concepts and activities associated with typical attempts to change the culture are not based on solid research and are not implemented in a way that demonstrates cause-and-effect relationships between what was done and what was achieved.

- *"Intrapreneuring."* Advancing the entrepreneurial spirit within a large corporation is a good idea if handled carefully. Too often, the approach is botched, creating tensions, jealousies, and motivational problems that exceed any potential benefits.

- *Employee participation.* Years ago, when People's Express and its innovative job rotation system prospered, many companies decided that "self-actualization," or "create your own job title" was the route to success. This idea disappeared almost as quickly as People's Express.

- *Strategic alliances.* Characterized by the notion, "If you can't beat 'em, join 'em," such efforts are creating scores of strange bedfellows. Sometimes the alliances work. More often, both parties wonder why they united in the first place.

- *"Management by Wandering Around."* This concept was popularized by Tom Peters' *In Search of Excellence.* The tactic of observing firsthand what's occurring on the shop floor is a good one. Mishandled—and it's easy to do—it often becomes "management by stumbling around." Well-meaning but unknowing managers can create morale problems among supervisors and other employees just by *where* they walk around and where they don't.

- *"Change Management."* The concept of managing change was presented to business as though change was something new and managing change was a science. In fact, most recommendations made by change management gurus presented commonsense solutions based on a false premise—that people resist all change. People only resist change at work because it usually is accompanied by immediate negative consequences. The reality is that change is natural and almost always accepted when it produces something positive for the performer.

From "My Own Style" to a Precise Procedure

As if management fads aren't dangerous enough, many managers proudly refer to their own "management style." What company can possibly succeed over the long term if hundreds of its managers have their own individual management style? How do you know that each manager's style is going to support the company's values and mission? What chance does such an approach have to bring out the best in the work force? One hundred different management styles yield confusion and inefficiency.

Imagine a doctor saying, "I've developed my own operational style. I'm going to operate on your brain a little differently than other surgeons would. No need to worry. I'm very comfortable with my style of operating, and I've had a couple of good successes."

Or suppose a pilot announces over the plane's public address system, "I'm going to land this plane a little differently than FAA procedures require; I've got my own method. I feel that today the runway assigned by the control tower is not the best so I'm going to use another. It will work out better, I assure you."

Performing surgery or landing a plane requires precision and the use of established procedures. With many businesses struggling to survive, and with large numbers of them failing, why do we tolerate so many subjective approaches to managing people?

Innovation in management is not wrong, but innovation without data, management by "hunch," or "let's give it a run and see what happens" techniques are too costly to tolerate any longer.

Bringing out the best in people and achieving measurably superior results requires a clear and precise understanding of human behavior. Yet most people understand the laws of human behavior at about the same level as they do the laws of gravity. They know that gravity keeps them on the earth, and they know not to walk off the top of a tall building. But they don't know enough to send astronauts to the moon and bring them back. Most managers know enough about human behavior to know that positive methods of management are preferred to negative ones. However, they usually know very little about how the selection, delivery, and timing of positive and negative consequences in the workplace influence the way people behave.

Many managers have an immediate negative reaction when they are told they need to study and understand human behavior. They don't believe it is necessary to managing a business effectively. They might as well say they don't believe in the laws of gravity. Believe in gravity or not, when they jump they will still come back to earth.

If you work with other human beings, you are subject to the laws of behavior. And if you don't understand them, more than likely you're impeding, possibly depressing, the performance of your employees, your peers, even yourself.

To obtain measurably superior results in the workplace, managers must understand why people behave as they do with the same depth that rocket scientists understand gravity.

Management by Sloshing Around Versus Precision Management

Very few managers use systematic, scientifically based management methods to bring out the best in people at work. Most try a variety of management approaches until they find one they like. But even when that approach seems to work, they don't know exactly why it did or why it works sometimes and sometimes doesn't.

Conversely, the approach described in this book is not something that I made up. It's based on over 80 years of research in human behavior. The body of knowledge is called *behavior analysis*. The application of these scientific findings to the workplace is called *Performance Management*. Once managers understand the principles of Performance Management, they can create the right environment and conditions to bring out the best in performers today, tomorrow, next month, and next year.

The senior managers I've known are not particularly impressed with one-time performance improvement in a job, in an office, or in a factory. They know that things occasionally get better. They get interested when things improve and continue to improve.

Organizations such as Eastman Chemical Company, Allied Systems, 3M Dental, Blue Cross/Blue Shield of Alabama, BP Amoco, and Preston Trucking Company (featured in Robert Levering's book, *A Great Place to Work*) have used Performance Management and thrived on its methods for over a decade. Other organizations have had the same experience.

Delta Faucet Company, for example, began applying Performance Management techniques almost 20 years ago. "Delta has had nothing but better years, every year," Don Ginder, retired vice president of human resources stated. Today, Delta leads the faucet industry in America and has begun exporting its products to Japan.

Performance Management is not a one-time management solution to a single problem at work. It provides a precise way of analyzing work and implementing a management system that will not only address the problems associated with inadequate performance, but will lead to practical ways to maximize performance in every aspect of the company's business. Because Performance Management is a precise, data-oriented approach, the solutions can be replicated in the same or similar settings and even extended to new settings with similar results.

Several years ago I visited a middle manager in a large manufacturing company. Ralph O. had been applying Performance Management in his department for about a year and had invited me to see the accomplishments of his team. The country was in a recession and the company was in the midst of its second downsizing in two years. Despite the doom and gloom prevalent in other departments occupying the same building, Ralph's team was enjoying dramatic successes, reducing labor and maintenance costs while demonstrating measurable quality improvement in their product.

Even more impressive was the fact that Ralph, reading the downsizing handwriting on the wall, had gathered his department together and offered them the challenge of improving their cost structure in a more constructive way than the usual method of mandated head-count cuts by corporate. Ralph's department found a way to reduce labor costs more than was requested, yet no one was laid off. All this improvement was accomplished through the use of Performance Management at a time when most people, including most of Ralph's peers and managers, thought any improvement was impossible.

During my flight home, I wrote a note to that company's manufacturing VP. I suggested that if the downsizing got to him and he needed a lift, he should go see Ralph and let him show how he was helping the company.

Most importantly, I wanted that VP to understand that what Ralph and his management team had done could be repeated in other areas. I wanted him to know that what was done was not dependent on Ralph's charisma or other personal attributes. Ralph had used a straightforward process that could be taught to all managers and supervisors.

Business Is Behavior

Performance Management teaches managers how to influence behavior. A company hires people because what needs to be done requires people to do it. The behavior of people is the only way anything is accomplished in business. If managers don't understand behavior management methods, and can't apply them consciously and correctly, they are almost certainly decreasing some behaviors that they want and increasing others that they don't want.

Every organizational accomplishment is dependent on behavior. Whenever an organization strives to improve quality, increase productivity, or boost creativity, it must ask people to change their behavior. People must then either do the same things they are currently doing *more or less often,* or do different things.

Consequently, the one thing executives, managers, and supervisors should know the most about is human behavior.

If they don't know the conditions under which people do their best, the organization will survive only through sheer luck.

Every management system ever devised was intended to bring out the best in people, but failed because it violated basic laws of human behavior.

Behavior Is a Function of Its Consequences

When most people see someone do something that is out of the ordinary, they ask, "Why does that person do that?" Most of us have been trained to look for the answer in what hap°pened *before* the behavior occurred. In other words, we think the behavior was caused—motivated—by some internal force, drive, need, or desire, or by some external order, request, or signal. Because some behavior appears to occur without an apparent external motivator, we are puzzled.

A behavior analyst, on the other hand, would respond, "A person does that because of what happens to that person when he or she does it." That is, the cause of the behavior lies, not in the conditions prior to the behavior, but in what happens immediately *after* the behavior.

For most people, this is a totally new way of looking at behavior, but it can be very helpful because it means you don't have to read minds or try "to figure people out."

You have everything you need to understand people when you *witness the behavior and observe the consequences of the behavior.*

Psychologists study the mind; behavior analysts study behavior and how to optimize desirable behaviors. Although *behavior is the window to the mind,* I prefer to leave people's minds alone. What goes on in other people's minds is, frankly, none of my business. The business of business is behavior.

A Most Practical Approach

Because Performance Management focuses on understanding behavior, we are able to tell what works and what doesn't simply by looking at the effect any intervention has on the behavior of people. Did the behavior increase or decrease, change or stay the same?

Performance Management uses scientific methods to change behavior. At first, a scientific method for managing behavior may not sound practical for line supervisors and managers, but in reality it is the *most* practical way to manage people.

Using scientific methods to manage behavior includes: precise specification of what we want to improve; the development of a baseline of current performance against which we can measure progress; and then a precise intervention and the evaluation of its impact on performance. This is no more than we would ask from any change in any other business process.

The best way to run an organization is also the best way to treat people.
SHERMAN ROBERTS
Harvard University

2
Management by Common Sense Is Not Management at All

She knows what her responsibilities are but she just can't seem to get the job done—she has absolutely no common sense.

Most of our organizational problems can be solved by applying a little common sense.

You'll catch on, it's just common sense.

If you had any common sense at all, you would have known that wouldn't work.

I'm on a crusade to stamp out the use of common sense in business. Contrary to popular belief there isn't too *little* common sense in business, there's too *much*.

Webster defines common sense as, "the unreflective opinions of ordinary people." Can organizations survive on management strategies based on the *unreflective* opinions of its leaders? No! Unreflective opinions are based on unanalyzed experience. Benjamin Franklin once said, "Experience keeps a dear school and fools will learn in no other."

A more modern equivalent was stated by W. Edwards Deming, the well-known quality guru. He said, "Experience teaches us nothing. If experience teaches us something, why are we in such a mess?"

If not common sense and not experience, then what?

I think Deming would say that *systematic, data-based* experience can teach us a lot. The alternative to common sense knowledge is scientific knowledge.

Common Sense Versus Scientific Knowledge

1. *Commonsense knowledge is acquired in ordinary business and living, while scientific knowledge must be pursued deliberately and systematically.*

No special effort is required to obtain common sense. As a matter of fact, you can't stop it. It occurs just from the fact that we are alive. No wonder it's so plentiful.

On the other hand, scientific knowledge requires a special effort to acquire.

2. *Commonsense knowledge is individual; scientific knowledge is universal.*

The biggest problem with so-called common sense is that it is not really common at all. It's drawn from personal experience and, as such, is as different as our lives. When someone asks, "Why didn't you use your common sense?" he or she is really asking, "Why didn't you do what I would have done?" The fact is that when you use your common sense, you always do what makes sense to *you*.

Scientific knowledge goes beyond the individual to look for that which is applicable across all situations.

3. *Commonsense knowledge accepts the obvious; scientific knowledge questions the obvious.*

This is probably the most distinguishing characteristic of the scientific mind versus the ordinary mind. Common sense always says, "Of course," while science asks, "Why?" In other words, the commonsense person always has an answer. Before science entered the picture, common sense told people that the sun came up, the stars came out at night, and the earth was flat.

Science eventually taught us that none of these things were true even though for centuries people conducted their affairs according to these common beliefs. The scientist *begins* his or her search for the truth with the commonsense answer.

4. *Commonsense knowledge is vague; scientific knowledge is precise.*

As a sports fan, one of my pet peeves is the way sportscasters inanely explain player motivation. When a player outperforms another on a play, for instance, the announcer says something like, "This player wanted it more than the other one." What does that *mean?* How would you tell the other player to succeed next time? "You need to want it more than the other player does."

When the home team is losing, many fans complain that the problem is that the athletes are paid too much. Maybe so, but their opinions don't help the coach develop a winning team. The behavior analyst would want to know precisely what actions the coach can take to create outstanding performance in those athletes regardless of their pay!

5. *Common sense cannot be counted on to produce consistent results; application of scientific knowledge yields the same results* every *time.*

This is the most compelling reason for people in business to abandon common sense and to seek scientific explanations to problems involving human performance in the workplace. No scientist would accept a one-time occurrence as cause-and-effect proof that the same results would occur the next time. Yet businesspeople constantly adopt policies and procedures that they have seen work at another company, accepting only a commonsense explanation of why those methods worked. Then, when they don't work in a new setting, they compound the error by adopting other unproven strategies.

With the fierce competition in business today, we have passed the time when we can rely on trial and error to produce a work force capable of doing the right thing every time. A business that is slow to attain high quality, bring new products to market, and respond to changing market conditions is on the road to an early demise. We must know that what we are doing will produce the desired performance *every* time.

6. *Common sense is gained through uncontrolled experience; scientific knowledge is gained through controlled experiment.*

This is probably the characteristic of science that causes the average businessperson to think that it is unrealistic for a business to use behavioral science in everyday management. This book will show you that it is not only possible, but the most cost-effective way to manage your business.

The Popularity of a Management Approach Guarantees Nothing

Tom Peters' book *In Search of Excellence* contains some valid observations, but it also stands as a good example of how people form (and follow) strong opinions and beliefs that are based on nonscientific information. Three years after *In Search of Excellence* became world renowned, *Business Week* magazine revisited the so-called excellent companies highlighted in the book and found that 14 of 43 companies no longer met the author's criteria for excellence.

In fact, several of the companies singled out for their successful management practices and commitment to customer service experienced considerable losses and underwent major reorganization after the ink was barely dry on the book.

Ironically, some of the companies the book urged American businesses to emulate were floundering. Companies touted as the "best of the best" no longer were. The experts failed to delve into what was going on behind the scenes at these organizations. Yet, consider the impact *In Search of Excellence* had, and continues to have, on American and worldwide business practices.

Managers around the world turned to this book to solve their management problems. Organizations spent millions of dollars to model their divisions and plants after those remarkably successful companies examined in the book. Yet, if the 14 companies that no longer meet the criteria really knew what they were doing to be successful, why would they abandon their own successful methods?

If It Ain't Broke, Find Out Why

An orthopedic surgeon was treating a patient for knee pain. The patient felt the pain periodically after participating in various sports activities. The doctor examined the man and could not find a specific cause for the pain. He prescribed some anti-inflammatory medicine, some antibiotics and some painkillers. Then he wrapped the knee and told the patient to stay off it for a couple of days. Within a few days, the pain was gone.

At his next checkup the patient said, "I'm completely cured. Doctor, you don't know how you have helped me." And the patient was right. The doctor hadn't a clue about which one of his treatments had ended the pain. Was it staying off the leg? the anti-inflammatory medicine? the antibiotics? the wrap? Perhaps even the painkillers helped. Or maybe it was a combination of everything he prescribed.

Would the pain have gone away on its own without the intervention of the doctor? Who knows? Certainly not the doctor or the patient. All they know is that the pain is gone and, to them, that's all that matters. Perhaps in a situation like this, not knowing the exact reason the pain dissipated is unimportant. On the other hand, what if some of the treatment has masked the symptoms of a serious disease? What if the pain returns and is even more intense?

Not knowing why things get better or worse is always a problem for a business. If it gets better "for no reason," later it will probably get worse "for no reason."

Let's look at a simple example of a computer operator who is having trouble advancing to the next screen. The computer screen has locked. The operator pounds and pounds on the keyboard, hitting virtually every key until the screen advances. The operator is happy to have arrived at the next screen, but he or she hasn't learned how to get there the next time, let alone with grace or ease.

The next time the computer locks up, undoubtedly the operator will pound away until the screen advances again. He or she has no idea which key or sequence of keys unlock the computer. By pushing keys, the operator hopes that eventually the correct screen will appear. How efficient is this? Not only is the performer not efficient, but the computer may be damaged in the process. More importantly, there may be a problem with the machine that, if repaired now, might save a lot of frustration as well as lost time and data in the future.

The point is, it's not enough to know that something works. It is vitally important to know *why* it works. For example, if your company is performing well and you think it's because you have an annual profit-sharing plan, you may be in for a surprise when suddenly you lose a big customer due to poor customer service. What happened? Did the profit-sharing plan quit working, or could it be that it never had anything to do with performance in the first place?

The following story illustrates the pitfalls of "popular solutions."

The Guru*

There once was an Indian chicken farmer who lived on the outskirts of Bombay. For years, he scratched out a reasonable living from raising his chickens and selling both chickens and eggs.

One morning when he went to feed his flock, he noticed several dead chickens. Not knowing what to do, he packed his bags and made a long trek into the Himalayas, climbed a mountain, and found a guru.

"Oh, guru," he moaned, "I am a poor chicken farmer. The other morning, I discovered several dead chickens. What should I do?"

"What do you feed them?" asked the guru.

"Wheat. I feed them wheat."

"That is your problem, my son. Corn! Feed them corn."

The man paid his tribute to the guru, climbed down the mountain, and journeyed home. When he arrived, he immediately changed the chickens' feed from wheat to corn. For three weeks, everything went

* Don Tobin, Digital Equipment, *Target Magazine*, Marlboro, Mass., March/April 1992.

fine. Then one morning, as he went to feed his flock, he found more dead chickens.

He packed his bags, made the trek to the Himalayas, and climbed the mountain once again. "Oh, guru!" he cried. "More of my chickens are dead!"

"How do you give them water?"

"I carved wooden bowls in which I gave them water."

"Troughs! You need troughs!"

The farmer made the long journey home and built troughs. For six months, everything went along fine. Then one morning, as he went to feed his flock, he found more dead chickens. So, again, he made the trek to the guru. "Oh, guru!" he cried. "More of my chickens are dead!"

"How do you house them?"

"I built a wooden shack in which they live."

"Ventilation! They need more ventilation!"

Back home, the farmer spent a small fortune putting a new ventilation system in his coop. For a year, everything went well. Then, one morning, he went out to discover that *all* of his chickens were dead.

Beside himself with grief, he packed his bags and again make his way to the mountain. "Oh, guru!" he wailed. "All of my chickens are dead!"

"That's a shame," replied the guru. "I had a lot more solutions."

There Are More Wrong Answers than Right Ones

Of all the many solutions that are proposed for solving the problems of business and industry today, how do you know what is right?

"Form self-directed teams."

"Empower the work force."

"Encourage participation."

"Change the culture."

"Create a learning organization."

"Set up a gainsharing program."

"Use the 7-habits of effective people."

And so it goes. These are only a few of the many answers that organizations are being told will make the work force more effective. Large numbers of companies, like the guru, are blindly throwing darts at the wall, hoping to hit the bull's-eye, or even the target!

The guru never systematically explored why the chickens died. The farmer received no concrete proof that the chickens' problems stemmed from their feed, or their water bowls, or even their ventilation system. He trusted the guru because he always had answers. Unfortunately, they weren't the right ones.

The guru story mirrors the search for truth by American businesses today. Management experts and theorists spew practical advice that ostensibly makes sense. Many managers today are so desperate to improve their operations or "save their chickens" that they are willing to try anything to make things better, whether it has a real effect or not. They often find themselves flooded with so many new approaches, and are so busy applying them to their working environment, they have no way of determining which strategies are effective and which are not.

Maybe the farmer's chickens were sick, or maybe they were old, who knows? No one took the time to find out what was going on in the chicken coop. Do you understand the cause-and-effect relationship between your performers' behaviors and the results they produce? Do you know what motivates your employees to work hard and smart and what discourages them? Understanding the principles of Performance Management will provide the key to improving your employees' performance, productivity, and satisfaction.

3
Louder, Longer, Meaner

It would really help if you would keep this file current.

How many times do I have to tell you to update this file?

I'm getting tired of talking to you about this file!

This is the last time I'm going to tell you this. Keep the files current or you're fired!

In most organizations we attempt to manage performance by telling people what to do. We tell them to work harder; we tell them to work better; we tell them to work smarter. We tell them to show more initiative, be more creative, be self-directed, be empowered.

We tell them to do these things in a variety of ways. We send memos, have meetings, write policies, hold classes, and make informational and inspirational speeches.

Interestingly, when these methods don't get the desired response or level of performance we want, we tell the same people again, usually in the same ways. Only this time we tell them a little louder, or a little longer, or perhaps a little meaner.

We send new memos around (with bolder type, capital letters, and even exclamation marks) about old memos that were ignored, or have meetings about why meetings don't seem to be productive. If we train people about the importance of doing it "right the first time, every time," and they don't, we bring them in and train them again. If we inspire them to reach for the heavens and they barely raise their hands, we make a more impassioned plea. If our first threat gets no response, we find a more severe punishment to hold over their heads. Let's face it, if threatening someone actually worked, would we need progressive discipline?

Surprise! People Don't Do What You Tell Them to Do

People frequently don't do what they are told. If we always did what we were told, we would eat only nutritious foods, never drink too much alcohol, and exercise regularly. We would always "put the customer first; focus on quality; take initiative; and do it right the first time."

Though we know that people don't do what they are told, we run our businesses as though the performance problems caused by people who don't know what to do, or don't want to do it, or simply don't care whether they do it can be solved by finding more and better ways of telling them what to do!

Several years ago, I conducted an informal survey and discovered that managers spend approximately 85 percent of their time either telling people what to do, figuring out what to tell them to do, or deciding what to do because employees didn't do what they told them to do. I don't think that has changed much in the intervening years.

Why Telling Alone Does Not Bring Out the Best in People

There are two ways to change behavior. Do something before the behavior occurs or do something after the behavior occurs. In the science of behavior analysis, the technical word for what comes before a behavior is *antecedent*. The word for what comes after a behavior is *consequence*.

Antecedents set the occasion for a behavior to occur and consequences alter the probability that the behavior will occur again. If you are to create an organization that consistently brings out the best in people, it is critical that you understand the specific role each of these elements plays in generating performance.

Since antecedents always come *before* the behavior of interest, they are referred to as *setting events*. In other words, an antecedent sets the stage for a behavior to occur; it does *not cause* the behavior to occur.

Consequences follow the behavior and alter the probability that the behavior will reoccur. That is, the consequence causes the behavior to occur more or less often in the future. While this sounds elementary, it is frequently violated in managing organizational performance.

Antecedents have limited control over behavior. *It is the role of an antecedent to get a behavior to occur once.*

It is the role of a consequence to get it to occur again.

Business success is dependent on getting lasting, consistent performance. Yet, as I've just described, business invests heavily in antecedent activity such as memos, training, policies, mission statements, slogans, posters, and buttons. Since antecedents get the behavior to occur once or a few times, it's apparent why businesses must continually repeat their messages. The antecedents are working, just as antecedents usually do.

Effective antecedents are necessary to initiate performance, but are not sufficient to *sustain* performance. Because of this they are a very inefficient and costly way to manage performance.

A Place for Antecedents

There are some valuable uses for antecedents. For example, we are all familiar with marketing antecedents: advertisements, attractive packaging, sales, direct mail, etc. The task of marketing is to get consumers to come into the store, or take a sample, or try the product "just one time."

Marketing people recognize the inefficiency of influencing behavior by using only antecedents. In fact, they plan for it.

Direct mail, for example, is considered a very effective way to sell some products and services. A company advertises a three-day seminar for $1000 and sends out 10,000 pieces of mail. To those not acquainted with this method of selling, you might be surprised to know that the company will be happy if the direct-mail campaign convinces a minimum of 20 people to attend the seminar.

This practice is considered effective because the organization sponsoring the seminar builds the inefficiency of the antecedent (eight responses per 1000 pieces of mail; two attendees per 1000) into the price of the seminar.

In day-to-day management, if only eight employees in 1000 respond to what we tell them, we have a major problem. Do you think we can overcome that problem by delivering the message 125 times so that everyone will finally respond? Of course that's ridiculous, but it is not far removed from actual practice.

One way to get people to continue to respond to antecedents is to continually change the antecedents. Novel antecedents are more effective than doing the same thing over and over. For example, *Candid Camera*, the hidden-camera television show, was extremely effective at getting people to do "strange things" by confronting them with unfamiliar circumstances (antecedents). On one show, drivers approaching the bridge going from New Jersey to Delaware were met by a sign that read "Delaware Closed." People stopped. They had never heard of a state being closed. What could it possibly mean? What would happen if they ignored it? Could they be killed because of some dangerous situation in the state? Would they be arrested? Because people didn't know the consequences, they were cautious and stopped. Temporarily.

Business Has Always Been Enamored of Novel Antecedents. A number of years ago, I interviewed employees of a furniture plant based in North Carolina. At the conclusion of the interview I opened the floor to questions or comments. A man spoke up, "What's all this about 'Quality is the only thing'?" I could tell there was an underlying agenda to his question.

"What do you mean?" I asked.

"They have all these signs all over the plant that say, 'QUALITY IS THE ONLY THING.' What does that mean?" he said.

I replied that I guessed it meant that quality was very important.

"If that's so, then why is it I see a chair that has a problem, and I set it off the line. It sits there all day 'til the end of the shift. My supervisor comes by and ain't got his production and says, 'What's wrong with that one?' I show him.

"He looks at it and says, 'Put it back. It'll run. Anyway, they'll probably catch it in the next department.' If he don't care, I don't care. I put it back."

What they should have had on the signs was "QUALITY IS OUR MOST IMPORTANT SLOGAN."

Many organizations have started using words like *associate* or *colleague* rather than *worker* or *employee* to try to cause some change in behavior. However, a person who is treated like just another pair of hands feels no different, and will behave no differently, just because he or she is suddenly called "associate."

Cigarette warnings are a classic example of dealing with problems through antecedent activity. Years ago, Congress debated the need for a warning on cigarettes to advise smokers of the health hazards. The debate centered first on whether to put a warning on the pack and then on what it should say. You may remember that the first message said, "Warning—the Surgeon General has determined that smoking *may be* dangerous to your health."

This had little impact. Subsequently, after much debate and many tax dollars, it was decided that the problem was the phrase, "may be." The new warning read, "Warning—the Surgeon General has determined that smoking *is* dangerous to your health." How many smokers do you know who pulled out their cigarettes to light up, looked at the new warning and said, "Whoa! Do you know these things are dangerous? I'm gonna stop." (The government doesn't know one either.) So, true to form, they debated again and decided they needed several different warnings defining the specific dangers. That was more effective, right? Of course not. There is no evidence that any of these printed warnings had any effect on smokers whatsoever.

Some people might point to the fact that cigarette smoking has declined rather dramatically from former levels. That's certainly true, but I suggest that what really changed smoking behavior was the change of consequences: no smoking on planes, in restaurants, or in public buildings. These changes and the negative social reactions to people who smoke have had more impact on smoking behavior than all the warnings ever printed.

Recently, I read a newspaper article with the title, "Alcohol and Pregnancy: Warnings Don't Work." I thought, *finally someone is getting the message about the weak effect of antecedents on behavior.* I was disappointed to learn that the article's author merely pointed out that the warnings were difficult to read. She then stated that the warning should be larger and more conspicuous. When will we ever learn?

The only thing that makes an antecedent effective is its *consistent pairing with a consequence.* People have to experience the pairing more than once or twice before they will respond reliably to the antecedent time and time again.

No matter how attractive or frightening an antecedent is, it will have a long-lasting effect only if it is consistently paired with a meaningful consequence.

For example, a sign that says "HANDICAPPED PARKING ONLY—VIOLATORS WILL BE FINED" is often ignored because the spaces are conveniently located for everyone, the parking lots are usually not well patrolled, and fines are rarely given for parking in a handicapped space.

On the other hand, signs that reliably predict consequences are reliably followed. Put a sign on a fence surrounding a generator that reads "DANGER—HIGH VOLTAGE" and the fence will likely not be touched—if the person can read and sees the sign. Most people learn early that electricity hurts *every time you touch it.*

This is the good news and bad news about antecedents. Antecedents can be found to get a behavior to occur one time. The bad news is they get the behavior to occur only once or a few times.

Since very few managers understand how or why antecedents work, or the need to pair them with the right consequences, they continue to search for new antecedents.

Threat as Antecedent— Not Consequence

The search for more effective antecedents has unfortunately led many supervisors and managers to use threats to get their people to perform.

Most people think of a threat as a consequence, since it implies punishment. But because the threat comes *before* the behavior you want, it is only an antecedent. For example, if you say, "Clean up this area by three o'clock, or you'll have to stay and finish it after everyone else has gone," the person may begin to clean up the area. However, if the person knows you never follow through on such threats, he or she may not finish cleaning before leaving. The threat is only an antecedent. The threat only sets the stage for the cleaning to begin.

Antecedents Get Us Going; Consequences Keep Us Going.   A number of years ago, when I worked more actively as a management consultant, I was asked to help a supervisor solve a quality problem on his shift. As I approached his work area, I saw that his manager had him cornered. The manager's face was red, his voice was loud and his language was abusive as he shook his finger in the supervisor's face. Witnessing this made me uncomfortable because, after the manager left, I had to talk to the supervisor about using positive reinforcement with his employees to improve quality— something his boss was definitely not doing with him.

When the manager left I said, "Boy, he got off to a rough start this morning, didn't he?" He replied, "Aw, don't pay him no mind. That's the way he is. If I'd been fired every time he told me I was going to be fired, I wouldn't work here a week. He threatens to fire me at least once a week."

Taking that kind of abuse was a part of the job as he saw it. It meant nothing. He had learned to ignore it.

Without consequences, threats are so much hot air. In the same way, promises of positive consequences, without follow-through, mean nothing. Without reinforcement, no behavior can survive for long.

Ultimately, the search for effective antecedents is never-ending and futile. Louder, longer, and meaner antecedents will not give us the consistent performance we require from our work force.

PART 2

The Astonishing Power of Positive Reinforcement

4

Behavior Is a Function of Its Consequences

People do what they do because of what
happens to them when they do it.

At the end of every working day people leave either more motivated to come back and do their jobs again tomorrow or less motivated as a result of what happens to them that day. Performance is about *what happens every day*.

Everything we do changes our environment in some way. When a behavior changes the environment in ways that we like, we repeat it. When our behavior changes the environment in ways we don't like, we stop. Everything we do produces a consequence for us.

Technically defined, *behavioral consequences are those things and events that follow a behavior and change the probability that the behavior will be repeated in the future*. This definition allows scientists to study and predict behavior through systematic observation. However, this concept is enormously useful to the nonscientist as well. Because we can observe the impact of a particular consequence on the rate or frequency of a behavior, we can begin to understand how to influence or change any behavior.

Consequences change the rate or frequency of a behavior. They cause a behavior to occur either more or less often in the future. There are only

25

four behavioral consequences. Two increase behavior and two decrease it. The two that increase behavior are called *positive reinforcement* and *negative reinforcement*. The two that decrease behavior are called *punishment* and *penalty*. (See Figure 4-1.)

Let's say an employee engages in 1000 behaviors per day at work. Each is followed by a consequence that will either strengthen or weaken that behavior. A large percentage of these consequences occur naturally and the employee gives them little thought. For example, he or she turns the key in the door to the building, pulls on the knob, and the door opens. The employee flicks the switch and the lights come on. These are natural consequences for these behaviors.

Another portion of the 1000 behaviors is followed by consequences provided by the people an employee works with. He or she smiles, says "Good morning," and receives a greeting in return. The employee shares a rumor, and receives the smiles and attention of peers.

Yet another portion of the 1000 behaviors is followed by consequences provided by supervisors and managers. These consequences should increase the behaviors that directly add value to the business and decrease those that interfere with value-added performance.

SUMMARY OF THE FOUR BEHAVIORAL CONSEQUENCES AND THEIR EFFECTS

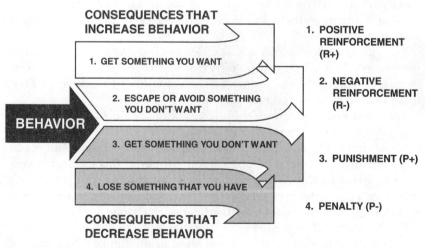

Figure 4-1

As a manager, could you explain to a visitor what you are doing to make sure that the right consequences are occurring every day for the right behaviors?

Think about your organization for a moment. Are only value-added behaviors being strengthened by consequences in the work environment? Or are off-task behaviors reinforced in some manner? Is it possible that some of the behaviors you want punished or penalized are actually strengthened?

I tell people that I can go into their organization and immediately see what is being reinforced. All I have to do is observe what people are doing. *What they do during the work day is what is being reinforced.*

Vic Dingus, technical associate at Eastman Chemical Co, points out that *a company is always perfectly designed to produce what it is producing.* If it has quality problems, cost problems, productivity problems, then the behaviors associated with those undesirable outcomes are being reinforced. This is not conjecture. This is the hard, cold reality of human behavior.

This is good news because it means that all we have to do to get the performance we want is to *identify behaviors that are producing the poor outcome and arrange consequences that will stop them. Then identify the behaviors that will produce the desirable outcomes and arrange consequences that will positively reinforce them.*

Can we introduce and arrange consequences in such a way that tasks that are now difficult, dull, or boring, become exciting, challenging and rewarding? Is that possible? It most definitely is.

Every Consequence Every Day

In everyday affairs all four of the behavioral consequences are at work. It is practically impossible to live a day without experiencing all of them.

For example, you are talking on your cell phone and you lose your connection (*penalty*).

When you tried to use a computer for the first time, you probably inadvertently deleted a document after working on it for hours (*punishment*). Now, you talk about how writing memos by hand for your secretary to type is still the best way for you to get your correspondence done.

You stay late on Thursday night to revise a presentation because you know that if the first draft isn't letter-perfect, the boss will chew you out (*negative reinforcement*).

You bought one of your staff members a cup of coffee while discussing the improved quality of his or her work, and the staff member's quality indicators went even higher the following week (*positive reinforcement*).

Each type of consequence has a different influence on the behavior it follows. A significant part of every manager's job is to identify those behaviors that are necessary and sufficient to accomplish the company's objectives, then plan and deliver consequences that support them.

Increasing Performance Through Reinforcement

The two kinds of reinforcement, positive and negative, increase behavior. Positive reinforcement causes a behavior to increase because a desired, meaningful consequence follows the behavior. Negative reinforcement causes a behavior to increase in order to escape or avoid some unpleasant consequence. It is important to know the difference, because the characteristics of the performance generated by each are *very* different.

Negative reinforcement generates enough behavior to escape or avoid punishment. The improvement is usually described as "just enough to get by."

Positive reinforcement generates more behavior than is minimally required. We call this *discretionary effort,* and its presence in the workplace is the only way an organization can maximize performance.

Since reinforcement is defined as any consequence that increases performance, it always works. If performance does not increase following the application of a consequence, then by definition the consequence was not a positive reinforcer. This means that an organization that uses reinforcement effectively will get improvement. Put another way, if performance is not improving, reinforcement is not occurring.

Consequences That Decrease Performance

As stated previously, just as there are two consequences that increase behavior, there are two consequences that decrease behavior: *punishment* and *penalty.* Since punishment, like positive reinforcement, is defined by its effect, we can say only that a particular thing or event is punishing when we see its effect on behavior. This is a very important principle for managers.

It means that a "chewing out" could be a reinforcer, rather than a punisher, if it resulted in an increase in performance. By the same token, a "pat on the back" is actually a punisher if it causes a decrease in performance, and it's not unusual for this to be the case.

Anyone in business who doesn't understand how consequences can vary greatly in impact can accidentally create problems while trying to improve performance. Without doubt, most of the punishment that goes on in the average organization is unintentional.

Most managers think that intention determines effect. That is to say, most managers think that if they intend to positively reinforce someone for good performance, then that is what they are doing. Unfortunately, that's not true. *The consequence is defined as positive or negative by the performer, the person who receives it.*

People live by their perceptions

Doing Nothing Is Doing Something to Performance

If inadvertent punishment is common, inadvertent extinction is epidemic. Extinction is technically defined as the withdrawal of positive reinforcement from a behavior, but it may be easier to understand this way: *the performer does something and nothing happens.* Ignoring is probably the most common example of extinction. We know extinction is occurring when we hear people say things like, "Nobody appreciates anything I do around here."

Most managers feel that doing nothing has no effect on performance. The fact is that when managers do nothing following employee performance, they may change that performance in one of two ways: (1) they put desired effort on extinction and (2) they open the door for some inappropriate behavior to be positively reinforced. And managers do this all the time!

If people are taking the initiative to go above and beyond what is required, then those behaviors, if they lack a favorable consequence, will at some point stop.

If people are taking shortcuts in areas such as safety and quality, the naturally occurring positive consequences associated with doing the job with less effort will cause the undesirable behaviors to continue.

Management changes behavior by its action and its inaction.

Let's say you have 30 people reporting to you. How many would be problem performers? Two, maybe three? Now look at how you spend your time. Is it possible that you might spend as much or more time with the 3 problem performers as you do with the other 27? It happens. This indicates that you are ignoring the good performance that makes your company successful, while giving your full attention to the poor performance. The extinction of good performance is a common complaint of business. It sounds something like this: *"People just don't have that old-fashioned work ethic anymore."*

Decades of ignoring good performance has taken its toll. We have put the "work ethic" on extinction.

A Change of Focus

A retired maintenance superintendent was called back to a Chrysler plant to train new employees involved in the manufacturing start-up of a new car. He was one of several people who made a presentation to plant management about the new product and the production training process.

He introduced himself by saying, "I'm Don F. Many of you don't know me, but I retired from this plant several years ago. Since I retired I've had a lot of time to think about my career here. I started as a mechanic in the maintenance department and after several years became maintenance superintendent for the entire plant. As I thought about those days, something bothered me. Of the hundreds of employees that I supervised and managed, I can remember the names of about 30 that I would classify as 'no good.'

"I can remember the names of about the same number who were 'outstanding.' That's 15 to 20 percent of everyone I managed. What really bothers me is the remaining 80 to 85 percent who came in and did their jobs every day. They were the most responsible for my success in the plant, and I can't even remember their names. I hope when you retire you don't bear that burden."

Bringing out the best in people requires that *all* performers get the right consequences *every day*. We shouldn't ignore poor performers, but if we are to have a high-performance organization, we *can't* ignore the good performers either.

The More Immediate, the Better

All four types of consequences are subject to impact erosion. This means the shelf life of a consequence is limited. The more immediate the consequence, the more effective it is in changing behavior. Everyone who has ever tried to change a bad habit understands this. We want to lose weight, but we eat high-fat, high-caloric foods today, vowing to change tomorrow. We vowed to start an exercise program tomorrow, but we tune in our favorite TV show instead. We want to quit smoking, but first we finish that last pack of cigarettes.

The immediate consequences—taste, amusement, comfort, and stress reduction—far outweigh the delayed and uncertain consequences of better health.

Consequences that are immediate and certain are very powerful in governing behavior. For example, if, when handling caustic chemicals, performers know a small drop on the skin will produce an immediate and painful blister, it will not be a problem to get them to wear gloves.

However, performers who handle lacquer products that may cause cancer and/or possible nerve damage with prolonged exposure may not consistently wear protective gloves. Many don't wear them at all.

Reinforcers Are More Effective than Rewards

The immediacy factor explains the difference between a reinforcer and a reward. Although that difference will be examined in more detail later in the book, for now you should remember that a reinforcer provided immediately for a behavior has much more effect on that behavior than a delayed reward.

Because a reward is usually in the future, there is always a degree of uncertainty associated with it. Those offering the reward may withdraw it or change the conditions necessary to get it. The performer might not be able to meet the conditions, could die, or otherwise not qualify for the reward. People typically respond more predictably to small, immediate, certain consequences than they do to large, future, uncertain ones.

The consequences that cause people to do their best every day occur every day. Yet experience has shown me that most organizations spend more time, energy, and money providing consequences that occur when employees get sick, retire, or die than on the ones that occur every day.

This has enormous implications for every firm. It means that bonuses, profit sharing, retirement benefits, and similar forms of compensation are future, uncertain consequences and, as such, do not bring out the best in people every day. These incentives are necessary, but not sufficient, to maximize performance. Certain forms of compensation facilitate performance better than others. However, compensation alone will not do the job of maximizing performance. Only effective and frequent positive reinforcement can do that.

Management Myth: People Resist Change

Another important implication of the effect of consequences on behavior involves the critical element of change. We are continually bombarded with rhetoric about the urgency and acceleration of change in today's "fast-paced business world." We are told that people naturally resist change. This has become a major concern for most businesses and many have invested millions learning how to "manage change."

The fact is *people don't resist change if the change provides immediate positive consequences for them.*

Nobody resists change when the immediate consequences favor it. "Do it this way, and you won't hurt your fingers." "Hold it this way, and you will be able to see it better." "Move your right hand this way, and you will be able to hit the ball straight." If the correct behavior follows these instructions, and positive consequences occur, we will not have a difficult time getting people to accept change in those situations. It is only in situations where the immediate consequences of change are punishing, or when the new behavior is not immediately reinforced, that we run into trouble.

Almost every corporate initiative impacts the performer negatively at first. While the performer may understand that there are long-term benefits to the company and to the performer personally, the immediate consequences of doing things differently are usually negative. New behaviors require extra effort to learn, result in increased mistakes, cause the performers to get behind in their other work, and create stress because people fear they won't be able to learn or perform as well under new conditions.

To make change a positive experience, we need to be less concerned with managing the change, and much more attentive to managing the consequences associated with change.

Everybody's Behavior Makes Sense to Them

As unbelievable as it may sometimes seem, every person's behavior makes sense to them. That's because everyone is reinforced in different ways. Initially, what is reinforcing to another person may not be obvious to us, but if we look a little deeper we can discover the consequences that maintain almost any behavior.

One of my associates once witnessed some of this seemingly inexplicable behavior when he helped a friend starting a new job. His friend had recently been appointed office manager of a government office in North Carolina. She soon discovered that her job wouldn't be an easy one. The office she managed had a statewide reputation for poor performance. When each office received monthly ratings on a variety of performance measures, her department invariably ranked near the bottom. She quickly asked my associate, a specialist in performance management, for help.

The two spent several weekends and evenings developing individual and group measures. They posted group feedback graphs, developed reinforcement plans, and celebrated improvement. In a short time, the office zoomed from near the bottom to close to the top in performance ratings.

Shortly after the dramatically improved ratings came out, the office manager's boss called her and said, "I don't know what it is you're doing down there, but I want you to stop."

The woman was shocked. Expecting praise, she received punishment instead! "This man must be crazy!" she thought. "Didn't he hire me to do the best possible job, to turn the office around?"

Not until several days later did she learn what had caused his unlikely reaction. Before she began her improvement efforts, her boss had spent considerable time trying to convince his boss that the only way to improve the situation was with more money and more people. She had accomplished the necessary improvement with neither of those organizational changes—changes that her boss anticipated would lead to his reinforcement and reward.

In retrospect, the reaction of the office manager's boss was perfectly understandable when considering the embarrassment her success caused him. His behavior was even easier for her to understand when she discovered that his pay grade was determined by the number of people in his department and the size of his budget. This is an example of an organization structure which provides positive consequences for the wrong behaviors and results!

No-Fault Performance:
Change—Not Blame

When you understand how consequences influence performance, you realize that finding fault with people for their inappropriate performance is unproductive and unfair. They are simply behaving in a manner consistent with the consequences they are receiving now and have received in the past.

The role of leaders in every organization is not to find fault or place blame, but to analyze why people are behaving as they are, and modify the consequences to promote the behavior they need.

This approach to management does not overlook poor performance. Nor does it seek to use only positive reinforcement to attempt to create some type of unrealistic, utopian organization. Quite the contrary.

The management system we should create employs all of the consequences appropriately and skillfully to stop problem performance and promote the kind of behavior that supports the organization's goals. The organization that can differentiate between, and effectively provide, all four types of consequences will quickly achieve levels of performance they may never have thought possible.

5
The ABCs of Performance Management

A Way of Seeing Things As Others See Them

In Chapter 4, I explained how apparently senseless behavior made sense to the performer because it was in some way positively reinforcing to that performer. However, as in the example of the department supervisor in the state government, it's often difficult to understand how some things that others do could make sense to anybody.

So, the first step when attempting to change the way people perform is to *understand why they are currently behaving the way they are.* We now know that people do what they do because of the consequences they experience following their actions. Therefore, it is helpful to discover what antecedents are setting the stage for the behavior to begin, and it is necessary to know what consequences are causing the behavior to continue.

The ABC (Antecedent-Behavior-Consequence) Analysis is a simple method for systematically analyzing the antecedents and consequences influencing a behavior. This analytic technique will allow you to understand behavior from the other person's perspective, even when it appears to be unproductive, irrational, or self-defeating. (See Figure 5-1.)

Antecedent: Something that comes before a behavior that sets the stage for the behavior to occur.

Behavior: What a person does.

Consequence: What happens to the performer as a result of the behavior.

The ABCs of Performance Management

Example

Antecedent:	Behavior	➡	Consequence
Your nose itches	You rub it		Stops itching
Gas gauge registers empty	Fill up		Continue your trip
Telephone rings	You answer		Customer places large order

Once you view performance in terms of Antecedent-Behavior-Consequence (ABC), you will be able to develop solutions to performance problems that you may never have attempted in the past.

Before you begin to analyze any performance problem, you should determine whether the problem is a motivational problem (won't do) or a skill problem (can't do).

Robert Mager popularized this important problem-solving step in his book, *Analyzing Performance Problems*. Mager suggested holding a loaded .45 caliber pistol to the performer's head and telling that performer to do what you ask or you'll pull the trigger. If he or she doesn't do it under these conditions, the previous lack of performance is a training problem. If the performer does it then (and wasn't doing it before), it is a motivational problem.

Of course, we can't practice this technique, but we can realize that most of the problems we face in day-to-day management *are* motivational problems. Nevertheless, we should always make the "won't do/can't do" determination before proceeding. One hint: If the person has done the behavior correctly in the recent past, but is no longer doing it or is doing it poorly, it's probably a motivational problem.

Motivational problems in the context of this book include all situations where the performer knows the correct behavior and can perform the correct behavior, but doesn't do it. Sometimes people may be able to do what is required but don't know it is time to do it. Or, they may be doing the correct behavior, but not at the correct rate. And, of course, sometimes they

ABC MODEL
of
BEHAVIOR CHANGE

ANTECEDENT	:	BEHAVIOR	➡	CONSEQUENCE
(Setting Event)		(Performance)		(Reinforcer/Punisher)

Figure 5-1

may know that it's the right time and can perform at the correct rate, but choose to do nothing. People always have the choice to vary their performance.

Keep in mind that the applicability of this analysis doesn't stop on the shoproom floor. Managers and executives also perform according to the consequences they receive.

In an ABC Analysis, consequences are classified on three dimensions:

1. *Positive* or *negative.*   This dimension answers the question, "Is the consequence positive or negative *from the perspective of the performer?*"

2. *Immediate* or *future.*   Here we want to know, "Does the consequence occur as the behavior is happening (immediate) or some time later (future)?"

3. *Certain* or *uncertain.*   This dimension expresses the probability that the performer will actually experience the consequence.

Let's look at an example. Some people don't wear seat belts. An objective analysis of this behavior shows that seat belts save lives and reduce injuries. Why, then, would a person not buckle up? Look at Figure 5-2. (In Figures 5-2 through 5-5, the designations P/N, I/F, and C/U refer to Positive or Negative, Immediate or Future, and Certain or Uncertain, respectively.)

What the analysis in Figure 5-2 tells us is that:

1. There are many antecedents that set the stage for *not buckling up seat belts.*

2. Although there are many serious negative consequences associated with *not buckling up seat belts,* those consequences tend to be in the future, or they are uncertain to occur, or both.

3. The positive consequences for *not buckling up seat belts,* such as "saves time," "freedom to move," and "doesn't wrinkle clothes" are small, but immediate and certain.

Let's look at what might happen if this same person who doesn't wear seat belts actually put them on, as shown in Figure 5-3.

If our non-seat-belt wearers were to put on the belts they would find that:

1. The positive consequences tend to be future and uncertain.

2. The negative consequences are immediate and certain.

This analysis points out the difficulty in changing any behavior. The present behavior or habit is receiving PICs and the desired behavior gets NICs. So, what we want this performer to do (wear seat belts when riding in a car) is associated with immediate punishment and the possibility of future ben-

Problem Behavior: Not Buckling Up Seat Belt

Antecedents	Consequences	P/N	I/F	C/U
Think they don't work	Death	N	F	U
Can't reach easily	Injury	N	F	U
Just going on short trip	Get ticket	N	F	U
	Saves time	P	I	C
In a hurry	Easier	P	I	C
Accident has never happened to me	Freedom to move in seat	P	I	C
	Won't be trapped by belt	P	I	C
	Clothes won't get wrinkled by belt	P	I	C

Figure 5-2

Desired Behavior: Buckling Up Seat Belt

Antecedents	Consequences	P/N	I/F	C/U
Saw accident	Less chance of dying in accident	P	F	U
Got a ticket	Less chance of injury	P	F	U
Passenger asked to put it on	Took more time to get started	N	I	C
Saw police officer	Restricted movement	N	I	C
	Wrinkling clothes	N	I	C
	Felt uncomfortable	N	I	C

Figure 5-3

efits. What we don't want this performer to do (ride in a car without wearing seat belts) is associated with immediate positive reinforcement and the uncertain possibility of some future, possibly serious, injury.

If you put any problem behavior through this analysis it will essentially come out the same, whether the problem is at home, work, or play. What you will most certainly find is PICs for the problem behavior and NICs for the desired behavior. Let's take a look at a common work-related behavior problem, as shown in Figure 5-4.

As you can see, the undesired behavior (processing claims fast, without concern for quality) is met with a number of naturally occurring PICs. There are even several provided *by management* which actually conflict with the consequences that management professes to support.

The desired behavior, processing claims accurately (shown in Figure 5-5), results in a number of NICs, and the only positive consequences are future and uncertain. In this case, it will be difficult to encourage this employee to change behavior.

When doing an ABC analysis it is important to understand that the classification of a single consequence may be unimportant. What *is* important is the *pattern* of PICs and NICs you can identify. You will quickly find out that some consequences can be accurately classified only after much study.

Undesired Behavior: Processing Claims without Attention to Quality

Antecedents	Consequences	P/N	I/F	C/U
Peers do it that way	Easier to do	P	I	C
No feedback on individual errors	Takes less time	P	I	C
	Every claim processed is accepted	P	I	C
Performance appraisal has quantity category	Get praised by boss for meeting quantity goal	P	I	U
Office has quantity goals and graphs on wall	Customers are unhappy with company and cancel policy	N	F	U
Got chewed out for missing quantity goal				

Figure 5-4

Some consequences can't be classified at all. Since we are trying to look at the problem from the other person's perspective, we can be 100 percent accurate only if we can read minds, which I confess I can't.

However, we can identify patterns which will enable us to rearrange consequences so they are more favorable for the desired behavior.

As one of our consultants accurately stated: "The ability to do a good ABC analysis is an indirect measure of empathy."

Building Trust

By now you should begin to see that understanding and managing consequences is the most effective way to improve performance. In the following chapters, I will explain how to create, arrange, and provide effective consequences in the workplace. However, before we go on I must say a few words about trust.

Understanding why people behave the way they do and then arranging consequences to influence that behavior is only the beginning. The major factor in determining whether you can change behavior in the long term is dependent on the extent to which you can consistently *pair antecedents with consequences*. We call this dependable pairing of antecedents with consequences *trust*.

Desired Behavior: Process All Claims Accurately

Antecedents	Consequences	P/N	I/F	C/U
Signs in office (Quality is key)	Takes more time	N	I	C
	Less time to socialize	N	I	C
Boss said "Be careful"	Requires more effort	N	I	C
Performance appraisal has quality as a category	Requires more concentration	N	I	C
	Good appraisal	P	F	U
Got chewed out for mistakes from last month	Raise	P	F	U
Received training	Missed quantity goal	N	F	U

Figure 5-5

In other words, to be trusted all you have to do *(consequence) is what you* say *you are going to do (antecedent).*

An old saying goes: "After all is said and done, more is said than done." This is not only the way some managers and supervisors behave, but a characteristic of many companies as well.

If we tell somebody that doing something a particular way will be easier for them and it's not, we've slightly eroded their trust. If we tell someone if they work hard they will be better off, and they are not, we lose more credibility. If we tell people that they will be promoted, get a raise, get a transfer, head up a project, be on a team, and these things do not come to pass, we destroy trust.

Organizations often think that poor communication is the biggest barrier to organizational effectiveness. In reality, some organizations communicate too much rather than too little. If the organization is communicating things that don't happen, for whatever reasons, employee trust of upper management will be eroded and eventually become nonexistent. More communication is not better if we communicate about things that don't happen. Whatever we communicate, we have to make sure it happens.

When people say we don't communicate, they aren't saying that we don't talk. They are saying that after we talk nothing changes.

I've chosen to make this point now because you are about to learn how to use Performance Management skills to manage your business and to bring out the best in people.

If you view these principles and techniques as tools to manipulate behavior in your favor without requiring you to use them in absolute good faith, you will fail.

Once trust is established, people will give you the benefit of the doubt if you make a mistake. If you are not trusted, they will not believe you even when you tell the truth.

6

The High Price of Negative Reinforcement

Be careful that victories do not carry the seeds of future defeats.
Bits & Pieces Magazine

We are all well aware of the many efforts being made to improve the way we manage the workplace today: employee participation, teams, empowerment, and so on. With this swirl of activity one would think that positive reinforcement has become the dominate way that organizations are managed. Unfortunately, such is not the case.

In my many visits to organizations of all kinds, I can tell you without a doubt that negative reinforcement is still the dominant management style. As a matter of fact, Robert Levering and Milton Moskowitz, in their all new edition of the national best seller, *The 100 Best Companies to Work for in America,* make the following comment:

> . . . Found in all parts of the country and in all types of industry, they [the 100 best companies] represent a signal departure from the hierarchical, dictatorial workplace that has prevailed for so long in American business. But they are also exceptional rather than typical. They stand out because they are so different. Most companies still offer dreadful work environments.

Let me give you an example where an organizational practice thought to be positive became instead a very negative experience.

Several years ago a man approached me during a break in one of my seminars and said, "Our company has gone crazy over teams. You can't do anything by yourself anymore. I was on a team with eight other chemical engineers for 18 months. It was the worst experience of my industrial life." (The team was a cross-functional team working on a quality problem at a large industrial site.)

He continued, "There was not one time during the entire 18 months that all nine of us agreed on anything! We fought like cats and dogs! It seemed that everybody was out for their own interests without regard for the rest of the team. I never was so happy as when we completed our final report and disbanded the team! About two weeks later we all got a note from our boss's boss thanking us for our teamwork and cooperation."

I won't tell you what he said his boss could do with the memo because it is not polite, but he continued, "That's just the problem around here. Nobody at the top has the slightest idea what we have to put up with at the bottom. If he thinks he can just sit up there and dash us off a note and think he's got us in his hip pocket, he's got another thought coming!"

If I were to talk to the boss's boss about positive reinforcement, he would tell me that he is already doing it. He would probably pull out copies of the memos he sent to each team member to illustrate his claim.

What happened here? Aren't teams one way to create a positive work environment? Maybe, but in this case, was there any positive reinforcement at work? Well, obviously the work itself was not reinforcing; the team members did not reinforce each other; the boss's boss was insincere and even inaccurate with his note, so he provided no positive reinforcement. In other words, little positive reinforcement was available for the team members' behaviors.

So why did they labor for 18 months on the project? Because they had to. The engineer in this example and millions like him are behaving in new ways, not because they want to, but because they have to. Doing things because you have to do them is a sure sign that negative reinforcement is the consequence at work.

From the foregoing description it is obvious that the boss thinks he is managing through positive reinforcement, but is using negative reinforcement instead. Of course, no one will tell him, so he will probably continue sending well-meaning, but meaningless, memos.

This is not an uncommon problem. While there are few managers these days who will not agree that it is better to manage with positive reinforcement than with negative reinforcement, there are very few who understand the difference.

Programmatic attempts at positive management techniques demonstrate this lack of understanding. Just because you have teams, participation, and empowerment does not mean you are getting results through positive reinforcement. In fact, if these initiatives are being managed in the same way work was managed before they were begun, negative reinforcement is undoubtedly the dominant consequence.

Positive or Negative Reinforcement: What Difference Does It Make?

There are only two ways to get organizational results. One is through positive reinforcement and the other is through negative reinforcement. If both get results, why should we care?

I believe everybody would agree that if both positive and negative reinforcement got exactly the same results, it would still be better to use positive reinforcement. Why? First of all, people like positive reinforcement better. It produces a less stressful workplace. For this reason alone, positive reinforcement should be preferred.

However, there is an even more compelling business reason. *Positive reinforcement maximizes performance, while negative reinforcement gets a level of performance that is just enough to get by,* just enough to escape or avoid some unpleasant consequence. For example, a team brings a tough project in on time but everyone on the team knows they could have done the job in a shorter period of time.

Because both kinds of reinforcement get improvement, it is important for management to know whether the improvement has been accomplished through positive or negative reinforcement. You see, if you are getting results with negative reinforcement, you are missing the substantially greater results you could be getting if positive reinforcement was the consequence at work.

How Can You Know? What are the indications that you are using negative reinforcement when you think you are using positive reinforcement?

When I walk into a workplace there are several clues I look for that tell me which consequence is driving performance. Before going into each one in detail, let's examine the way negative reinforcement works to improve performance.

Let's say that due to a recent job change someone is assigned to you who is performing very poorly. Let's also say that you know the person is capable of good performance because that individual has performed much better in the past, but for a variety of reasons this person's performance dropped below satisfactory. Because the person has worked for the company for a long time, the previous supervisor tolerated the poor performance. Now, because of increased competitive pressures, everyone has to improve, so you cannot tolerate this individual's substandard performance.

You go to the employee and say, "Seventy parts per hour is entirely unsatisfactory, and if you can't get performance up to 100 parts per hour by 30 days from today, I will have to terminate you." Now let's say that the person believes you because he or she knows that you have terminated others in the past. In other words the person "is motivated" to change his or her performance to avoid some unpleasant consequence—termination. When will this employee get to the goal? Will it happen on day one? If you understand how consequences work, you know that it won't. Why not?

Deadlines give people permission to wait. By setting the goal 30 days away, you have told the person that it's okay to wait until the end of that time to get to the goal. That may not be what you meant, but if the person did wait and got to goal level on the last day, he or she would have avoided being fired under the conditions that you stated. Figure 6-1 shows graphically what this performance looks like.

Under these conditions, performance will get to goal only in the last few days of the established time period. Look at this situation from the employee's viewpoint. If he or she gets to goal in the first few days of the month, the only thing that the employee will get is to keep his or her

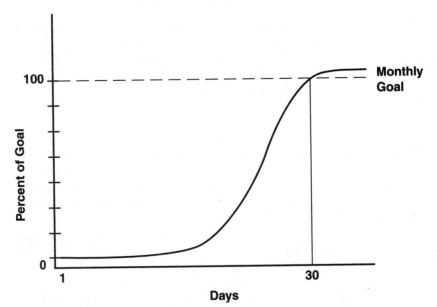

Figure 6-1

job—the same consequence that would transpire by waiting until the last day. In some cases, people fear that if they get to the goal too early, someone will raise it even higher. Under those conditions, most people will wait.

Goal attainment gives people permission to stop. Now let's suppose this "problem performer" gets to 100 parts per hour. What will the individual do now? He or she will probably hover around 100. The individual knows that even if he or she can do more, it's best to wait, because before long the goal will probably be raised anyway. If the employee holds back now, most likely it will be easier to reach the next goal.

W. Edwards Deming had observed this goal/performance phenomenon and frequently exhorts management to eliminate goals and standards. He says they limit performance. Could it be that setting goals actually does limit performance? Yes and no. It depends on whether the goal is a negative reinforcer or an antecedent for positive reinforcement.

To summarize, performance motivated by negative reinforcement will tend to increase only at the last minute, and then only to the "just enough to get by" level.

Five Easy Clues That Indicate Negative Reinforcement Is Present

The following indicators constitute a checklist for you to use to see if performance in your company or department is being driven by positive or negative reinforcement.

1. *The "J curve."* If performance shows a sharp rise just before a deadline, suspect negative reinforcement. If people are always scrambling at the last minute, working late and overtime to meet a deadline, check one for negative reinforcement.

2. *Negative talk.* If you hear people saying things like, "I hate this place," you don't have to look any further for your answer to the kind of motivation that's present.

However, more subtle negative talk will probably be the more common indicator. You may hear comments like:

"We work under a lot of pressure here."

"I've got too much on my plate."

"They expect too much."

"That's too hard."

"Why are we always the ones? Why not ask them?"

"That's not my job."

Management may say things like:

"That's what they are paid for."

"They oughta want to."

"It's their job. It's their responsibility."

"It's their fault."

Negative reinforcement produces negative talk. Positive reinforcement produces positive talk like:

"Let us go first."

"We can do it."

"Let me try."

"Is there anything I can do to help."

Check negative reinforcement if you hear negative talk.

3. *Performance goes flat after reaching goal.* The only way this would occur with positive reinforcement is if the goal represents the highest performance possible. In practically every case where you have significant improvement to get to goal and then improvement stops, you can be fairly sure that it was attained through negative reinforcement.

The use of stretch goals is also an indicator of negative reinforcement. I believe that stretch goals came about because managers noticed that unless they set additional goals, performance improvement stopped when the first goal was attained. By setting goals beyond the actual requirement, they were initially able to get more improvement. Stretch goals are used extensively, and I have unintentionally alienated a fair number of managers by criticizing them. However, if performance is driven by negative reinforcement, I cannot recommend stretch goals.

Another attempt at making goal setting more positive is to involve the performers in the development of their own goals. But even using performer participation to set goals does not guarantee that you are using positive reinforcement to attain them.

You may get the idea that I am against goal setting. I am not. Significant space will be devoted to the proper use of goals in Chapter 14.

4. *There is no plan for positive reinforcement.* If there is no plan to celebrate the achievement of a specific goal or the successful completion of an important project, the only consequence for completion is to start work on something else.

On the other hand, when the successful completion of some important task is an antecedent for positive reinforcement, people want to get started on another. If planning a celebration for achievement is not part of your planning and goal-setting process, and celebrations do not actually take place, you can probably put another check in the negative reinforcement column.

5. *If you remove a performance requirement and performance drops.* For example, if you announce to your work group or team that their involvement on a quality improvement team was purely voluntary and they stopped participating, you can bet that they were doing it only because they felt they had to do it.

Years ago, when I was consulting with the public schools, I would ask the classroom teacher to give the students an assignment and leave the room. When the teacher left, if the students stopped working and started talking, walking about the room, putting on makeup, throwing spitballs and erasers, or reading comic books, it indicated to me that they were studying only because they had to. If the students continued to study after the teacher left, it tended to indicate that they were studying because they wanted to.

George Halas, the legendary coach of the Chicago Bears football team was asked when he was 79 years old how much longer he intended to work. He replied, "It is only work if you had rather be somewhere else." It is a sad fact that large numbers of people at work today would rather be somewhere else.

Is Negative Reinforcement Ever Appropriate?   Everybody is negatively reinforced many times every day. We go to the dentist when we have to; we pay our taxes when we have to; we put on the brakes to avoid running into the car in front of us; we scratch when we itch; we put up our umbrellas when the rain starts falling. The list is long. *Negative reinforcement serves us well in those circumstances where all we need is compliance or minimum performance.*

Today, every business I know of is interested in world-class performance. *Attaining these goals requires much more than minimum performance.* Negative reinforcement will give you only incremental improvement. Breakthrough performance rarely occurs with negative reinforcement, but negative reinforcement does have application in business.

Sometimes There Is Nothing to Positively Reinforce.   If you have to look hard for something to reinforce, and the best you can come up with is, "You sure do have a neat, clean desk," you may have a performer in serious need of some negative reinforcement. If that individual is not performing in a way that gives you something to reinforce, the use of negative reinforcement may be very appropriate to start some behavior.

If someone is clearly not doing the job, and you know they are capable of doing it, it is appropriate to go to that person and say, "Your work is entirely unsatisfactory, and if you don't get your performance up to standard by this time next week you won't have a job here," or some other meaningful—and legitimate—threat.

Most of you reading this chapter are nodding your heads in agreement with this action, remembering times you used such a tactic, probably with some success. However, my experience is that most managers wait too long before dealing with poor performers. They hesitate before introducing this "do it or else" directive. However, once the manager does motivate the performer to improve by using this negative reinforcement approach, the manager must be prepared to positively reinforce every improvement that occurs. Unfortunately, most managers find it difficult to reinforce small improvements by a performer who has been the source of problems in the workplace.

If you manage someone, and you can't bring yourself to deliver any form of positive reinforcement for improvements that occur because you feel he or she doesn't deserve it, or you are angry at the person, you would be better served to find another place for that person to work, either inside or outside the company.

Without the addition of positive reinforcement for improved performance, the improvements you get through negative reinforcement will soon disappear. The past problems will resurface, and they will probably be worse.

Management Is No Place to Hold a Grudge.   If you truly want your people to improve their performance, you have to forget the problems of the past and focus on the improved performance occurring in the present. Negative reinforcement can start a poor performer moving in the right direction, but only positive reinforcement can keep that person going. If you can't respond to performance as it is happening today, you will not be able to develop people. As Benjamin Franklin once said,

"Write people's accomplishments in stone and their faults in the sand."

Negative Reinforcement and the Illusion of Control

The fact that negative reinforcement seems to work better than positive reinforcement is an illusion. It gives the illusion of saving time, money, and effort. In reality, it does none of those things. This illusion is grounded only in personal experience, not in scientific fact. Let me expose the illusion.

Negative Reinforcement and Control

Technically, managers get things done through either positive or negative reinforcement, which are the only behavioral consequences that increase behavior. Although most people think they use positive reinforcement to get things done, the fact is that, most of the time, they don't.

Negative reinforcement is most easily recognized as the "do it or else" management approach. However, it is often difficult to spot today because modern negative reinforcement methods are much more subtle than in days gone by. The picture of a red-faced supervisor yelling threats laced with obscenities used to be a daily affair that is etched in the memories of many old-timers. This scene has all but disappeared from the workplace, but negative reinforcement hasn't. Today, it is found most often in the use of stretch goals, threats of layoff, increased workloads, and the lack of positive reinforcement.

Because there are only a few businesses that have not been touched by a series of layoffs, the threat is always there that "you could be next," no matter what your position or performance level. Under negative reinforcement, people work because they "have to," not because they "want to." Doing a "good job" is what you are expected to do and not doing one is a cause for management intervention. Under this management style, the motivation is to avoid some negative consequence rather than to get a positive one.

Managers who use this style talk of control, authority, and accountability. They want people to take individual responsibility and be held personally accountable. These are code words and phrases for needing the ability to use negative consequences on people who fail to live up to their responsibilities.

I have heard it said many times that managers are afraid they will "lose control" with positive reinforcement. The fact is that they don't have control with negative reinforcement in the first place. With negative reinforcement you lose control of the following:

1. *You don't have control of your time.* For negative reinforcement to work at all, the threat of punishment for the wrong behavior must be imminent. That is, as long as the boss is physically present, he can get a certain performance. When the threat is removed by absence of this punisher, performance drops. This means that the negative reinforcement manager must be always vigilant and present in person or by representation. Some companies have installed video cameras to monitor performers. Computer pro-

grams are set up to monitor whether computers are being used for business or personal use. Telephone bills are printed out by telephone, by individual phones, and by call to be sure they are being used only for business. The interesting thing about this is that all of it requires management to add considerable monitoring time to their already busy days.

Because under negative reinforcement control, you can't trust people to monitor themselves, you must do those things that guarantee that the company is getting what it is paying for. Checking up on people by meetings, by wandering around, by watching videotapes, or by analyzing telephone bills ties management down and eats up time. As it relates to control the question is, who is controlling whom? I know a sales manager who holds a sales meeting every Friday afternoon to make sure that all the salespeople work a full day on Friday. Whether they are working is an open question, but at least they are there. But guess what, so is he! The sales manager never gets a Friday afternoon off.

2. *You don't have control of your budget.* Because there is no positive reinforcement for beating your budget under negative reinforcement control, the incentive is to spend it all. The manager thinks that he is exercising fiscal control when he monitors spending closely, and applies negative consequences to any that exceed allotted amounts. In reality, he is not being fiscally responsible if fiscally responsible means getting the best value for the dollar spent. The first time I had responsibility for a budget in my job at the hospital, I thought saving money while meeting my departmental objectives was actually a good thing. My first year I actually beat my budget by a substantial amount. I was pleased until I realized that my budget for the following year was reduced by almost the same amount as the savings. What made it worse was that another department that I thought wasted money and practically always overspent their budget got an increase! It was the last time I had any savings. Need I say more?

Everybody who has done business with the government knows about the last-minute spending at the end of the fiscal year. Even though a manager in this situation seems to be in control, it is certainly illusory because money is often being spent before it needs to, and in some cases, it is spent foolishly.

3. *You don't have control of performance.* A dead giveaway of negative reinforcement is when performance stops when the goal is reached. This is such a common occurrence that it has led to widespread use of "stretch goals" to let performers know that they are not through when they get to their first goal. This gives the illusion that the manager is in control when the goals are met. In reality, the performers are in control because they have typically "saved some performance for a rainy day."

"Banking" is a term often used in sales to describe a salesperson who reaches quota and stops turning in additional sales in that period, saving them for the next one. Although not as obvious in other work situations, it is more common than usually thought. Deming actually advised managers to "eliminate goals and standards" because he saw that they capped performance. That is, if you have a standard of 20 units per hour, the most you usually get is 20 per hour. It is not the goals and standards that cap performance, it is that they are used as negative reinforcers. With negative reinforcement you never know what people are capable of doing; you only know what they did, because at best they only give you a little more than is needed to avoid some undesirable consequence. A plant's manufacturing department had never met engineered standards. In labor negotiations the company put in an incentive for meeting standard. When they met standard they could quit work for the day. They consistently finished before noon!

A manager of a motel, a retired Army master sergeant, could not have been more negative in his management style unless he had packed a 45-caliber pistol on his belt and threatened to shoot people when they didn't perform to his standards. When I pointed this out to the VP of operations for the motel chain, he replied that "Gene has the best back-of-the-house cost in the company." I simply replied that I thought he was a problem, but it was the VP's decision as to whether any action was taken. None was. The other 10 motels in the company implemented a positive reinforcement system in their properties, and by the end of the year, Gene was on the bottom of the list. His performance had not slipped, the others had improved. By relying on negative reinforcement, there was no way that Gene could get more out of his employees.

A similar situation occurred with the manager of street sales for a newspaper. When the manager's negative style was pointed out to upper management, they informed the consultant working with them that this man was a legend in the newspaper industry. He gave talks to industry meetings about how to manage street sales. He was completely dedicated to his job. As management began to see the progress other managers were making when they changed their management behavior from negative to positive, they moved him to another position at the paper. Within the next six months, street sales increased almost 30 percent.

4. *You don't have control of your feelings and your health.* Because negative reinforcement cannot occur without some degree of fear, the work environment is filled with stress. Keeping employees on their toes with negative reinforcement takes its toll on the manager as well as the employees. Short tempers, hurt feelings, and hostile interactions are a daily occurrence. The pressure created by lackluster performance, negative talk, and meeting goals just in time takes its toll, resulting in frayed nerves and stress-related

illnesses. The best antidote to stress in the workplace is positive reinforcement. Positive reinforcement neutralizes most harmful stress.

Why, then, is it that the use of negative consequences is by far the more common way of getting things done in business, industry, and government? It is very simple. Mother Nature pulls a trick on us. Negative reinforcement is more likely to provide a PIC for the user than is positive reinforcement. If you positively reinforce a behavior, you will have to wait until the next time there is an opportunity for that behavior to occur to see if your positive reinforcement effort worked (PFU). If you use negative reinforcement, you are likely to see increased activity immediately (PIC).

This trick of nature hides the fact that when a substantial performance improvement is needed, the best and fastest way to get it is with positive reinforcement. Remember that positive reinforcement *accelerates* behavior. It is the only consequence that does.

Tough, competitive times demand positive reinforcement.

7

Capturing Discretionary Effort Through Positive Reinforcement

Most people only know what happened;
only those who know this technology,
know what's possible.
                    HANK PENNYPACKER, PhD.
                    University of Florida

Most American workers admit they could do a better job if they were properly motivated.

In a "Public Agenda Report on Restoring America's Competitive Vitality," Yankelovich and Immerwahr (1983) reported that fewer than one out of four employees, 23 percent, said they were performing to their full potential and capacity. The majority agreed that they could increase their effectiveness significantly. Nearly half of the work force, 44 percent, revealed that they did what is required of them and held back any extra effort.

Can you imagine what could be accomplished by our work force if every employee worked up to their full potential every day?

The question every business leader should be asking is how do we motivate people to do their best because they "want to" rather than doing only what they "have to"? To answer that question you need to understand the concept of *discretionary effort.*

Discretionary effort is defined as *that level of effort people could give if they wanted to,* but which is beyond what is required. In other words, since discretionary effort is above and beyond what is expected, demanded, paid for, planned for, there would be no punishment to the performers if they didn't do it. Discretionary effort is what is possible. In many organizations today, management is happy just to get what is expected.

Discretionary effort is within the power of every individual to give or withhold. All of us have "given a little extra" on many occasions, usually on projects that held some special interest for us. Most often, this extra effort was expended on a project at home or in some activity that we enjoy.

The only way business can capture discretionary effort is through the effective use of positive reinforcement. As Russell Justice of Eastman Chemicals has said:

> Discretionary effort is like loose change in a person's pocket. It is management's job to get them to want to spend it all every day.

Positive reinforcement is clearly the most effective way to manage any business. Nevertheless, of all the ways to manage, it is the most misunderstood and misused.

When most people hear the words "positive reinforcement" they immediately think of things like "atta-boys," a pat on the back, a service plaque, a round of applause at a company meeting, or some kind of public recognition like "Employee of the Month."

"Isn't that what you are talking about when you say positive reinforcement?" they ask me. My reply is always the same. "Absolutely not!" This shallow understanding of positive reinforcement is what prevents many managers from using it to motivate people and improve performance.

What Does Positive Reinforcement Look Like?

Let me remind you of the definition of positive reinforcement. *Positive reinforcement is any consequence that follows a behavior and increases its frequency in the future.* The fact is that most of what motivates us day to day are little things that people do or do not do that make a big difference.

If you ask people if they got any positive reinforcement at work yesterday, most would say no. In fact everybody at work gets positive reinforcement thousands of times every day.

When you walk into your office and flip on the light switch, you get positively reinforced when the light comes on. When you pull on a desk drawer, your behavior is positively reinforced by the drawer opening. When you press your pen on a piece of paper and it makes a mark, you are positively reinforced for using the pen. When you call somebody's name, you get positively reinforced by the person responding. Every time I push a key on my computer and the correct letter appears on the screen, my key-press behavior is positively reinforced.

When you understand positive reinforcement in this context, you see how frequently it occurs in everyday functioning. If reinforcement were not built into these performances, the behavior would stop. If I pushed a key and never got the right letter on the screen or no letter appeared, I would quickly stop pressing the keys. If I flipped a light switch and the light never came on, I would quickly stop flipping the switch.

Apple Computer, Inc., gets the credit for coming up with the concept of "user-friendly." This was a stroke of genius because early in the development of computers most people were not positively reinforced for trying to use them. "User-friendly" is another word for positive reinforcement. At some level at least, the developers at Apple understood that if their computers were easier to use (more positively reinforcing to the user), their market would be greatly expanded.

The mouse, menus, and windows are all attempts to put positive reinforcement into using the computer. These days many computer programs are so reinforcing that if you know how to turn the computer on you can use it. The antecedent "Press any key to start" guarantees that anyone who can read will get reinforced.

Positive reinforcement occurs every time a behavior produces a favorable change in the environment for the performer.

The problem with most work is that it has not been designed so that positive reinforcement occurs as a natural part of the process. For example, a clerk processing insurance claims does not get positively reinforced every time he or she processes a claim. Why?

Because while the clerk was completing one claim, two more were added to the pile. The only natural consequence for processing the claims faster is getting more to do. It is easy to see why someone who has been processing claims for any period of time would lose their sense of urgency.

In tasks like these, management has to do something to put positive reinforcement into the job, or people will never do their best. At Blue Cross/ Blue Shield of Alabama, when management engineered positive reinforcement into the claims adjudication process, performance increased almost 300 percent! Although this result is outstanding, it has been duplicated many times in many different jobs.

Kinds of Positive Reinforcement

There are two ways for positive reinforcement to occur: naturally and created. The examples of reinforcement illustrated earlier were natural reinforcement. Natural reinforcement occurs when the behavior automatically produces it. Pushing the button on a water fountain automatically produces reinforcement in the form of water.

Created reinforcement does not occur automatically, but must be added by a person. A congratulatory note, praise, public acknowledgment, money, a plaque, or a trophy are all forms of created reinforcement.

Social or Tangible.   The two most common forms of created reinforcement are: social and tangible. Social reinforcement is reinforcement that involves doing or saying something to another. Social reinforcement includes symbolic reinforcement and anything that has *trophy value*. In this context, trophy value means that the trophy or symbolic reinforcer would have value only to the person or persons receiving it. Tangible reinforcement is a positive reinforcer that has *salvage value,* that is, something that would have value to someone else.

The most available form of created reinforcement is social reinforcement. You do not have to have a budget for it; you do not need permission to give it; and, when given correctly, people never tire of it.

Tangible reinforcement should serve as a backup to social reinforcement—not a substitute for it. A client of ours knew that early attempts at positive reinforcement were in trouble when a supervisor, handing out merchandise earned with points for improved quality, told an employee, "Here's your damn toaster. Now get your butt back to work!"

I'll bet toast from that toaster never tasted good. In all likelihood, every time that employee looked at the toaster it reminded him of somebody he hated.

All tangible reinforcers should be paired with social reinforcement.

I will talk more about this in Chapter 24.

It's an Individual Thing.   Whether natural or created, what is reinforcing to a person is highly individualistic. Some people like mechanical things; others hate them. Some like sports; others don't. Some like to be with people; others like to be alone. Whatever you can name, you will find people who like it and people who don't.

This means that in order to effectively reinforce, you must first understand what people want. Because reinforcement is an individual thing, this approach to management is the most employee-focused of all the current approaches. What works with one person may not work with another. If you are looking for something that will work for everybody, stop. You won't find it. It doesn't exist.

This may sound too hard or time-consuming, but it's not. The advantages you gain from increased performance make it well worth treating people as individuals—not to mention the improvement in interpersonal relationships that will result.

What Do They Want Anyway? Finding Reinforcers. There are three ways of finding out what is reinforcing: ask, try, and observe. Although common sense tells most people that the first thing you would do is ask, common sense would fail you again.

Try Something. Usually, the best way to start positive reinforcement is to try something that you think might work. The majority of the time, it *will* work, because people generally find attempts at reinforcement to be reinforcing. If you make a mistake trying to positively reinforce, people will generally forgive you.

What do you try? You try things that others have found to be effective. Attention is usually a positive reinforcer because it shows you are interested in what a person is doing. If you give approval for a particular action taken, it will probably be received as positive reinforcement. Most people like to be appreciated, so anything that demonstrates that you value them and their efforts will likely be reinforcing. Remember, you will know you have positively reinforced a particular behavior if you try and the behavior increases. If it doesn't, try again.

Ask. The reason asking should not be the first thing you do to discover what is reinforcing is that you may run into one or more of the following problems: (1) people may not know, (2) they may not want to tell you, (3) they may tell you what they think you want them to say rather than what they really want, and (4) asking may set up false expectations.

1. If you ask most people what their positive reinforcers are, they probably won't know what you are talking about. In addition, what a person thinks is a positive reinforcer may not be one. What they think they would work for and what they would actually work for may be very different.

2. Because of the way many people have been treated at work, they may be suspicious of your motives if you ask them what they like. If they have been managed with punishment and negative reinforcement, they may not trust you to use the information to their benefit.

3. In the climate of uncertainty created by reorganization and downsizing, people tend to "hold back." They may try to tell you what they think you want to hear rather than risk saying something that might label them as unambitious or put them in the category of "problem employee."

4. It is not unusual for managers, who think positive reinforcement is easy, to walk into a meeting and ask people what they want. This approach is very dangerous because it may set expectations that whatever is requested will be forthcoming. Obviously, all the things that people want will not be available at work, but this casual approach to identifying reinforcers may lead people to believe they will be. When, subsequently, what they asked for does not become available, they become disappointed and even angry.

For these reasons, asking is not the first way to find reinforcers. Rather, after you have tried something, ask them how they liked what you did. At this point they have a frame of reference against which to suggest other things that are likely to be acceptable. For example, if you bought lunch to reward some specific improvement in performance, when you ask what other things would be reinforcing, it is unlikely they will say "an extra week off with pay." In other words, your initial attempt will establish realistic expectations for positive reinforcement.

Observe. You can discover a lot of potential reinforcers simply by observing what people spend their time doing when they have a choice. Many reinforcers can also be discovered just by talking to people or, better yet, by listening to them.

Unfortunately, we are so busy telling people what we want that we have little time left to listen to what they want.

Grandma's Law

David Premack, a psychologist, discovered in his research that when people are given a choice of things to do, whatever they consistently choose can be used as a reinforcer for the behaviors not chosen. His discovery is called "the Premack principle." This has been more simply translated by Ogden Lindsley, who calls this principle "Grandma's law."

Grandma's law states, "If you eat your vegetables, you can have dessert." Eating vegetables is a low-frequency choice for most children. Eating dessert is a high-frequency choice. When the high-frequency choice is made contingent on the low-frequency choice, children not only eat more vegetables, but may learn over time to like them.

At work this means that if we watch how people spend their time when they have a choice, we can identify reinforcers for them. If a mechanic spends most of his or her unassigned time repairing electric motors instead of doing something else, we can assume that repairing electric motors is a reinforcer to that mechanic. When given a choice of leads, a salesperson always chooses to call on large companies rather than small ones. That would tell us that the opportunity to call on a large client could be used as a reinforcer for that salesperson.

Grandma's law has some personal applications too. In fact, it represents the best time-management technique available today. Here's how it works. Make a list of all the things you need to do. Rank them from the things you most want to do or enjoy doing to the things you least like to do. *Then start working at the bottom of the list.*

If you do this you will notice an interesting phenomena as you complete tasks. When you start at the bottom, every time you finish a task the next one on the list is more desirable, enjoyable, or interesting. If you start at the top, where most people start, the consequence of completing a task is that the next one is more undesirable, difficult, boring, etc. In the latter approach, you look for an excuse to quit. In the former, you don't want to quit until all the tasks are done, and if you stop in the middle, you can't wait to get started again.

Case Study

Gary Lorgan, department manager of Kodak's Image Loops and Sundries Department, put Grandma's law to the test. The Image Loops and Sundries Department produces image loops for Kodak's Ektaprint copiers.

Lorgan observed that the operators in his department enjoyed working on special work-related projects, usually team activities aimed at improving production quality and the production process. Of course, improvement in both areas is beneficial to the organization, so Lorgan and production supervisor, Karyn Johnson, decided to use team activities to reinforce the operators for meeting weekly production and quality standards.

"When the operators reach their weekly goal for each type of loop, we shut down production and let them work on other projects," explains Lorgan. In these small team activities the operators, at their own initiative, develop ideas for improving the operation and break into teams of two to ten people to implement them.

"We have had 15 or 20 improvements that have been made right on the production line as a result of the operators' team activities," Lorgan notes. Our production quotas are not easy to meet, but there have been times when we've made the goal late on Thursday and had the entire day Friday for team activities. Other times we've made goal just before the end of the shift or didn't make the weekly quota at all. There is no guarantee they will make it every week, but when they do, we turn them loose on their special interest projects.

"The operators thrive on the challenge. They monitor their own progress on a large 6- by 10-foot bar graph. Their graphs reflect cumulative effort, and each team has its own color to designate its contribution to production. The color-coded production measures make each team's results visible. This way, they get feedback on how they are doing and how they are contributing toward the weekly goal. Highly visible daily feedback toward a common goal has inspired the operators to find ways to help each other eliminate unnecessary activities, for example, paperwork and testing.

"They are so anxious to move on to their special projects that on three occasions, some operators have finished early and *volunteered* to continue working to make up a previous week's shortfall. They were able to get to their team activities those weeks, and they seemed to enjoy catching up. So that quality doesn't take a back seat to quantity, the operators perform random daily quality audits, graphing those results as well."

Since starting the team activities, production has gone up, but Lorgan sees that as the side benefit of Grandma's law. He is pleased with the production increase, but remarks, "Our primary goal is not to increase productivity, but to maintain it while emphasizing quality." Operational improvements made by the teams are the real plus for day-to-day operations. "The best thing about it is, the improvements are their ideas, and they feel good about it in the end."

Sources of Positive Reinforcement

As I discussed earlier, positive reinforcement surrounds us at work. As illustrated by Grandma's law, it can even come from the work itself. But it also comes from peers, from supervisors and managers, and from the environment.

Work-Related Reinforcement.   The term *operant conditioning* was introduced by B. F. Skinner to explain the primary way in which we learn. What he meant was that a behavior that *operates* on the environment to produce a desirable effect for the person will be strengthened (i.e., it will occur more frequently in the future).

When we do things that "work" we are positively reinforced by the task itself. Things that go smoother or are easier when done a certain way will typically always be done that way. The "user-friendly" computer example described earlier is a good example of work-related reinforcement. Anytime we can arrange a task so that reinforcement is automatically associated with the task, we will be more likely to get that task repeated.

The concept of "job enrichment" was a well-intentioned attempt to put reinforcement into the work, but it generally has failed to meet that objective. Job simplification and job enlargement have met similar fates. Whether a clerk completes part of a form or all of the form makes little difference if the only consequence is that he or she has another one to do. Whether a person on an assembly line puts the door on a car or builds the whole car makes little difference if good performance is taken for granted and poor performance is criticized. Building the complete car can be just as boring as putting on doors—after you've done it 20,000 times.

These efforts at making work more interesting have not succeeded, because rearranging or changing the tasks is not (and never was) the issue. What has to be rearranged in the work process is positive reinforcement. Finding ways to put reinforcement into the work itself is a great first step, and one that should be taken by every manager and supervisor. Grandma's law is worth trying. I will give some additional direction on how to make work more reinforcing in Chapter 20. However, even if reinforcement is built into the job, it will rarely be enough to bring out the best in people. Other sources of reinforcement must be tapped.

Peer-Related Reinforcement.   Peers are the most effective source of reinforcement at work—and the most underutilized. They are in the best position to deliver positive and immediate reinforcement (PICs) because they can observe performance more closely and more often than most supervisors and managers.

This source of reinforcement is rarely tapped by the organization. The problem is that most employees have never learned that it is a part of their responsibility to provide reinforcement to their peers. Worse, they are not reinforced by management when they do. The whole concept of teams has missed the mark on peer reinforcement and, as a result, has had little measurable success in improving organizational performance. Instead of using the proximity of peers to provide one another with positive reinforcement for work-related behaviors, organizations have focused teams on making process improvements. Process improvement is, of course, very important. However without attention to the reinforcement of team members by team members, teams produce relatively few improvements and never achieve their potential. Often teams stay together but are a team in name only.

When peers recognize that they can and should be a major source of reinforcement for each other, improvements occur more frequently, much faster, and last much longer.

Management-Related Reinforcement.   Since management has the overall responsibility for performance, it also has the responsibility for coordinating reinforcement. This is not to say that managers are responsible for providing all reinforcement. As we've noted, managers are responsible for providing the appropriate consequences for performance, and the most important consequence they can provide is positive reinforcement. But it is not practical and, in fact, it is not possible for managers and supervisors to provide all the reinforcement employees will receive. The job of management is to ensure that reinforcement occurs for the right behavior, at the necessary frequency, and from all sources available. Planning and delivering reinforcement are the two most important behaviors of supervisors and managers.

The manager who can harness the power of positive reinforcement for value-added performance will be the manager who can capture and enjoy the benefits of discretionary effort.

8

Decreasing Behavior— Intentionally or Otherwise

By now you know that if behaviors are occurring there must be some reinforcement for them somewhere in the environment. No reinforcement equals no behavior. And you have known for a long time that the behavior that occurs is not always the behavior that you want. We have spent the last two chapters talking about how to increase and even maximize behavior. We will spend this chapter talking about how to reduce or even stop behavior.

I described the consequences that stop or reduce behavior briefly in Chapter 4. They are referred to as *punishment* and *penalty*. Like all four consequences, when appropriately applied, they do work. Obviously, you would like to be able to stop behavior you don't want. Unfortunately, consequences always affect behavior, so just as you can inadvertently reinforce behavior you don't want, you can also inadvertently punish and extinguish behavior you do want. If you and others in your organization are unaware of the effect of consequences on behavior, it is possible that you are stopping behavior that you want people to do. In order to understand more fully what is happening in your company, let's discuss the effects of punishment and penalty in detail.

Punishment and Penalty— Stopping Behavior

What do you do when people do things that are unsafe, unhealthy, unfair, unethical, or illegal? If possible, you act to stop these kinds of actions immediately because of the high level of potential damage they represent.

Punishment and penalty are active consequences that follow behavior and decrease its frequency in the future. As described in Chapter 4, punishment occurs when a behavior produces something the performer does not want. Penalty occurs when a behavior results in the performer losing something that he has.

Although it is necessary to use punishment and penalty from time to time, they should be used sparingly. Both are difficult to use. Although they may decrease or stop behavior, they do not predict what behavior will replace the one you have stopped. Punishment and penalty should always be used in conjunction with positive reinforcement for the desired alternative behavior.

> *Warning: Stopping problem behavior does not mean that a positive or productive behavior will take its place.*

Much of the punishment that occurs in business is not planned; it's inadvertent.

Everybody is familiar with the manager who "fusses at" the person who brings bad news, and can't understand why, after a while, no one will reveal problems.

Take the case of a fiberglass plant where they were having a difficult time producing a particular product. The line had not met standard for almost two years and was running at a significant loss. The engineers had been unsuccessful in correcting the problem.

Finally, management decided to try a different approach. They got the employees from each shift together and asked for their input.

On the first shift, when someone would make a suggestion, the engineer who was writing down the suggestions would ask follow-up questions to make sure he knew exactly what the person was talking about.

In the second shift, everything was the same, but in this case the department superintendent, an acknowledged expert in fiberglass manufacturing, was in attendance. Within the first 10 minutes he jumped up three different times to show people why what they had suggested wouldn't work.

The first group produced over 50 suggestions. The second group produced only six. The difference? In the second shift the superintendent punished people for their ideas. He didn't intend to; he just wanted to use this opportunity to teach the group something. Instead, every worker who offered an idea was made to feel stupid in front of his or her peers. The idea-giving behavior was stopped cold.

Different Strokes . . .

Some of the same characteristics that make positive reinforcement effective also make punishment effective. Just as with positive reinforcement, what is punishing to one may not be punishing to others. Believe it or not, getting chewed out may be punishing to one person and positively reinforcing to another. The only way you can really tell is by what happens to the behavior after the chewing out.

In the same vein, delayed punishment is no more effective than delayed reinforcement. One of the things that reduces the effectiveness of the criminal justice system is the long delay between the commission of a crime and the start of the sentence.

In organizations that have progressive discipline systems, the fact that someone progresses through the system tells you that the consequences are not punishing. But the amount of time that it takes to mete out the punishment is probably more important.

Look at your system and see what the average interval is from the infraction of the rules to the punishing consequence. Immediate consequences are the most effective, and any lengthy interval diminishes the effectiveness considerably.

Punishment Never Solves a Problem

Because punishment only stops behavior, it does not add value to a business. The only reason we would want a person to stop an unproductive behavior is to replace it with a productive one. *Punishment doesn't tell people what you want them to do; it only tells them what not to do.* It is quite possible that you could stop one undesirable behavior and have another equally undesirable one take its place.

For this reason, you should never punish one behavior without knowing what you want in its place and reinforcing the desirable one as soon as it occurs.

Recovery

One of the problems with the use of punishment and penalty to stop behavior is that when they stop, if an alternate behavior is not reinforced, the old behavior will recover. Technically, recovery refers to the fact that punished behavior will return to nonpunished levels when the punishment or penalty is stopped.

The effect of getting a speeding ticket may last only until the trooper is out of sight. Why do most criminals go to jail many times over their lifetimes? Prison obviously did not stop the criminal activity permanently. When behaviors incompatible with criminal activity are not reinforced, you can expect that the old behavior will recover soon after getting in an environment where there is no immediate threat of punishment or penalty. Punishment and penalty never solve a problem. At best they stop behavior long enough for you to find a way to reinforce behavior that is productive.

Extinction—Doing Nothing Changes Behavior

There is another way behavior is stopped, and it is the most common way organizations unintentionally demotivate people.

Extinction is what happens when a behavior occurs with no reinforcement. In other words, *extinction means withholding or not delivering reinforcement for previously reinforced behavior.*

Someone tells what he or she thinks is a funny joke. After the joke, the teller starts laughing hysterically. Then the individual suddenly realizes no one else is laughing. Immediately, the joke teller stops laughing as well. If the same joke is told a couple more times with the same response, the individual will no doubt eliminate it from his or her repertoire.

In the same way, a new employee arrives on the scene believing that his or her best work is what is required and is more than willing to oblige. After a few months on the job, "going the extra mile," the employee realizes that nobody notices. Like the joker in the first example, this person soon eliminates extra effort from his or her repertoire.

If you want a behavior or performance to continue, you must make sure that it is being reinforced. Since failing to reinforce productive performance is tantamount to extinction, it's easy to see why performance and motivation drop off in even the best people.

They are simply not getting the reinforcement they need to continue doing a good job. This is why in work environments where management is not making a conscious attempt to positively reinforce, the extinction of discretionary effort is almost assured.

But there are behaviors we want to eliminate, and at those times the intentional use of extinction can be very helpful. We are all familiar with the saying, "Just ignore it, and it'll go away." That's basically how extinction works. However, as you might imagine, if it were that easy, we wouldn't have to deal with it in this book. To bring out the best in people you need a much more complete understanding of extinction.

Let's look at an example to which everybody can relate. Mom and Dad are having trouble getting Johnny to sleep alone. When they put him to bed he starts crying. His parents ignore him for a while, but after a few minutes of crying they go get him and bring him into their bed. They admonish him all the while that he must learn to sleep in his own bed, but he continues to sleep in theirs. A helpful relative suggests that it will not hurt the little boy if he is allowed to cry, and assures the parent that if they leave him in his bed he will stop crying after only a few nights.

What actually does happen is known to almost everybody. It goes like this.

1. The parents let the child cry for longer than usual.

2. He cries louder than usual.

3. The parents think something must be wrong.

4. They give in to him at this point; he ends up in their bed.

You probably know that the next night, he will cry louder and longer. Let's assume they don't go to him, but rather they stick it out.

If crying louder doesn't bring the parents, the child may begin to flail about in his crib, crying all the while. If the parents don't go in, he will eventually stop crying. After he is quiet for a few minutes he may start crying again, but this time if his parents don't come in to get him, he will stop sooner than the night before. This may go on for a few nights, but each night the crying will get shorter, and in a relatively short time he will stop—if the parents can stick with their plan for ignoring the crying.

While this is not a business example, when you understand the different aspects of extinction in this problem, you will understand how to fix some of your motivational problems at work.

Extinction Burst. The first thing that happens when a well-developed behavior is ignored is an increase in the behavior. In other words, the behavior that is being extinguished will actually occur more often. We witness this in our everyday affairs. If we push the button for an elevator and it is slow to arrive, we will push the button several times in succession, although this has no effect on the elevator.

If we lose something, we probably look in the same places over and over. In an election, when a candidate begins to slip in the polls, he or she tries harder, makes more appearances, criticizes the opponent more vehemently. If someone is a chronic complainer and you ignore the complaints, he or she may actually complain about more things, and with more agitation. This is a predictable and naturally occurring phenomenon. You can see it at every level of society.

At work, when you hear things like, "We've got to get back to basics," or "We've got to try harder," you are hearing an extinction burst. People get comfortable with the way they have always done things, and initially will try to do more of it when it stops being reinforced.

Doing the same things harder will rarely solve problems. If what was being done all along could have solved the problem, it would have already been solved. Doing the same thing harder is often an indication that the behavior is undergoing extinction.

Emotional Behavior.   Following the extinction burst, you will usually see negative emotional behavior. The child flails about in his crib, the candidate gets more venomous, an individual kicks the elevator when it doesn't arrive.

If you are not prepared to handle the emotional behavior, you better not try to use extinction. It is not uncommon to see strikes settled during the emotional behavior phase, which of course increases the probability of violence in future strikes.

Negative emotional behavior is further evidence that extinction is occurring.

Erratic Behavior.   After the emotional behavior has run its course, the behavior will continue to occur at various, irregular intervals until it stops altogether.

Sometimes the behavior will be replaced by a similar behavior. It is during this period of erratic behavior that you must be careful not to reinforce new, undesired behavior. The amount of time it takes for the behavior to finally stop is affected by a number of variables but, in general, the more reinforcement the person has received for the behavior in the past, the more time required for extinction.

Resurgence.   When the old behavior has stopped for a period of time, it is not unusual for it to occur again, seemingly out of nowhere. This has led many of us to believe that people don't really change. You see someone try to eliminate a habit, quit for a while, but eventually go back to the old ways.

The resurgence of the old habit is an indication that the behavior(s) that replaced it are not getting enough reinforcement to maintain them.

We see this occur in many people who try to quit smoking or drinking or who are trying to lose weight. They will have some initial success only to revert to the old habit.

The key to making the consequence of extinction work to eliminate an unwanted behavior is to *introduce positive reinforcement for a productive alternative behavior.* For example, at work there may be a person who constantly interrupts meetings with sarcastic, hostile comments. The group could put these comments on extinction by ignoring them. Then they should positively reinforce constructive comments and questions. When you want to extinguish behavior, you need to be prepared for the four previously mentioned aspects of extinction. If you don't think you will be able to handle them all, you need to chose another consequence.

> *Problems in the workplace are often created not by what we do, but by what we fail to do.*

Bringing out the best in people is not only about getting more of what you want, but getting less of what you don't want. All four consequences I have presented have appropriate application at work. But like any skill, the use of behavioral consequences to manage people takes time to learn. There are right ways to use them, and there are attempts that fall short. We are going to present some very specific applications for all four consequences in the remainder of this book.

9
Effective Delivery of Reinforcement

If people are not told they are appreciated
they will assume the opposite.

If positive reinforcement is so effective, why is it not more commonly used in business?

One reason is that managers are more likely to be positively reinforced when they punish or use negative reinforcement than when they use positive reinforcement. Think back to the chapter on consequences (Chapter 4). You may recall that consequences that are Positive-Immediate-Certain (PICs) are much more powerful than those that are delayed. A manager is more likely to receive positive immediate consequences when delivering punishment than when delivering positive reinforcement. The reason? If punishment is going to work, it will typically work right away. The manager gets what he or she wants (usually some inappropriate behavior stops immediately), and this provides the manager with a PIC. The manager, like all of us, will tend to repeat that punishing behavior because it was reinforced. Likewise, negative reinforcement ("Do it or else!") will result in an increase in activity, providing positive reinforcement for the manager again.

When that same manager uses positive reinforcement, he or she will have to wait until there is an occasion for the behavior to occur again to know whether the reinforcement had any effect on the performer. In this case, the consequence for the manager is a PFU (Positive-Future-Uncertain), not a powerful consequence.

Another reason positive reinforcement is not the predominant consequence at work is that many managers have tried to use it and have been unsuccessful. I've heard many times, "Oh, I tried to reinforce them and it didn't work." Of course, by now you know that can't happen. Reinforcement always works! It is defined that way. It has to increase behavior or it isn't a reinforcer.

Common Mistakes in the Delivery of Positive Reinforcement

What I have discovered is that when managers complain that positive reinforcement doesn't work they have made one of the following errors: perception, contingency, immediacy, frequency. Let's discuss each of these.

The Perception Error. As stated earlier, what works as a reinforcer for one person may not work for another. Many people will choose to use reinforcers they like, rather than finding what others like.

At times we make the mistake of thinking people *should* want things that we want them to want. In other words, they should respond positively to the things we give them.

There are many things managers think are reinforcing that are not. For example, most people assume money is a reinforcer to everybody. Do you think Ross Perot would find $100 reinforcing?

Many people do not find money reinforcing under certain circumstances. We have all said at one time or another, "You couldn't pay me enough to do that" or, "I wouldn't work there for any amount of money."

Some managers think that if $1000 is reinforcing to someone, then $100 would be *somewhat reinforcing* to that person. This is erroneous thinking. There are some things that you would be happy to do for $1000 but wouldn't even lift a finger to do for $100. This mistake is also seen in the way we give raises and bonuses. The top performers get 5 percent increases and the level below them get 4 percent. Many outstanding performers have been heard to say in this situation, "If they think I'm going to break my back for a lousy 1 percent, they're crazy."

Similarly, have you ever heard someone say, "Everybody likes public recognition"? The fact is that in surveys we have done, most employees say they don't like it. They give various reasons, but most of those reasons center on concern about what peers might think about them. The effective manager or supervisor knows which people like public recognition and which people don't.

The most basic element in Performance Management is that you must first have a reinforcer. Make sure you use some of the ways discussed in Chapter 7 to find an effective reinforcer.

Once you have a reinforcer, you are on your way, but there are still some things that could cause it to be ineffective.

The Contingency Error.   This error relates to the relationship between a behavior and a reinforcer. If you can get a reinforcer without engaging in a prerequisite behavior, then that reinforcer is said to be noncontingent. If the *only* way you can get a reinforcer is to do a particular behavior, that reinforcer is said to be contingent on that behavior.

For example, in the average company an increase in fringe benefits will not increase performance because fringe benefits are provided to everyone, regardless of performance. Improved fringe benefits are given whether or not performance increases. They are noncontingent.

To say that hard work pays off implies that there is a reinforcement contingency between hard work and pay and/or promotions. Many people will tell you that if there is a contingency between work and pay, it is a loose one.

Profit-sharing and gainsharing programs are other examples of the contingency error. One reason they lose their effectiveness is that there is only an indirect contingency between profit and the performance of any given individual. In many companies, if there is profit it is shared on the basis of some predetermined formula. Unfortunately, the formula does not usually include a performance contingency. Therefore, if there is a profit, everyone will share just because they are on the payroll.

Salespeople sometimes "earn" commissions not because of what they did, but because they were lucky enough to have a customer who uses the company's product. If they were not using sound sales behaviors to cause the sale to close, the commission may inadvertently reinforce behaviors that represent poor sales techniques and will lead to poor performance in the future.

Make a list of reinforcers and rewards in your organization and state the behavioral contingency in the following format:

"You can get _____ if and only if you _____."

To use a previous example, "You can get *fringe benefits* if and only if you *are on the payroll.* If you make such a list you will be surprised at how few reinforcers are contingent on the behaviors we want. You will be enlightened and reinforced at the same time because you will immediately see solutions to some of your problems.

The Delay Error.   I explained the importance of immediate reinforcement earlier. I have had it said to me, "I don't have time to reinforce." My response is, "In that case, you better reinforce immediately." The longer you wait after the behavior, the less effective it will be. The error is delaying the positive reinforcement. If you have a limited amount of time to spend in the activity of reinforcing, spend it reinforcing behavior while the behavior is occurring.

Most leadership research is based on what leaders *say* they do. Dr. Judi Komaki (1986) is one of very few people who has done research on what leaders *do*.

What Dr. Komaki has found is that the most effective leaders, managers, and supervisors do not necessarily reinforce more often than the ineffective ones. What they do is *reinforce while people are performing*. To be able to do this they spend more time in the work area. Where do you think the ineffective supervisors spend their time? You guessed it. In their offices.

The only behavior a supervisor can reinforce in his or her office would be whatever the person is doing in the supervisor's office. Ironically, most supervisory duties today take the supervisor out of the workplace and into an office or a meeting room.

When reinforcement is immediate, you know what you are reinforcing because it is happening before your eyes. The performer receiving the reinforcement is almost certain to know which behavior is being reinforced. The longer reinforcement is delayed, the less sure you are of which behavior is actually being reinforced.

The greatest advantage of teams (and one that is almost always overlooked) is that team members can provide immediate reinforcement to each other. If team members are taught to deliver positive reinforcement, they are in the best position to make it immediate. In most cases, they are also in the best position to know which behaviors merit reinforcement.

The Frequency Error. *One positive reinforcer will not change your life.* "I reinforced him but he didn't change," is an oft-stated complaint. It is not that managers don't understand the need for reinforcement and recognition; it is that they don't have an understanding of the amount of reinforcement that is needed to create peak performers and a high-performance organization.

A case can be made for the fact that a little reinforcement is better than none at all, but in the amounts given in many organizations it is not much better. To give you a perspective on frequency, in *The Technology of Teaching*, B. F. Skinner states that it may take as many as 50,000 reinforcers to teach competence in basic math—roughly the first four grades.

This works out to more than 70 reinforcers per hour per student. The number of *attempts at* verbal reinforcement varies widely from teacher to teacher, but the median number found in several studies is about six per hour. When you understand this relationship of reinforcement to learning you can understand the problems we are experiencing in the schools today. There is simply not enough reinforcement to maximize learning.

I would not want to suggest that the number of reinforcers that adults need to acquire a new skill or make substantial improvement in an existing way of doing something is equal to what a child needs in school. However, it certainly gives you a perspective on what it takes to make significant changes in behavior. With this frame of reference everybody should understand that an occasional reinforcer at work will make only a small difference in performance.

The way that many organizations think about frequency may be seen in *annual* performance appraisals, *annual* recognition dinners, *quarterly* bonuses, employee of the *month*, etc. This low frequency of reinforcement will have no impact on organizational performance. Positive reinforcement needs to be a daily affair.

4 to 1 Rule

Years ago when I first started working in industry, I was often asked, "What is the proper balance between positive reinforcement and punishment?" That question was sometimes phrased as, "How many 'atta-boys' does it take to erase one 'You really screwed that up!' " In researching the literature I found two studies that I think have some bearing on the question.

Madsen (1974), in training classroom teachers, found that those that had positive reinforcement to punishment ratios of 4:1 or better had good discipline and high achievement in their classrooms. Below these ratios they had problems. Stuart (1971) in a study of delinquent children found similar ratios with parents of nondelinquent and delinquent children. Hart and Risley (1995) found that vocabulary development in young children was dramatically accelerated in families where the ratio of positive to negative interactions was high, approximately 6 to 1.

White (1975) and Thomas (1968) studied naturally occurring ratios in classrooms and found ratios in the range of 1:2. Self-reports by supervisors and managers revealed ratios of 2:1 at best. The ratios reported are probably more positive than the naturally occurring rates since the rates were taken as a part of a class in Performance Management. Few would disagree that there is a lot of room for improving the ratio of positive reinforcement to punishment in most organizations.

Some people have misunderstood the 4 to 1 rule. It does not mean that if you reinforce four times you have to punish something. The ratio can be higher than 4 to 1. In a high-performing organization, punishment may be infrequent indeed, but it is unrealistic to expect that there will be no occasion for negative consequences in any organization over a period of time. If you have a work environment where there are never any negatives, it probably means that you are positively reinforcing some poor performance.

Check your own ratios. Keep a 3 by 5 card and tally all of your attempts at reinforcement and punishment each day. If the ratio is less than 4:1, work on increasing your attempts at positive reinforcement. The card will be an antecedent for looking for opportunities to reinforce. Remember to reinforce only behavior or performance that warrants it. Many improvements have been reported in quality and productivity when supervisors simply increased their daily frequency of contingent positive reinforcement.

Competition for Positive Reinforcement

When there is too little reinforcement to go around, people will compete with each other to get it. Competition for significant reinforcers and rewards, financial or social, can generate behavior that is incompatible with the team-oriented work environment most organizations are trying to promote. Infrequent reinforcement promotes the kind of "political" behaviors with which we are all familiar: blaming others, covering your rear, and even sabotaging the initiatives of others.

People should not be exerting effort competing for reinforcement within your company. If we want employees to compete, we should focus them on external competitors. Because we have all grown up in a competitive society, we assume internal competition is an acceptable model for business.

I suggest that internal competition isn't a good model. In obviously competitive circumstances (like sports), within the team, competition becomes visibly counterproductive very quickly. When a basketball player takes a shot that should have been passed to a teammate, everybody on the team and in the stands knows it. In football, when a teammate steps in front of the intended receiver to catch a pass, everyone clearly sees it.

At work it is not as easy to see behaviors that cause others to fail or to have a more difficult job.

We certainly want our employees to be competitive. But we want them competing within our industry, not within our company. We don't want people to fight for reinforcement. We want reinforcement to be available for all who earn it.

Employee of the Month

When you think about the principles described in this chapter, it becomes obvious that *Employee of the Month* (EOM) and other such recognition programs violate every rule of effective positive reinforcement. In Chapter 19,

I will describe how to fix EOM and other recognition and reward programs, but for now let me just say that EOM not only doesn't reinforce performance, it may in fact be punishing it.

If you have such a program in your organization think about the following: Does the award go to the best performer every month? Does the performance of the recipient improve after he or she receives the award? Can you identify the specific behaviors that the award is reinforcing? Do you know if the actual award given is something that the recipient likes? If you answered no to these questions, cancel the EOM program now. If you answered "I don't know," take a closer look and be prepared to alter your approach after you read Chapter 18.

Two Attempts at Positive Reinforcers That Aren't

The "No But" Rule.   When supervisors and managers are asked, "Do you tell people that they are doing a good job?" they practically always say they do. When you ask employees, "Do your supervisors tell you that you do a good job?" they practically always respond, "They don't."

My analysis of this is that managers actually say the words, "You did a good job," or "I appreciate what you did." However, they don't stop there. Frequently they go on to say something like, "*. . . but you could have done . . .*"

A complete example may sound something like this: "*You did a good job compiling the final project report, but it would have been even better if you had included the original documents as an appendix.*" From the perspective of the supervisor making this statement, he or she has taken the time to reinforce the behavior of "compiling the final project report" and mentioned a little helpful hint: "next time include the original documents as an appendix." Although well intended, this statement would probably be more punishing than reinforcing.

John Domenick has said it well:

"Good intentions are terrible things to waste."

When the supervisor added the word *but,* he or she eliminated the positive statement from the memory of the person intended to be complimented. You see, "*but*" *is a verbal eraser* when used in an attempt to praise. It erases everything that preceded it. The reinforcement is gone. The criticism remains.

The president of a nationally known dairy products company once told me that he received a call from the chairman of the board of their holding company. The call started off, "John, I was just looking at your financial results from last year. You set a record. It was the best the company has ever done." At this point the president said he was feeling great. However, the chairman went on to say, ". . . but if you had a better handle on your inventory during the second quarter, you could have done even better." John said he was devastated immediately and got angry later. I'm quite sure the chairman is certain he complimented John for a good job. If asked, he would probably say that John knows how much he appreciates his work. I know that John did not feel either complimented or appreciated.

Do not use the occasion for praise as an opportunity to prompt or instruct.

The Sandwich. The so-called sandwich method of correcting performance is probably the most widely taught concept in basic supervisory training. A variation of the "no-but" rule, the "sandwich" is a negative between two positives. It goes like this:

Positive. "Thad, you are one of the best employees I've got."

Negative. "But if your attendance doesn't improve I'm going to have to terminate you."

Positive. "You know, you have more talent in your little finger than most people have in their whole body. I would hate to lose you."

Some psychologists say this method preserves one's self-esteem in the process of correcting. I know of no experimental data that demonstrates that fact. I think it helps the punisher—not the punished. At best it is confusing to the performer. After all, there were two positive comments and only one negative. In addition, when do you think Thad will hear positive statements like this again? Probably not until he is in trouble again.

Sandwiching is not a good practice. Criticism should be short and to the point. You should be very clear regarding which behavior must increase or stop, and what will happen if it does or doesn't. Positives should be saved until there is some improvement in performance.

Do not pair positive reinforcement with punishment.

Our example would have been better handled like this: "Thad your attendance has put your employment in jeopardy. If you miss one more day during the rest of this quarter you will be terminated. I hope this will not be necessary. If there is anything I can do to help you, let me know."

Later that day, when he is doing his job, you could approach Thad and say something like, "Thad, I hated to have to get on you this morning. You're one of the best employees I've got. . . ."

While this may appear to be a trivial difference, I assure you it will produce a very different result. Since showing concern is usually positive to most people, the pairing of concern with good work will probably act as a positive reinforcer for the productive performance. If concern is paired only with problem performance, you will likely get more problem performance.

A Case of Positive Imprecision

A plant manager once asked me if I would talk to one of his department supervisors to see if he was "cut out to be in management." The plant manager thought that because I was a psychologist, I would be able to analyze the supervisor's management potential. As a matter of fact, the management staff had already decided to terminate this supervisor because the general foreman didn't think he was management material.

I explained that it would be difficult to make a recommendation just by talking with the supervisor. I suggested that, if they were serious about making an informed decision, they should put the supervisor through Performance Management training and see how he did. I would then have some data about his effectiveness and could help them make a better judgment.

As it turned out, the young supervisor was *too* positive. That is, he reinforced everything, violating the contingency principle many times a day. When his reinforcement attempts didn't work, he started using the negative management style of most of his peers. Since he didn't like managing that way, his heart was not in it, and he had become totally ineffective.

When he learned about contingency, immediacy, and frequency, the performance of his shift changed dramatically, almost overnight. I don't know the end of this story because it hasn't been written yet, but the last I heard the young supervisor was a plant manager.

Most managers using "atta-boys," "pats on the back," and other "positive management techniques" typically commit some or all the reinforcement errors mentioned in this chapter. They are usually well-meaning individuals who are not aware of the precision required in the effective delivery of positive reinforcement. Because of this they are usually ineffective in bringing out the best in people.

However, these managers are usually predisposed toward being positive. When they learn to avoid these errors, they are able to increase their personal effectiveness dramatically, and in a short period of time.

PART 3
The Scientific Approach to Leadership

10

Pinpoint Precision

If you don't know where you are going, any
road will take you there.   ANONYMOUS

The president of a manufacturing company, aware of my experience as a clinical psychologist, asked me to explain why a really top performer would "become almost useless overnight." "Could it be drugs, alcohol, stress, family problems, or something like that?" he asked. I said it was possible, but I needed to know more.

He then described a performance problem in a plant in Louisiana, and continued. "We decided the plant manager had failed to take any action so we let him go and promoted the assistant plant manager to take his place. He did a great job, and things turned around almost immediately. Not too long after that, we began having trouble with a larger plant in Virginia, so we moved him there. Shortly after his arrival the plant was doing much better.

Now we've brought him to our home base where we have our largest plant and his performance is a disaster. I can't believe how unorganized he is. He doesn't plan well; he doesn't follow through; he changes priorities from day to day. He seems confused. What would cause such a change?"

"What did he do to turn the plant around in Louisiana?" I asked.

"I don't know," he replied.

"What did he do to turn the plant around in Virginia?"

"I don't know," he repeated.

"Then what makes you think he is doing anything different now?"

"I don't know," he said.

I don't think the plant manager was doing anything different in his third assignment than he had done in the first two plants. Circumstances, rather than his behavior, probably accounted for the difference in results.

This company was managed solely by results. As long as the results were there, little attention was paid to how the results were attained. In many organizations in this country, if you are getting results, management leaves you alone, and they spend their time with those who are not getting results. This is an ineffective and very risky management practice.

As a lieutenant in the Army I heard many times, "I don't care how you get it—just get it!" In the 1950s and 1960s, organizations using this same strategy seemed unconcerned with how results were achieved. Business was booming and getting results at almost any personnel or production cost. The increased costs were simply passed on to the consumer. In the 1990s, with tougher competition and heightened social awareness, organizations must be vigilant about *how* results are attained or face serious economic, social, and legal consequences.

Today it is not enough to know that something is working. We need to know why it works. That point is very clear. If you don't know why something works, how will you know how to fix it when things go wrong or circumstances change?

You cannot truly manage by results alone. Getting results is critical to an organization's survival and success. No organization can survive without them. However, short-term results can be achieved by using totally inappropriate behavior. The sales representative who cuts a deal that is impossible for the company to honor and the manager who fudges on the numbers to make production figures look good are just a couple of examples in which the ends are not justified by the means. Short-term results can be achieved in ways that will drive up costs and damage quality later. We must always be interested in and very much aware of how results are attained.

Unfortunately, we sometimes pay attention to behaviors only when the results turn sour. The cause of the Exxon Valdez oil spill was inappropriate behavior that had been tolerated or ignored for some time.

The crew and the captain engaged in behaviors other than those that would safely guide the oil tanker through the waters. The press reported that the captain had an alcohol problem, but his past results were sufficient, and Exxon officials had ignored the behaviors related to this problem until it was too late. Other disastrous examples of results-only management include the savings and loan and insider trading scandals which signaled the end of the winner-takes-all mentality of the 1980s. In every one of these cases, inappropriate behaviors produced positive short-term results, and long-lasting negative ones.

Sustaining results requires precise management. Managers need to know precisely which outcomes are required *and precisely what the acceptable behaviors are that produce them.*

The procedure for specifying results *and* behaviors is *pinpointing*. Pinpointing means being specific about a result you want and then being very specific about the behaviors you require to achieve that result.

Beware of the Activity Trap: Pinpoint Results First

At the annual Governor's conference in August 1993, President Clinton commented that when he was Governor of Arkansas, he was excited about going to work every day because he knew he would be able to accomplish some things that day. He observed that when he went to Washington, people seemed to be more concerned with the process of getting something done than they were with the product. He commented, "It's the darnest [*sic*] thing I've ever seen."

Although the element most often missing in the pinpointing process is the behavior pinpoint, it is still very important to pinpoint results first. You need both, but you should *always pinpoint results before you pinpoint behaviors*. While this sounds obvious, it's commonplace today for organizations to start programs that require people to change the way they work, with only a general idea of the results they want to achieve.

This is particularly true in the human relations area, where certain behaviors are assumed to have value. Teams, participative management, and employee involvement programs, for example, often are "sacred cows," whose real value to the organization is seldom questioned.

Frequently these programs are initiated without any direct ties to specific results. Many organizations have found themselves spending a lot of time and money with little or no return.

For example, the 1992 IQS study, showed that cross-functional teams that include the customer did not always result in improved performance. An unpublished study conducted at Auburn University in 1991 by Dr. Bill Hopkins also found no evidence that self-directed teams are an effective means of achieving important organizational objectives. He further reported that, "We have not found one published paper that reports clear increases in areas such as productivity, quality of production, or sales or clear declines in areas such as absenteeism, scrap, or maintenance costs."

General statements like "improved morale," "better decisions," and "personal pride" make great slogans, but they don't represent tangible pinpointed results. Programs are rarely measured and evaluated against such nonspecific outcomes.

Pinpoint the specific results you want first. Then identify the behaviors necessary to produce those results. If you know precisely which result you want, you can then test the relationship between the behaviors you think will get it and the actual accomplishment. You should never assume that you already know the behaviors that will produce the results. *Always evaluate changes in behavior against changes in results.*

One of our clients, an electrical connector manufacturer made the error of thinking they knew the critical selling behaviors for their product. Sales management directed its sales force to call on architects to persuade them to specify their product in their architectural drawings and design. They assumed that this behavior was the best way to sell more of the product. But it was difficult to get appointments with the architects, and the sales managers had to constantly prod their salespeople to keep after the architects, chiding them for not obtaining appointments with the architects more often.

As a part of our work on improving the effectiveness of the company's sales management, we audited the sales reps' performance. One of the things we did was follow the best salespeople to observe what they did to make sales. The audit results shocked management because the data showed that their best salespeople spent very little time with architects. They spent most of their time with distributors.

The behavior that produced the best sales results was calling on the distributors and convincing them to use the client's product regardless of what had been specified by the architect. The assumption of which behaviors would result in sales was based on someone's intuition rather than on actual observation and solid evidence.

Pinpoints Are Not Inside the Person

To use pinpointing effectively it is necessary to remember one very important rule: *Pinpoints are real.* They are tangible, observable results and behaviors, not beliefs, attitudes, or anything else internal, subjective, or abstract. Terms such as motivation, personality, communication, and rapport are useful when we are communicating informally, but when we need to change performance they are not only not useful, they create prejudice and build obstacles to progress. Correcting or improving some performance or outcome requires precise pinpointing.

Labels such as "lazy," "lacks drive," and "bad attitude" imply that the problem, and therefore the solution to the problem, is within the person. Using labels to describe performance not only can't help change the performance, it also produces blame. We blame the performer for being unmotivated, having a bad attitude, needing too much attention, not having enough drive. When you approach problem performance this way, the only solution is to tell the person to "shape up or ship out."

Another problem with these performer sterotypes is that even if, as a manager, you accept the responsibility to "change someone," you don't know which behavior to change. The reason most people think you can't change a person's attitude or personality is that what is generally referred to as *personality* is actually a collection of many behaviors. To change someone's attitude requires that you pinpoint the behaviors that make up the attitude. If you can pinpoint the behaviors, you can change them one at a time. If over time you change some or all of the specific behaviors, you certainly will change an individual's personality. The process of pinpointing gives you a realistic place to start the change process.

In the Eye of the Beholder.   What do we mean when we say a person has a positive attitude? We could be referring to the fact that the individual is always on time, or seldom complains, or keeps the work area exceptionally clean, or volunteers to help others, or smiles and jokes, or maintains high productivity and quality.

In other words, we could characterize a person as having a positive attitude if he or she did any one of those things, or all of them.

The same is also true for performers with a "bad attitude." They, too, demonstrate a pattern of behaviors that result in a negative label. Once you realize that a "bad attitude" is composed of many behaviors, it's easy to understand why that "attitude" is so difficult to change or remedy. Flushing out and pinpointing the specific and individual behaviors that make up the "bad attitude" or cause you to label the person as negative or uncooperative is essential if you are to effectively change the performer's "attitude."

Labels Don't Provide Answers.   Using vague phrases or labels to describe problem performance does nothing to change or improve performance. Calling someone lazy or worthless fails to provide the necessary information needed to change behavior. The productive question to ask is, "Which specific behaviors cause me to label this person lazy?" Turning in projects late? Turning in messy work? Failing to follow through with customers and coworkers on important assignments? These are specific questions that can lead to specific answers.

What to Do . . .   For some managers, pinpointing is the most difficult part of managing performance.

We always seem to know more about what we don't want people to do than what we want them to do. We issue directives like: Don't make errors; Don't have accidents; Don't be late. What we must keep in mind is that people are hired to *do* things. Active behavior gets things done. If, for example, someone is making mistakes in data entry on an assembly procedure, telling the person to stop making errors will not solve your problem because *one way of not making errors is to do nothing.* Errors are a measure of something other than the behavior of interest, so you will not necessarily get what you want by stopping what you don't want. If you tell people to stop making personal phone calls, for example, they may stop the calls, but talk to coworkers instead. Pinpointing behavior requires finding what people do, not what they don't do.

The importance of pinpointing *active behaviors* was made clear by Dr. Ogden Lindsley. In 1965 he developed the "dead-man's test" which is: "If a dead man can do it, it isn't behavior, and you shouldn't waste your time trying to produce it."

Yet much of what we typically track in quality and safety violates the dead-man's test. "Zero defects" and "days without a lost-time accident" are prime examples of popular goals that violate the dead-man's test. Dead men never have accidents and they never produce defective parts.

If you examine typical business, you'll see numerous examples of management focusing on inactive behavior or behavior that leads to no accomplishment.

Some people think this active versus inactive dimension of pinpointing is really two sides of the same coin; that it's more a problem of semantics than a real one. Not so.

One day I looked out the window of my office and saw two young carpenters just as they finished shingling the roof of a building in our office park.

As crazy as it may sound, one of them proceeded to do a handstand on the crown of the roof. He then walked on his hands from one end of the building to the other, a distance of about 60 feet. Not to be outdone, his coworker followed close behind. Obviously this was something the two athletic young men had done many times before. It was certainly not safe behavior, but neither fell and they ended the job with no lost-time accidents.

Using the criteria of the usual safety program, these two could easily qualify as participants at their employer's safety celebration, commemorating a million hours without a lost-time accident. As you can see, no "lost-time accidents" doesn't necessarily reflect the level of safe behaviors on the job; it just reflects a fortunate result. In the same way, zero defects does not equal careful quality-oriented behavior.

If It Doesn't Move, It's a Result

Like behaviors, results can also be more precisely pinpointed. Gilbert (1978) developed a test for determining if you have an accomplishment. He called his test the "leave-it test." The leave-it test works this way: If you can leave it behind when you walk out of the office or plant, it is a result. If it's something you take with you, it is not. For example, safety awareness cannot be left behind at the end of the day and therefore would not meet Gilbert's definition of a result.

Safety awareness, better communication, and increased teamwork are not pinpointed results, and effort spent trying to produce them may consume considerable financial and personnel resources, generating little value to the organization. These phrases are descriptions of a problem and, as such, represent only a beginning. You must pinpoint the desired result more precisely if you are to solve problems reliably and efficiently.

Behaviors and results define performance, and you need both to run an efficient and effective organization. So how do you pinpoint?

Precision Pinpointing

Pinpointing means being specific about results and behaviors. It requires *precise descriptions* of results and behaviors that are *observable, measurable, and reliable.*

Observability

Seeing is believing. In the final analysis, business has to be interested in results and behaviors that can be seen. Pinpointing observable results is relatively easy. This is why we have focused on them for so long. The problem of observability comes up when we try to pinpoint behavior. Factors that affect behavior but are not observable, such as thoughts and emotions, are not the province of management. We can't expect line managers, or anyone for that matter, to delve into the inner feelings of others. The good news is we don't have to. You can manage yourself and others very successfully by limiting yourself to pinpointing behaviors you can see and hear.

Measurability

Many people, when faced with these characteristics of good pinpoints, immediately complain that these criteria (especially measurement) will limit the pinpoints they can identify. This is not the case.

The fact is, if something is happening it can be measured. Every behavior can be measured in terms of frequency or duration, or both. Even when something is not happening, it is being measured. The measure is zero. Some things may not be worth measuring, but if it is important, it can be measured. (Measurement will be explained in detail in the next chapter.)

Reliability

The third characteristic of a valid pinpoint is reliability. When two or more people can observe a behavior or result and come up with the same count or measure, you have a true pinpoint.

Have you ever heard someone described as "friendly" by one coworker and then described as "aloof" by someone else? They are either observing or measuring different things or their measures are not reliable.

This example from the *American Journalism Review* will show you what I mean:

> *From the Washington Post, Jan. 15:*
> "Donna E. Shalala . . . at her confirmation hearing . . . faced little in the way of tough questioning . . ."
> *From the New York Times, same day:*
> ". . . Shalala encountered tough questioning today . . ."
> *From the Washington Post, Jan. 16:*
> Diary Says Bush Knew 'Details' of Iran Arms Deal
> *From the New York Times, same day:*
> Entries Suggest [Bush] Did Not Know Details . . .

Refining observations to the point of reliability is an important skill in pinpointing. We may often start with a pinpoint that is not totally reliable but, as we use it, measure it, and discuss our observations, we can refine it until it becomes more and more reliable. Even journalists could be trained to do this.

Counts of Behaviors Versus Results

As I pointed out at the beginning of this chapter, behavior is what a person does and a result is what is produced by the behaviors. Differentiating the two is sometimes difficult when you first begin pinpointing.

A count of behavior is sometimes confused with important organizational results. Behavior counts (e.g., number of times one of your staff gets reports in on time, number of times one of your peers disrupts a staff meeting with jokes, number of days an employee arrives on time) are important measures of behavior if your goal is to reduce or increase that behavior, but they are not results.

Some organizations require employees to attend a fixed number of hours of training each year. Is that a valuable result or a count of behaviors? I consider attendance at training as merely a count of behaviors. The valuable result should be measured in terms of on-the-job performance.

Results are usually defined as some outcome valuable to the organization: number of defect-free items produced, increased revenue per sale, and reduction of cycle time. Of course, it is important to measure both behaviors and results, but you should avoid confusing the two.

Figure 10-1, from *Performance Management: Improving Quality Productivity through Positive Reinforcement,* will help you differentiate behaviors from results.

Control of the Pinpoint

One of the important considerations in pinpointing a behavior or result you would like to change is to make sure the behaviors and/or results are under the performer's *control.* Care must be given to identify pinpoints which are within the influence of the performer.

Two examples come to mind. On the production floor, frontline employees do not typically control cost. Someone in purchasing does that. Employees control use of materials and supplies which impact cost.

Frontline employees don't usually control units produced per day either. Production control may cut the production schedule or increase it. The performer controls only the number of units produced per hour when material is available.

When developing pinpoints, it's important to specify the results performers control. *A rule of thumb is to describe the results that are as close as possible to the behaviors that produce them.*

POINTS FOR DISTINGUISHING BEHAVIORS FROM RESULTS

Behavior	Results
1. What people are doing.	1. What people have produced.
2. What you see people do when they are working.	2. What you see after people stop working.
3. Must see people working.	3. Not necessary to see people working.
4. Tends to be expressed in present tense, verbs ending in "ing."	4. Tends to be expressed in the past tense by noun-adjective pairings: "documents filed."
5. Cue words: by, through, to.	5. Cue words and phrases: in order to, so that, to achieve, to be able to.
6. Commonly used terms: input, process, activity, means.	6. Commonly used terms: output, product, outcome, achievement, ends.
7. Examples: inspecting, designing, conducting meetings, reinforcing, giving feedback.	7. Examples: Production, yield, run time, milestones met, suggestions made.

Figure 10-1

Although few people in business today have total control over results, the control requirement is usually satisfied if a person or group has more control over the pinpoint than anyone else. One test for control is to ask, "If the performer did nothing would the result change dramatically?"

Another way to determine if a performer has control over results is to look at the data. If there are wild swings in the data from day to day, the performer probably doesn't have control. Also, if the data never varies, the performer probably doesn't have control either. If there are minor variations from shift to shift, or performer to performer, then the performer likely is in control of much of the result. The only way you can know if the performer is really in control is to correlate change in behavior with changes in results.

In summary, when you can pinpoint results and behaviors that are active, measurable, observable, reliable, and under the control of the performers, you will have taken the first step toward being able to bring out the best in people.

11

The Effective Use of Measurement

When I worked as a clinical psychologist I never had a patient complain about being measured. The reason: they never doubted that measurement was being used to help them with their problems.

In business, measurement is also used to solve problems, to help the company perform better, but one of the most frequent uses of measurement is to identify performers who aren't measuring up. Based on the measurement, negative action is usually taken to correct the performance problem. No wonder employees avoid measurement whenever they can. It's no fun being identified as the problem.

The purpose of measurement in a Performance Management system is different. Rather than using measurement to find problem employees, *measurement is used to enable employees to do better,* which of course should help the company perform better. When you understand the difference between the way measurement is traditionally used and the way it should be used, you will understand how to create conditions where people seek measurement rather than avoid it.

Myth: What Gets Measured Gets Done

In my performance management seminars, the item on the agenda that attracts the most interest is measurement. A great many people in business think that measuring a problem is tantamount to solving it. But as important as measurement is, measurement alone will not change behavior.

91

If measurement changed behavior there would be no fat people, no one would smoke, and everyone would exercise, because all of these behaviors and their results can be easily measured. Many people know exactly how much they weigh and want to weigh less; know how many cigarettes they smoke and want to smoke less. But measuring doesn't change a thing. So what does measurement do for us?

In most cases, measurement is an antecedent. Unfortunately, in business it is most often an antecedent to punishment. About every year or so the *Wall Street Journal* carries a story about a company having problems as a result of a new measurement system. Employees complain that they don't even have time to go to the bathroom, or that they are being watched every moment. Yet these new measurement systems seem to get improvements almost immediately.

By now you should know how they typically get it—with *negative reinforcement*. If the company establishes a range of acceptable performance, and if that range is higher than previous expectations, the company will see improvement because the employees quickly realize that by maintaining their performance within that range, they can avoid punishment. You know that measurement is a negative reinforcer when you hear comments like, "You can't measure what I do." This is not an attempt to avoid measurement; it's an attempt to avoid punishment.

The ability to measure is not now, nor has it ever been, the problem. We can measure any performance. The problem in measurement comes from the way it is used. If it is used to punish, people will go to extraordinary lengths to avoid being measured. Falsification of data is a more common problem than many upper managers realize, and its main purpose is to avoid punishment.

When It's Done Right

Believe it or not, you can create an environment where people will want to be measured. I have seen it time and time again. When measurement is used to increase positive reinforcement, people will look forward to being measured. In these cases, if management doesn't provide measurement, people will devise it for themselves.

Preston Trucking Company developed a positive measurement environment. When I visited there several years ago, a mechanic showed me a graph and with obvious pride pointed out that his group had found ways to reduce (by more than half) the number of hours it took to rebuild an engine. In addition, the quality was so good they guaranteed the engines for more miles than the original equipment.

In Preston's tire recapping department the recappers showed me a similar result. When old tires came in, the first thing they did was check the serial number and truck odometer to see how many miles the recapped tires had run.

A supervisor in the Preston accounting department showed me a note from a part-time employee. It read, "Mr. Smith, can I please have a graph like Mary Jo? P.S. I did 32 invoices in 45 minutes. I timed myself."

Obviously, measurement held no fear for these employees.

In another case, I sat in on a Performance Management review at AG Communications company and heard a senior engineer report on his progress. He displayed a graph which indicated had more than doubled his productivity on software development. He commented to the group, "I'm pleased with the increase in productivity, but it has caused me to worry that I may be sacrificing quality. I don't think I am, but to make sure, I have figured out a way to measure my quality and will start using that measurement on Monday."

Overcoming Resistance to Measurement

If people in your organization try to avoid or delay attempts to install job measurement, and you want to begin measuring more precisely, there are two things you should do:

1. Increase the frequency of positive reinforcement for desirable behaviors as they occur in the workplace.
2. Pair reinforcement with existing measures.

The length of time you must do these two things before introducing the new measures will vary depending on your history of using measurement to punish and your ability to increase effective positive reinforcement. However, if you use these two techniques for a couple of months, in most cases you will have a much easier time installing a new measurement system.

How to Measure

There are two basic ways to measure: counting and judging. Counting is generally recognized as the best way to measure because it is more objective. Frequency counts are generally the most desirable data.

Judging is generally thought to be more subjective and takes a backseat to counting as a measurement method in business. However, if counting is not possible in certain situations, judging can be very useful in helping people improve.

Counting

When we can, we should count. In business we are usually interested in the *rate* of doing something. We typically want to increase such things as quality parts per hour, sales per week, and customer inquiry calls completed per day.

These things are usually thought of as easy to measure. However, nothing is easy to measure if the performer doesn't want to be measured. If people don't want to be measured, they can find many reasons why what you have chosen to measure is not a valid indicator of their performance. Counts that are not paired with positive reinforcement when improvement occurs will give you only marginal improvement.

Raw versus Cooked. When you establish a measurement using counting, consider using the raw data rather than some mathematical function like percent. Lindsley (1993) puts forth a convincing argument that percent correct or incorrect is the wrong measurement method for business, because it is a way of "cooking the data." The further you move away from raw data, the more data you lose.

For example, he points out that percent change is not symmetrical: ". . . many of us do not realize that if you add 20 percent and then subtract 20 percent, you are not back to where you started; you are actually below where you started."

Typically used as a way of reporting such things as manufacturing efficiencies, yields, and quality, percent treats "corrects" and "incorrects" as dependent entities. In fact, they are independent of one another. As such, percent obscures some useful data. As an example, if someone produced 1000 units with 100 defects, they would have 90 percent good parts and 10 percent errors. If the next day they produced 1200 units and 110 were defects, they would have 90.8 percent good parts and 9.2 percent defects. Quality would appear to have improved but, in fact, more defective units were produced. This could not be detected from the percent data.

· By examining the raw frequencies (uncooked data) you might be able to spot a problem and correct it much earlier than if you had only percent measures. For example, Lindsley has discovered 11 patterns of correct and incorrect performance that can be detected by plotting responses. He calls these patterns "Learning Pictures." Seven of these are illustrated in Figure 11-1. By studying these pictures you can see how corrects and incorrects are independent, the relative frequency of each and any change in performance. Percentage does not add any new information and practically always masks useful data.

Percent can be particularly misleading if you don't know the frequency of the behavior being counted. One of something can be 100 percent, and

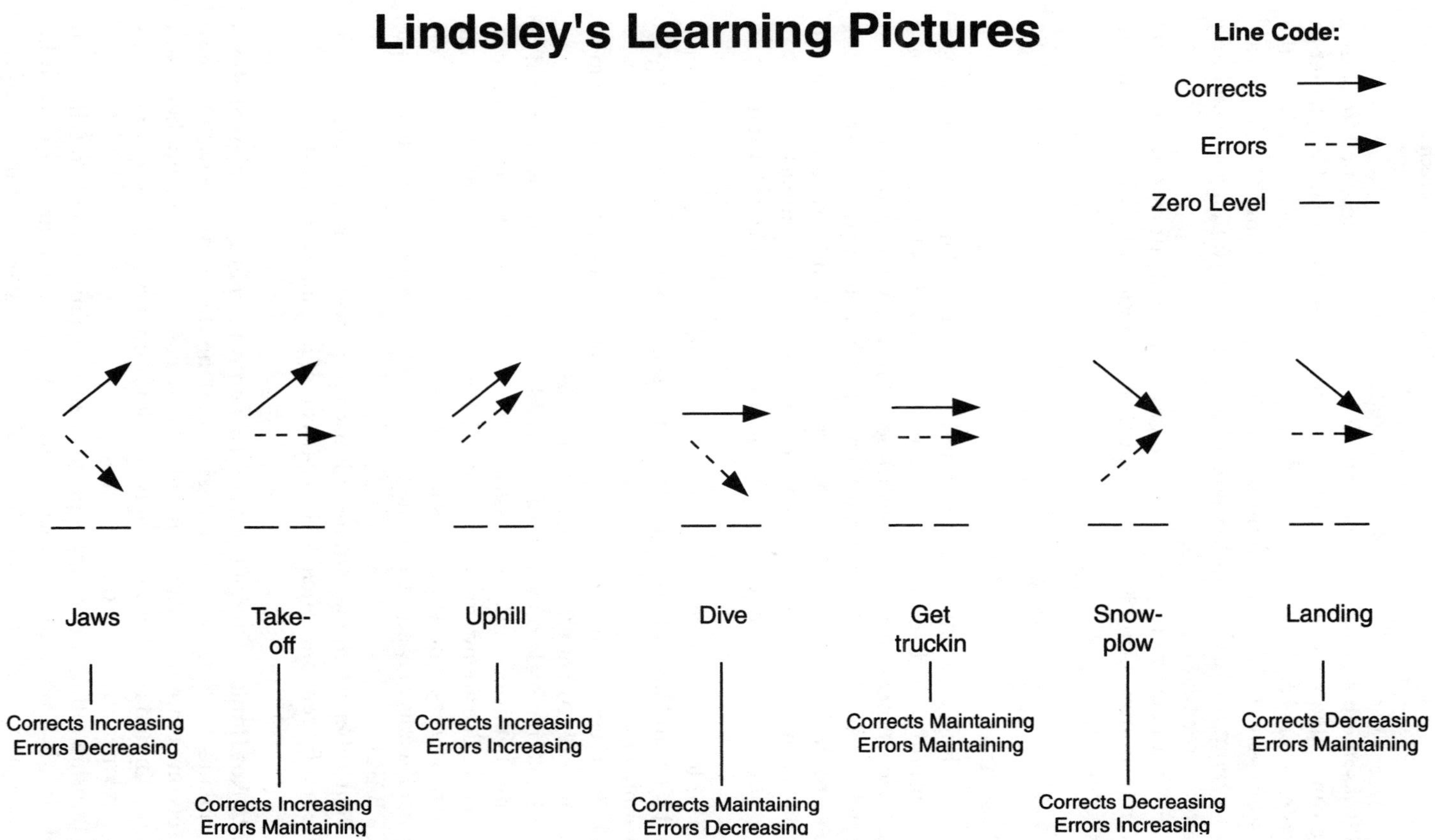

Lindsley's Learning Pictures

Line Code:

Corrects ——→

Errors - - →

Zero Level ———

Jaws
Corrects Increasing
Errors Decreasing

Take-off
Corrects Increasing
Errors Maintaining

Uphill
Corrects Increasing
Errors Increasing

Dive
Corrects Maintaining
Errors Decreasing

Get truckin
Corrects Maintaining
Errors Maintaining

Snow-plow
Corrects Decreasing
Errors Increasing

Landing
Corrects Decreasing
Errors Maintaining

Figure 11-1

95

100 of something can be 100 percent. If we don't know the actual frequency we can't adequately evaluate performance. It's not unusual for a batter in professional baseball to carry a very high batting average early in the season—say, .667. Does this mean that he is a great hitter? You'd be cautious about declaring him the next Ted Williams if you knew he had only batted three times.

Use raw data where you can. It will give you more information, generate more hypotheses, and lead you to quicker resolution of problems than will percent.

Judging

Many things in business are not readily countable. This makes judging a very useful tool. The biggest problem with measures based on judging is that they appear in many cases to be arbitrary. What is being evaluated seems to vary from one measurement to the next. A way of overcoming this problem is to establish specific criteria that can be reliably observed by two or more people. Many athletic events, such as gymnastics, ice skating, and diving to name a few, rely on judging to determine winners and losers.

The legal profession has long wrestled with the subjectivity of judging and seeks to build a body of evidence to assist in making decisions of guilt or innocence.

In business we can overcome the subjectivity of judging by constructing a Behaviorally Anchored Rating Scale (BARS).

A BARS is a scale on which each variable to be measured is anchored by specific behaviors and accomplishments. Quality performance and customer service are two areas where BARS have been used to assist in the evaluation process. The scale is usually constructed by performers and their boss, or teams may construct one for themselves. Figure 11-2 is an example of a BARS.

Remember, when measurement is used to provide opportunities for positive reinforcement, much of the criticism of judging is reduced.

Rate Not Rank.   One of the most frequently used measurement methods is ranking. I strongly advise against it. Ranking should not be used because it sets one employee against another. There can be only one number 1 and only a limited number of winners. We don't intentionally hire losers. Let's not use measurement to create them.

By using ratings we compare performance against established criteria. In this way, it is possible for everyone who meets the required criteria to be rated as a top performer. A company of winners will be a winning company.

Preventive Maintenance Technician

Behaviors: Perform required tests, identify problems, schedule repairs.

Performs **all** tests on **all** equipment as scheduled.

Identify **all** problems.

Coordinates assignments with repair supervisor.

weight _____
score _____

Performs no tests. Makes repair assignments based on past data. Turns over to repair supervisor with no discussion.	Performs less than 50% of required tests on 75-100% of required equipment. Turns over to repair supervisor with no discussion.	Performs 75-100% of required tests on 75-100% of required equipment on time. Turns over to repair supervisor with no discussion.	Performs 100% of required tests on 100% of required equipment on time. Turns over to repair supervisor with no discussion.	Performs 100% of required tests on 100% of required equipment on time. Discusses with repair supervisor before completing repair schedule.

Performs 100% of required tests on 100% of required equipment on time. Discusses with repair supervisor before completing repair schedule. Follows up to be sure work has been done as scheduled.

Performs 100% of required tests on 100% of required equipment on time. Discusses with repair supervisor before completing repair schedule. Follows up to be sure work has been done as scheduled. Identifies potential problems not on maintenance list.

Scale: 1 — 3 — 5 — 7 — 10

Figure 11-2

97

Validating Behavioral Measures

When measuring behavior, it is important to compare behavioral measures against results. If behaviors are judged to be good but the results are not, you may have the wrong pinpoints. You should reinforce the performer for behaving the way he or she was asked to, but refine the behavioral pinpoints until they correlate with required results. Remember, the behaviors you originally pinpoint may have to be revised and/or refined a number of times until they give you the desired pinpointed result.

A sales division of a grocery products company developed a checklist for salespeople to complete after every sales call. The checklist included items such as: Did I sell a promotion? Did I ask for the order? Did I ask for additional facings? Did I cross-sell our new product? The sales reps tallied their scores and plotted them on a graph at the end of each day. At the end of the week they sent the graph of their completed checklists to their supervisor. The sales supervisor also plotted their scores on the checklist against "cases sold." He was pleasantly surprised to find a high correlation between behaviors and results.

Because there was a high overall correlation, the scores helped diagnose individual performance problems. If someone had high scores on the checklist and no increase in sales, it indicated there might be a problem in how the person was setting up and conducting the sales call. During the time the division used this checklist and correlated behaviors with results, they experienced record sales.

In another case, an accounting manager wanted to focus on past-due accounts as a way of improving cash flow. He had two clerks who were working on this job. His checklist was called "Positive Credit Calls" and included only behaviors the clerks could control. To earn credit for a call the clerks had to (1) find the name of a person in the company who could take action on the bill, (2) call and talk to that person, (3) get some form of commitment to take action on the bill, and (4) record the action on a log at their desks. The accounting manager then checked the number of calls against the number of past-due accounts that were paid each week. The clerks doubled the number of positive credit calls per day. The results were up almost 30 percent.

Measurement Helps You See Small Changes

One of the most important reasons for establishing a good measurement system is to enable you to see small, incremental changes. Most improvements do not occur suddenly. Frequently improvement has begun and you hardly notice it. Many initiatives have been canceled when progress was under way, but there was no measurement system in place to let anybody know about it. Since American business is noted for its impatience and a desire for a "quick fix," having a way to measure small improvements is critical.

Years ago I worked with a teacher who asked for help with a student who would suddenly yell out for no apparent reason. She told me she had him tested by the school psychologist, who diagnosed him as "having a need to scream."

The teacher also told me that the student was driving her crazy. She never knew when he would yell. "How often does he yell," I asked. "All the time," she responded. Knowing that he could not be yelling *all the time,* I asked her to record the number of times he yelled in class during the next week.

When I visited her the following week, even I was shocked by the data. He averaged yelling out once every six minutes—about 50 times a day. I suggested an intervention which she faithfully implemented.

Let us say that she obtained the following results:

Time frame	Yells per day
Baseline	**52**
Monday	49
Tuesday	47
Wednesday	46
Thursday	41
Friday	39

If you were the teacher and I asked you if the student was getting better, what would you say? The teacher said he was getting better. As a matter of fact, he did scream less every day. "Do you think we should continue for another week?" I asked. "Yes, of course," she responded.

Suppose for a moment that I told this teacher to try the same intervention, *but didn't ask her to count the yells per day.* What do you think she would have told me the next week? I'm sure she would have said that there was no improvement, because without measurement the difference between screaming 52 times a day and 39 times a day would probably have gone unnoticed. Thirty-nine yells per day is still a lot of yells.

In case you were wondering, the intervention we used was to set a timer on the student's desk. For every 10 minutes he could go without yelling he got to spend 1 minute with the teacher after school, a positive reinforcer for this student. This allowed the teacher to reinforce him a minimum of once every 10 minutes, and it allowed her to see progress at the same time. A good measurement system should provide reinforcement opportunities for both the measurer and the measuree.

By the way, at the end of the day on Friday of the first week, he came to the teacher and said, "Next week can I go 20 minutes without yelling?" By the end of the second week he had stopped yelling and did not yell a single time the rest of the year.

I'm sure I don't have to sell you on the importance of measurement in business. In business, we have to keep score. But measurement used to set the occasion for positive reinforcement has benefits that you may never have imagined. More than keeping score, measurement can add significantly to bringing out the best in people.

12
Performance Feedback

Pinpointing defines the results you want and the behaviors you need to get them. Measurement tells you how much of each you are getting. Once you have those two Performance Management elements in place you are ready to turn that information into feedback.

The term *feedback* is not to be confused with general information or data. *Feedback is information about performance that allows an individual to adjust his or her performance.* Feedback shows a performer where current performance is in relation to past performance and usually some goal.

Without feedback there is no learning. You can't learn to talk, walk, write, ride a bicycle, or learn to play a musical instrument without feedback. *Learning requires specific information about how your behavior is affecting the environment.*

For the most part, feedback is such an integral part of everyday life that we take it for granted. Our senses constantly provide us with information that helps us adjust our behavior in order to walk safely, type correctly, hammer a nail, fill a cup with coffee, or pick up the phone.

Although much of the feedback we experience in daily life is built into our biology and physiology, in most jobs we do not get the feedback we need to perform optimally.

Ordinary performance data alone does not necessarily tell you what to do to improve performance. A golfer who sees a ball slice wildly from the tee into the woods certainly has information about performance, but may not have the slightest idea what he or she did wrong. To this golfer the information is not helpful, it's punishing. Because there are many things that cause a golf ball to slice, to the novice golfer simply observing the ball careening off in the wrong direction is not helpful to his or her game.

However, the consequence of having the ball go into the woods may eventually (or in some cases immediately) cause that individual to give up the game.

Similar situations exist in businesses, where industrially engineered standards may be so complex that beginning performers don't benefit from seeing this data. Performance feedback, by behavioral definition, is specific information or data about performance that will allow you to change your performance.

If you have a job processing insurance claims, for example, there is nothing in the job that automatically causes you to adjust the pace or the accuracy of your work. When there is no naturally occurring feedback, some mechanism must be developed by which this kind of information is generated and presented to the performer. Performers need to know how they are doing, if they should pick up the pace, slow down, be more careful.

In his lectures on improving quality, Dr. Edwards Deming repeatedly asked, "How could they know?" He was referring to the sad fact that most performers do not receive or have access to the feedback they need to do a quality job.

Feedback deficiencies are a major contributor to virtually all problems of low performance, yet most organizations today have no real system for providing performance feedback to their employees. Even those companies which are now sharing production figures or quality indicators with employees are typically providing information, not feedback. This kind of information gives performers only a vague idea of how they are doing. It has little impact on their job performance. With effective feedback, improvements ranging from 20 to 600 percent aren't unusual.

Feedback Is an Antecedent

Once again, I must point out that feedback is very important, but alone will not sustain behavior change. In a large number of documented cases, performance has doubled in a short period of time following the introduction of performance feedback. This causes many managers to think that feedback produces some kind of performance magic. However, they are often disappointed when several weeks or even days later the performance drops to prefeedback levels.

The surge in performance occurs because feedback is an antecedent, and you'll recall that antecedents can get almost any behavior to start. Feedback tells the performer what needs to change in his or her performance. How the performers choose to respond to that antecedent depends on the consequences they experience, have experienced, or expect to experience.

Feedback Doesn't Always Improve Performance. It is possible that for some performers, feedback could be an antecedent to limit their performance. They may be afraid they will run out of work and lose their jobs, or they may be concerned that feedback will illustrate their superior work, causing other workers to be jealous. Peer pressure is a powerful consequence.

In a Performance Management system, improving performance is an occasion for positive reinforcement. Feedback is an excellent format for the performer and the manager to know when positive reinforcement is due.

The reinforcement for the behavior that is associated with the feedback sustains the performance improvement.

Feedback in Graphs

Although feedback is technically defined here as *any* information about performance that will allow you to change that performance, in this chapter I am going to emphasize feedback presented in graphic format. Graphed data has many advantages over charts, text, or data presented verbally.

Graphs show you at a glance where you are in relation to where you have been and where you are going. Graphed data allows you to see performance trends earlier, permitting a more timely response to potential problems and more immediate positive reinforcement.

Dean Tapp, owner of a label-printing company, reports a case where press operators were given verbal feedback in an effort to increase sheets per hour on a printing job.

Verbal feedback on today's performance (usually given the following day) sounded something like this: "You ran 14,156 sheets per hour yesterday." As you can see from Figure 12-1, performance deteriorated. As you will recognize, "verbal feedback" was actually a punisher, since it caused performance to decrease. When they began using systematic graphic feedback and reinforcement, it improved dramatically.

Feedback Interval

Obviously, immediate feedback on performance is preferred. With immediate and frequent feedback people learn more quickly because they are provided more opportunities for reinforcement than less frequent, more delayed feedback would permit. Many managers and supervisors say that it's impossible to provide immediate feedback.

The question I ask in such circumstances is, "Then what is the shortest practical interval?" Hourly feedback is better than daily, and daily feedback

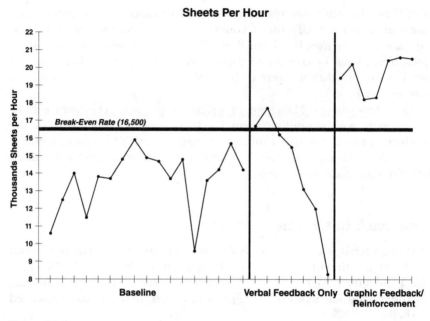

Figure 12-1

is preferable to weekly feedback. Feedback delivered less often than weekly is better than nothing, but not much better. Monthly feedback is much too delayed to have any significant impact on performance. After all, monthly feedback only provides 11 opportunities a year to reinforce or correct performance.

Daily feedback is the most common feedback interval in most Performance Management applications. Daily feedback is possible on more jobs than you might imagine. Employees on production jobs, office jobs, and even creative jobs such as software development can easily arrange a system for daily feedback. Once again, I am referring to graphic feedback. Using graphs makes frequent feedback possible.

Individual Versus Group Feedback

Individual feedback is more effective than group feedback. As you might imagine, managers will say, "I can't get data by individual performer." If you can't do it, don't do it. But get it for the smallest group possible.

When you have individual feedback, you should graph group performance as well. This provides increased opportunities for reinforcement for the individuals in the group while increasing reinforcement opportunities for cooperation and other teamwork behaviors.

Public or Private.   Post group performance publicly; provide individual feedback privately. We encourage individuals to keep a notebook of their performance and show it to their supervisors daily. This gives the supervisor the opportunity to reinforce, if appropriate, and offer help if needed. This is a powerful way to maximize performance.

Supervisors should keep individual performance data private. Resist the temptation to compare one performer to another. Don't say, "Courtney completed 123 documents yesterday, and I know you can do as well." This sets Courtney up as a punisher to the others and does not foster teamwork. On the other hand, if a person asks, "How many did Courtney do yesterday?" the proper response is, "Ask Courtney." Voluntarily sharing feedback among peers offers many opportunities for peer reinforcement.

In an organization where measurement is being used to provide positive reinforcement, it is not unusual for individuals to post their own graphs publicly. If they choose to do so, great, but don't ask them to do it. Remember, public recognition can be punishing for some people, and you could be setting up a negative reinforcement situation if you post individual graphs when the performers would rather you didn't.

Sales organizations often publish a newsletter or memo ranking each salesperson. Just because this is frequently done doesn't mean it's an effective procedure. I strongly discourage this practice. Listing the names of those above goal is a preferred alternative. A graph showing the highest performance (without naming the performer), and the average and lowest performances (again without the name) will produce the same results as ranking, without the negative side effects.

On the other hand, always publish group results publicly. When group graphs are posted publicly, it increases reinforcement between members of the group and also encourages positive remarks from visitors to the department.

Performer-Controlled Feedback

Just as with pinpointing and measurement, don't give feedback on variables that are not under the control of the individual or the group. There is no advantage to be gained, and it may be frustrating for the performers if you post a graph over which they have little or no control.

I recall an incident in the production area of a furniture manufacturing plant. The plant manager pointed to a huge graph on the wall, and said,

"Here is our feedback graph." I looked at it and noticed there was no apparent trend, so I asked, "How are you doing?" He replied, "Good!" I pointed to a high point on the graph and said, "Boy, you knocked the top out this day, didn't you?" "Naw," he responded, "We worked 10 hours that day."

"What happened here?" I asked as I pointed to the low point on the graph. "We had some equipment problems that day," he replied.

Contrary to what the plant manager thought, this graph was not feedback to the production employees. It may have been feedback to the production controller, production superintendent, and the plant manager, but not to the line employees. The line employees needed feedback on the number of chairs they finished per hour *when the line was running*. That way, they could see the difference their pace and skill made. The graph being used did not help individuals improve their performance. An employee on the production floor might have had a personally productive day only to be disappointed by a graph that showed no improvement. That kind of feedback provided the individual with no opportunity for reinforcement, no opportunity for learning.

By the way, a large production graph in the plant is a good idea. Even though this particular graph was not performance feedback for the employees, with the addition of group and individual feedback, as well as controllable variables, it could become a source of reinforcement and reward for the general plant population.

I saw a second example of a performer-control error in another furniture plant. In this case, management was concerned about the amount of money being spent on sandpaper. One manager organized a work team to reduce the dollars spent on sandpaper. The team worked really hard for a month, coming up with many ideas and implementing them successfully.

The group was stunned when, at the end of the month, they saw that *the amount of money spent for sandpaper had essentially stayed the same.* It turned out that the vendor had two price increases for sandpaper that month. No amount of explaining by the manager could offset the disappointment the group felt when they saw no change in the costs they worked so hard to reduce.

The manager could have assured success if he had given feedback on "increasing board feet per sandpaper belt." That was something they could control.

Feedback and Reinforcement

Feedback and positive reinforcement form the most powerful combination of techniques you can use to bring out the best in people. To have effective feedback, you must have the right pinpoints. Then add feedback and reinforcement and you will have the right mix to maximize performance.

The plant manager of a company based in St. Paul, Minnesota, recently told me that as he posted record group data on a plant graph, one of the most militant union members walked by, saw the graph, and shouted, "Alright!" as he threw his arms up in the air. "Seeing such a change in that man made all the effort of Performance Management worthwhile," the manager said with a big smile.

To be most effective, feedback must be established as an antecedent for positive reinforcement. Although feedback is not a natural reinforcer, when performers know that positive reinforcement is consistently paired with improved performance, simply watching the graphed data move in the right direction can become a source of considerable reinforcement.

13
A Model for Problem Solving

The Model

All the individual elements necessary to bring out the best in people must be applied in a systematic format for solving performance problems and maximizing performance. In the early 1960s Ogden Lindsley (1991) developed such a model and used it effectively in his work with parents, teachers, and students. He wanted a way of solving problems that would be simple for parents to use and to teach to their children.

The original model was comprised of four steps:

1. Pinpoint
2. Record
3. Consequate
4. Evaluate

In 1968 I modified the model slightly for use in business. I divided the second step, Record, into the substeps of Measure and Feedback. My version looks like this:

1. Pinpoint
2. Measure
3. Feedback
4. Reinforce
5. Evaluate

Differences in these two versions are slight. Lindsley asked the people he worked with to record their data on six-cycle log paper (called a *standard celeration chart*), which would automatically give them a graphic display of their data. However, if I had asked frontline supervisors and managers to record data on a log chart in addition to everything else I asked them to do, I knew they'd kick me out of their companies.

Another slight difference in the two models is the word *Consequate.* Lindsley coined this word to mean simply that there should be an application of consequences—positive or negative. My original thought was that managers don't need to be told to punish more, but should be encouraged to find solutions that are positively reinforcing.

Since business is interested in increasing performance, I knew that reinforcement had to be the emphasis. Some people mistakenly think that Performance Management doesn't use punishment. Punishment is a consequence that has a place in managing performance. Yet, after using positive consequences correctly, you'll find that punishment begins to play a smaller and smaller role in your management practice.

The power of the Performance Management problem-solving model lies in its systematic use. You can't use the pinpointing technique alone and expect to get any lasting change. You can't measure, and then use it as a way to punish. You can't give feedback without reinforcement, and expect to see sustained improvement. You can't even reinforce without the other steps because, if you do, you will probably reinforce the wrong behaviors at the wrong time. The problem-solving model starts with pinpointing and ends with evaluation for an important reason. All steps must be used, in that order, to take full advantage of its power to improve performance.

One of the most important actions for management is to *positively reinforce those who use the model* to improve performance. Don't wait until employees get improved performance (a result). Initially reinforce the behavior of using the model to solve problems or improve performance at work.

This Model Works on *All* Performance Problems. One of the main obstacles I have encountered over the years when trying to get companies to use this behavioral model as the total way to approach their business is the reaction that "It's too simple for our complex problems." When I hear that statement I remember what Sam Jenkins, a retired executive with International Paper, once said: "Managers consistently refuse to accept simple answers to complex problems." The model is simple. Applying it is not.

This model applies to any aspect of business—from downsizing to cycle time reduction. If you need to increase sales, this model works. If you need more new products from the lab, this model works.

Dr. Glenn Latham, a behavior analyst at Utah State University, stated in his article, "The Application of Behaviorological Principles":

> It is my experience that eventually, reasonable, honest, and effective solutions can be found *for every single problem. No exceptions!* I have become absolutely unequivocal and fearless on that point, so much so that I am willing to bet anyone $10,000 that, relative to any behavioral problem, if they will be honest about it, and do what I tell them to do, an effective intervention will be found and within a reasonable period of time.

Implementing the Model

To implement this model, you must select a pinpoint and begin measurement prior to a performance intervention. This allows you to collect a baseline, a starting point, against which you can evaluate the effect of the intervention. In Performance Management, an *intervention* is typically defined as the introduction of systematic feedback and reinforcement.

If you evaluate your results and see that your intervention of systematic feedback and reinforcement is not working, you should reexamine the reinforcer step to determine if the consequence you are providing is really a reinforcer to the recipient(s). If changing the reinforcer doesn't solve the problem, you have probably selected the wrong pinpoint. In any event, to be successful you must complete all the steps of the model. If you don't get the results you want, change one element at a time and monitor your results—the same procedure a scientist follows—until you solve the problem.

Can We Do Science at Work?   The model described in this chapter lends itself to scientific analysis. Because of the precision of the pinpointing, measurement, and intervention, you can easily measure pre- and postintervention performance. Then you can use one of several research designs to evaluate the effects of your Performance Management intervention.

Evaluating the Impact of a Performance Management Intervention

B Design

In this evaluation design, you decide what you want to do to change performance, you do it, and then track the results. Most people in business are content if things get better. However, this is the least powerful design for testing whether your intervention was responsible for any change. This approach is weak because you have no baseline against which you can evaluate your intervention. (See Figure 13-1.)

B Design
Reruns as a Percent of Completed Jobs

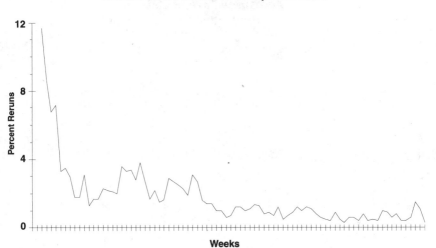

Figure 13-1

AB Design

This design requires that you collect baseline data on current performance. This data allows you to show that the performance was not moving in the right direction until after the intervention. Then, if improvement starts after your intervention, you have some evidence that your intervention is responsible for the change. A critic could claim (and often will) that the improvement was due to another change in the working conditions that occurred simultaneously with your intervention. They point to environmental, economic, seasonal, or other such changes to explain the differences. Although this test is more powerful than the B design, it's still considered relatively weak as far as scientific proof is concerned. (See Figure 13-2.)

ABA Design

This is a more powerful design than either the B or AB designs because it involves a return to baseline conditions. For example, if your intervention consisted of introducing some form of reinforcement, *after a period of time you withdraw the reinforcement and see if the performance returns to its previous level.*

The problem with this design is that, in an ongoing business, rarely would a manager want to stop something that is working just to prove that the intervention is really the cause of the improvement. (See Figure 13-3.)

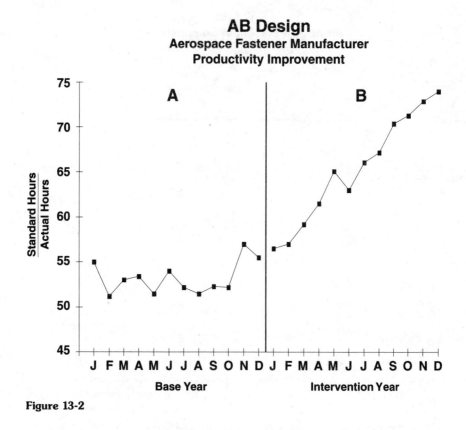

Figure 13-2

Multiple Baseline Design

A multiple baseline design is several AB designs implemented at varied times. This is one of the most powerful designs because you can do as many AB designs as you need to determine cause and effect. This is easy to do and in my opinion should be standard operating procedure with any new program designed to affect performance. (See Figure 13-4.)

All of these evaluation designs can be applied in the workplace. I call them *noninvasive*. That means you do not have to disrupt the normal conduct of business to test the efficacy of your intervention.

The usual social science and psychological model requires that you set up control and experimental groups. This means that you balance the two groups on all variables (age, sex, education, experience, etc.) that might affect the outcome. It also usually requires that you either set up an artificial situation or that you reassign people. As you might imagine, very little of this type of research is done in real work situations. The designs

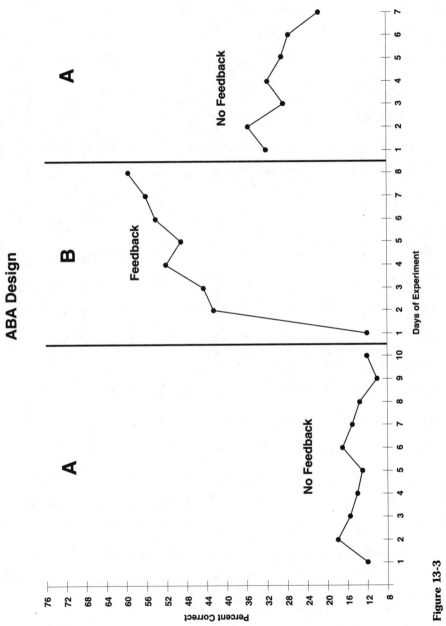

Figure 13-3

113

Multiple-Baseline Design

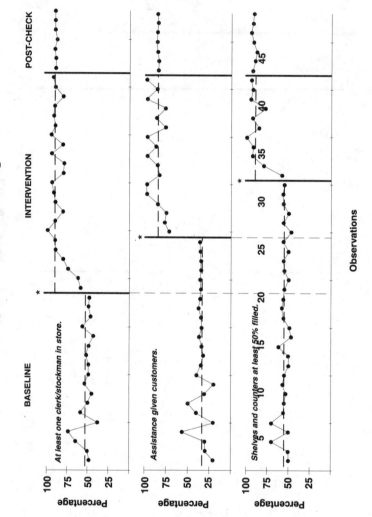

ADAPTED FROM: Komaki, Judi; Alternative execution strategies to management performance improvement. JOBM Vol. 1, No. 1 (1977), pg. 63.

Figure 13-4

described in this chapter use the group (or individual) as its own control, eliminating the need for any change that could be disruptive or nonproductive.

Once again, this method should be standard operating procedure for evaluating any effort to change any aspect of performance. If this approach is used routinely, it *will* save organizations millions of dollars over the years by eliminating commonsense solutions that don't work, but are not usually evaluated.

Hopkins, et al. (1992), suggest there are so many ineffective strategies being sold to businesses that some sort of business protection agency needs to be formed "to protect vulnerable and unwitting corporate and agency executives from unscrupulous or unwitting social scientists, consultants, and personnel staff members who promise salvation but, in fact, deliver unproven and possibly completely useless or even harmful technology."

PART 4

Turning Good Intentions into High Performance

14
Goal Setting
to Shape Behavior

Make haste slowly.

BENJAMIN FRANKLIN

Few things consume more management time than goal setting. Establishing "realistic, attainable, yet challenging goals" has been a battle cry for legions of managers—and management consultants. In fact, training courses in goal setting and the accompanying "Conducting an Effective Performance Appraisal Meeting" are second only to sales management skills as the most popular nontechnical training courses offered by most companies.

You'd think that as often as goals are discussed, developed, and used by managers there would be agreement on how to set goals and document their value to business. Yet there is not.

As I've mentioned previously, noted quality expert W. Edwards Deming advised us to eliminate goals altogether. Deming had observed how, in actual practice, goals and standards limit performance. He said that people who are capable of more reach their goal level and stop. In other words, performers typically give only what is asked for, even when they are capable of more.

Remember, in earlier chapters I described this same scenario as a sign of management by negative reinforcement.

What Deming saw in many organizations was that the majority of people attain goals in order to escape or avoid the consequences of not meeting the goals, rather than attaining or exceeding their goals as a means of receiving positive reinforcement.

119

Understanding the True
Nature of Goals

Goals are antecedents for either reinforcement or punishment. If people are punished when they fail to reach a goal, people will reach the goal only to avoid the punishment. On the other hand, if people reach their goals and receive positive reinforcement, they will not stop when they get to goal but will continue to perform at their best, knowing that more positive reinforcement will be forthcoming.

The belief that goals improve performance interferes with their effective use. If goals are set but there are no consequences for either success or failure, the goals will produce no improvement and will ultimately be a waste of time.

A textile sales organization in New York used a goal-setting process called *targeting* with their salespeople. This process consumed several months of management time each year. It involved the sales manager sitting with each salesperson, reviewing every account, and setting sales targets for each season.

When asked how many targets were met each season, the most common response by far was, "about 75 percent." The actual data was available but was not routinely reviewed. When we actually examined results for the previous season, we discovered that only 8 percent of the targets had actually been met! Management was shocked. They were sure the data was wrong. We then looked at the data from the season before and found that goal attainment was only 11 percent.

Management had mistakenly assumed that good participative goal setting would surely produce improvement.

Goals Get Results (a Management Myth).   What we know by now is that the setting event will not produce the outcome if the consequences don't favor it. Goals, no matter how well conceived, are antecedents. Only if they are antecedents for positive reinforcement will people be enthusiastic about reaching them, and willing to set more.

The Best Mistake.   When Deming encouraged management to eliminate goal setting, he was really calling for the *elimination of goals as they are currently used. And I agree.* However, I know that goal setting does have the potential to contribute to improved performance if used in the correct way.

Very clearly, *the purpose of setting goals should be to increase opportunities for positive reinforcement.*

If this is the purpose, *we should want many, not few, goals.* And, contrary to common sense, the best mistake to make in goal setting is to *set the goals too low.* The reasons for these techniques may be obvious to you by now:

1. If the goal is low, it increases the probability of success. If the goal is reached *and success is celebrated,* the motivation to do even more the next time is increased.

2. If goals become the antecedent for positive reinforcement, then the more goals you have, the more occasions for positive reinforcement.

The mistake that is most commonly made when setting goals is associated with the word *challenging.* The concept of "challenging goals" usually causes managers to set fewer goals and to set them too high. Fewer goals, harder to attain, equals very few opportunities for positive reinforcement and reward.

The Challenge of "Stretch" Goals.   I hope by this time your company has discontinued the practice of setting *stretch* goals.

Stretch goals reduce the probability of success because they are too difficult, maybe even impossible, to attain. Depending on how far your performers are stretching, the probability of success may be less than 50 percent. No business can survive these days by reaching its goals only 50 percent of the time.

Stretch goals evolved as a means of avoiding the phenomenon Deming observed. That is, people get to the goal and wait for the next one before starting to improve again. When there is a goal and then a stretch goal beyond it, people know they can't quit, but they also know that failing to reach the stretch goal won't be "the end of the world" because management is admitting that the probability of attainment is low. Using stretch goals to try to fool people into superior performance just doesn't work.

As I mentioned previously, when I talk negatively about stretch goals I annoy many managers because they have used them successfully. Rather than being annoyed, they should be excited about the possibilities that using better methods provide.

Make Haste Slowly.   You may have gotten the idea that when I say things like "set goals that are relatively easy to achieve," I don't understand the urgent demand for dramatic improvement in the marketplace today. To the contrary, I understand that the urgency is so great that we can't afford any more mistakes in the use of goals and standards, whether applied to individuals or the organization as a whole. We can't afford to waste another decade guessing about goal setting. We can't afford to waste another day.

Let's stop guessing and look at what we know.

Equal Goals Are Unfair to All

Nothing is more unequal than the equal treatment of unequals.
     Attributed to VINCE LOMBARDI

Across-the-board goals are unfair to everybody. For example, if we ask for 10 percent improvement in productivity from everybody, it will generally be too difficult for the lowest performers, too easy for the average performers, and too difficult for the best performers.

The learning curve shown in Figure 14-1 illustrates the proper way to set goals. At the lower end of the curve, notice that the goals are modest. In the middle ranges, the goals are more moderate. At the upper end, the goals are once again smaller.

Let me explain. Low performers won't be able to achieve the first level of performance where the reinforcement is available if they are expected to increase their performance at a rate equal to everybody else. They will quickly give up. For them, average improvement is asking too much.

Average performers will tend to meet the goals and then, if there is no positive reinforcement in place, settle back into a level of performance that is comfortable for them to maintain, but not their best.

Top performers, already operating at a high level, when asked to give the same percent of improvement as lower achievers, will often become resentful and feel that they are being punished for being the best.

Goal Setting in a Training Situation

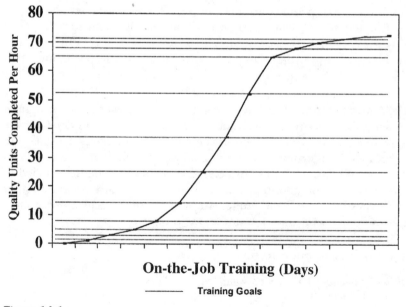

On-the-Job Training (Days)

——— **Training Goals**

Figure 14-1

For each performer, you should set the first goal slightly ahead of his or her current performance. You will make much more progress if you use short time frames (days, weeks) and smaller goals than you will if you set high goals and longer time frames (month, quarter, year).

The process of setting attainable goals based on current performance allows you to reinforce everyone for their individual performance. It also allows all performers to progress at their own pace.

Take the case of an individual in a group performing at 73 units per day when he or she should be at 110 per day. Don't hesitate to start with an initial goal of 75, even if others in the group are producing at much higher levels. The next goal might be 77 or 78 and the next after that, 83 or 85.

If you use daily or weekly goals, it won't take long for a reinforced performer to reach the ultimate goal; when he or she gets there, you will have a turned-on, fired-up individual. Compare that approach to one where you tell the entire work group that everybody needs to produce at 110, 120, or more and then wait until they do before you provide any reinforcement. You might wait a long time.

Slow and Steady Wins the Race—More than a Fable. The fastest way to change individual behavior is to set small goals, reinforce effort, and celebrate attainment. Remember, positive reinforcement accelerates the rate of improvement. The only way we can achieve dramatic improvement in anything is with lots of reinforcement.

Think about your organization. Think about yourself. If you can't visualize how you and the rest of management are going to act when the organization is successful, you will probably not be in a position to celebrate effectively when you are. The Japanese have a saying, "Many raindrops make an ocean." This means that every improvement, no matter how small, is valuable.

We Americans seem to have a hard time with that. We want large, rapid changes, and we want them now! Our motto seems to be, "If you can't give me want I want right now, I will get someone who can."

Well, that approach is a trap. The resources to make dramatic change are most likely already at your fingertips. Consider this. Suppose you have 1000 people in your company. At the end of the day as everybody is leaving you ask them, "Tomorrow, do you think you could do your job this much better?" as you hold your index finger and thumb a quarter inch apart. What do you think people will say? The overwhelming majority will say, "Sure!"

Let's say all 1000 say yes, and then actually make some small improvement. And you, in some way, let them know you noticed and appreciated the improvement. At the end of the next workday you ask the same question. You will probably get another, "Yes." How many days would you have to do this before the company's performance improved dramatically?

Three weeks? A month? Surely not longer, because you would be compounding 1000 improvements every day.

Think many small improvements; think frequent positive reinforcement.

Shaping: The Fastest Way to Change

The fastest way to improve performance actually seems slow. It involves positively reinforcing *small* improvements. Since positive reinforcement increases the rate of behavior by reinforcing small changes in performance, you are able to accelerate performance early and often.

If we reinforced every behavior in a learning situation, we would generate a lot more excitement, enthusiasm, and improvement than if we reinforced only every 100 behaviors.

The rate of change is directly related to the number of reinforcers received.

The technical name for this process is *shaping. Shaping is the process of positively reinforcing successive approximations toward a goal.* The ability to shape behavior is the essence of effective teaching, coaching, managing, or supervising. Shaping is at the heart of bringing out the best in people. To shape effectively requires the ability to break down a task into small steps, the patience to reinforce very small changes, and the celebration of reaching the final goal.

Creating Rubik's Fanatics.   Years ago I used to demonstrate how I could teach everybody to do the Rubik's cube, a popular three-dimensional puzzle. All I needed to "hook" them was 30 minutes with their hands on the cube. It was easy. I was able to generate so much enthusiasm with this shaping exercise that, eventually, I had to give it up as a classroom exercise because the class became so involved in practicing the cube they wouldn't pay attention to the class work.

The way I created this enthusiasm was first to teach the students to find the "top" of the cube. I showed them how to determine the top, tossed it to them, and asked them to find it themselves. A simple verbal reinforcer, "Good," was sufficient when they were successful with this first step. I repeated this process again and again until they were always successful finding the top. Then I showed them the next step of finding the colored blocks that should go on the top; then how to move those blocks to the top, etc. Using this step-by-step approach, I arranged for them to receive several hundred reinforcers in 30 minutes. This was enough to keep many of them awake late into the night, practicing. The next morning they showed up early to ask my help with a step they couldn't remember, always eager to learn the next step.

I liked this problem as a class exercise because moving the sides of the Rubik's cube is about as meaningless a task as you can devise. And when you're successful the only thing to do is mess it up and start over again. It clearly demonstrates how *meaning resides in consequences—not behavior.*

The result of a completed cube was too far away from the initial tasks to provide any meaningful reinforcement. *It was only the many positive consequences that were provided for making one block at a time go into place that not only kept the students working on the cube in class, but induced them to continue to work on it for hours into the evening.*

This example of shaping which I have just described may sound impractical for the real world of work. But, in fact, it is very pragmatic and efficient. It requires only two things: (1) the final outcome must be important to you and/or the company, and (2) there must be positive recognition for very small increments of change.

If the change is important, it is worth the investment of your time. And, if you will invest the time and effort in reinforcing often in the early stages of improvement, you will have to reinforce much less often later on. In other words, it takes a lot of reinforcement to establish a habit, but only an occasional reinforcer to keep it going.

You have probably heard the expression, "Pay me now or pay me later." The effective use of shaping costs you more time and effort now, but will pay you many dividends in improved performance and reduction in turnover, in retraining time and disciplinary action later.

Organizational Goals and Benchmarking

IQS Study Explained.   The International Quality Study (IQS, 1992) commissioned by the American Quality Foundation found that benchmarking, the practice of tracking business processes considered to be the best in a given sphere of influence ("best in industry," or "best in the world," for example), produced positive results on bottom-line variables only in the best-performing companies. Companies rated medium- or low-performing showed no performance improvement. The study showed that, "In fact, low performers who benchmark their marketing and sales systems can actually expect their performance to suffer."

When you understand how the average company uses goal setting, it is easy to see why the IQS found such results. The best-performing companies probably find the levels of performance of the benchmark companies to be easily attainable. As such, they could get a lot of reinforcement from the knowledge that attainable improvement resulted in being on track to be the "best in the world," "best in the industry," and so on.

On the other hand, many of the medium- and low-performers were probably overwhelmed by the gap between their performance and that of the benchmark. Indeed, some managers probably used the data to punish low performers.

These lower-performing companies must focus first on incremental gains with small goals. This will increase confidence in their ability to improve. As small gains are made, the subsequent gains will be bigger and bigger. Soon they will be in a position to compete with, even challenge, the best in the world.

Remember, where you set goals in relation to present performance is critical, but the most important thing is the celebration of goal attainment. The celebration of attainment is what makes goals motivating.

David McClelland, a Harvard psychologist, has studied achievement for many years. His research determined that the highest achievers in our society set *moderate* goals. Being the highest achievers probably means that they have high *aims*, but that they use moderate goals to manage their performance day to day. Our people are no different. They can and will operate at their best every day. What we have to do is help them get to that point one step at a time. Asking for quantum leaps in performance will only discourage the performer and disappoint the manager who is asking. Goals can play a part in bringing out the best in people, but only when they are used as opportunities to recognize progress toward being the best. *Goals that are celebrated are records waiting to be broken.*

15

The Missing Link in Quality

Quality efforts fail to deliver superior results because the only thing that has changed about quality is the way we talk about it. Everything else has remained the same. Washington Post

As I grow older, I pay less attention to what men say. I just watch what they do.
ANDREW CARNEGIE

Never before has there been so much emphasis on quality in American business. Nearly every company in the United States has launched a bigger, bolder quality program designed to deliver the best products and services available. However, companies are discovering that these promising new programs are failing to produce the superior results originally expected.

Today managers across all organizations are asked to champion the new quality control and improvement effort. They are challenged to "sponsor change," "support the quality vision," and "lead the continuous improvement movement."

Often managers and executives are left wondering how to accomplish these directives and, in desperation, do what they've always done when called upon to adopt a new management change:

- Invest heavily in training programs
- Appoint quality trainers and staff
- Hold numerous meetings on quality improvement techniques
- Publish and circulate informational brochures and pamphlets
- Give testimonials to employees whenever possible
- Distribute quality policies and procedures
- Print inspiring stories and announcements in the company newsletter and paper

As you may have already recognized, all of the preceding items are antecedents to engage in quality improvement behaviors. Antecedents do nothing to increase quality behaviors and results (or any behaviors and results) for more than a short period of time. Antecedents most definitely will not sustain those behaviors until the highest levels of quality are attained.

Meetings, literature, policies, procedures, and training work only when they are paired with meaningful consequences—when something happens to people when they follow, or don't follow, the quality processes.

Total quality programs have come under attack because of their relative ineffectiveness. The biggest complaint is that they bring about only short-term gains and, at worst, are impossible to measure with any real certainty. By now you know why.

Fatally Flawed Notions of Quality

The *Wall Street Journal* recently reported that the total quality movement, "one of the biggest fads in corporate management, is floundering." The newspaper cited an Ernst & Young study of 584 companies in the United States, Canada, Germany, and Japan which reveals a wide range of failings in quality improvement activities in the auto, computer, banking, and health care industries. The *Wall Street Journal* concluded that, despite plenty of talk and much action, many American companies were stumbling because their implementation efforts at quality improvement are "simply too amorphous to generate better products and services."

The American Quality Foundation expressed the opinion that a proliferation of consultants, each preaching their own pet strategy, ". . . confuse and confound . . ." the companies that hire them. The Ernst & Young study showed that in the 584 companies they examined, 945 different quality management tactics were employed.

Many TQM programs attempt to take a shotgun approach to fixing everything all at once within a company.

Even the Malcolm Baldrige National Quality Award encourages companies to ride off in all directions implementing dozens of new practices simultaneously.

In almost every company, the quality effort emphasizes awareness of quality and ignores the importance of reinforcing the specific performance required to bring about quality improvement and make it last.

In several companies with quality programs, managers were asked which quality tools the department used and what was monitored now that wasn't monitored before the programs began. The managers' general response was typically, "More than anything, we really have an appreciation of the quality thing. We're not doing anything basically different, but we're more aware of how important quality is." One wonders how they can expect to get different results without changing the methods they use to get them.

Most quality improvement programs usually show some results when the program is first started, but that improvement soon levels off and, in some cases, drops even lower than previous levels. Why does this happen time and time again? Most often, quality improvement programs fail because they don't take into account the most important element in attaining and sustaining quality—the human element.

Phil Crosby, with the publication of his book, *Quality Is Free,* probably did more than anyone to bring quality to the attention of company executives in this country. He pointed out that most companies spend roughly 25 cents of every sales dollar on quality, either in producing quality products and services or fixing problems. Thousands of executives and managers rushed to his seminars to find out how to save money by producing quality.

"Do it right the first time, every time," was the slogan on everybody's lips. However, many people soon became disenchanted when the slogans didn't transform reality.

Crosby developed the following 14 points for producing quality:

1. *Management commitment.* To make it clear where management stands on quality

2. *The quality improvement team.* To run the quality improvement program

3. *Quality measurement.* To provide a display of current and potential nonconformance problems in a manner that permits objective evaluation and corrective action

4. *The cost of quality.* To define the ingredients of the cost of quality and explain its use as a management tool

5. *Quality awareness.* To provide a method of raising the personal concern felt by all personnel in the company toward the conformance of the product or service and the quality reputation of the company

6. *Corrective action.* To provide a systematic method of resolving forever the problems that are identified through previous action steps

7. *Zero-defects planning.* To examine the various activities that must be conducted in preparation for formally launching the zero-defects program

8. *Supervisor training.* To define the type of training that supervisors need in order to actively carry out their part of the quality improvement program

9. *ZD day.* To create an event that will let all employees realize through a personal experience that there has been a change

10. *Goal setting.* To turn pledges and commitments into action by encouraging individuals to establish improvement goals for themselves and their groups

11. *Error-cause removal.* To give the individual employee a method of communicating to management the situations that make it difficult for the employee to meet the pledge to improve

12. *Recognition.* To appreciate those who participate

13. *Quality councils.* To bring together the professional quality people for planned communication on a regular basis

14. *Do it over again.* To emphasize that the quality improvement program never ends

If you examine these points from the perspective of what you have read in this book, you can see that only one—*recognition*—has anything to do with consequences for performance. If you read Crosby's work you will understand that his definition of recognition is a PFU (Positive-Future-Uncertain) consequence for the performer and, as such, is very weak in sustaining new behavior.

Crosby's message includes some important guidelines that every company could profit from following—but, if these things are worth doing, companies must build in some PIC (Positive-Immediate-Certain) consequences and PFC (Positive-Future-Certain) consequences to generate these behaviors and continue them at high and steady rates.

If Crosby attracted the attention of big business, Deming captured it. Probably no other individual is discussed more in business today than W. Edwards Deming.

As a businessperson, if I had to choose among all the various approaches to quality management available today, I would choose Deming's. His system is data-based with a bias toward application at the company's front line.

I've often said that Performance Management is to the management process what Deming is to manufacturing and service processes. Deming attempts to discover root causes of variance in the manufacturing process so the variance can be reduced. Performance Management discovers the root causes of variance in the human performance process and reduces those variances through systematic behavioral intervention.

The shortcoming in Deming's system is similar to that of Crosby's. Assuming that everything he tells companies to do is valid, how do you get people to do it? He addresses this question in only the vaguest way in his exhortation to "drive out fear."

Deming, like Crosby, developed 14 points for the management of quality. I don't disagree with any of them. But the question remains, "How does Deming propose to get people to carry out these directives?" People often ask me how Performance Management and Deming relate. My response is that any time Deming says, "Do this," it's a place to use Performance Management.

Following, I have listed Deming's 14 points with my interpretation of what each point means in Performance Management terms.

Deming's 14 Points

1. *Establish constancy of purpose.* Pinpoint those behaviors that support the quality initiative and reinforce *only* those behaviors.

2. *Improve constantly and forever every system of production and service.* Always reinforce improvement—no matter how small.

3. *Eliminate numerical goals and quotas, including management by objectives.* Negative reinforcement limits performance. Use goals to increase opportunities for positive reinforcement.

4. *Drive out fear so that everyone may work effectively for the company.* Make positive reinforcement the primary consequence for getting things done. Positively reinforce managers and supervisors who get results through positive means.

5. *Institute leadership.* Determine the behaviors that support the quality initiative and make your support clear by what you reinforce. Make it very clear via personnel promotions and choice assignments that those who successfully implement the program are the models for leadership in your organization.

6. *End the practice of awarding business largely on the basis of price.* Develop a measure for vendors that weights quality and reliability more heavily than price. Reinforce quality by giving your business to vendors who produce quality goods and services.

7. *Break down the barriers between departments.* Positively reinforce cooperation. Be sure you are not inadvertently reinforcing internal competition. Define winning as "everyone wins."

8. *Institute training on the job.* Invest in the development of people, but be sure that training results in improved performance. Evaluate how well people use new skills, not how many classes or hours of training they attended.

9. *Eliminate the annual rating or merit system.* Delayed consequences are ineffective. Develop performance measures that can be tracked daily, weekly, or monthly. Put reinforcement in place for improved behaviors when they occur; reward results when they occur, not months later. Remember, small rewards can have more impact on performance than large ones when they are provided sooner rather than later.

10. *Institute a vigorous program of education and self-improvement.* Develop reinforcers and rewards for formal and informal study and educational accomplishment.

11. *Eliminate slogans and exhortations.* Antecedents don't work to bring about lasting change. Motivate by reinforcement. People are not motivated by slogans. It won't take too many false starts to destroy credibility.

12. *Cease dependence on mass inspection.* Put consequences for quality as close to the performance as possible, and reinforce individuals for taking responsibility for their own quality control.

13. *Adopt the new philosophy.* Develop a reinforcement plan to reinforce all behaviors related to the new way of doing business. Ensure consistency of behavior by being consistent in reinforcement.

14. *Create a structure in top management to accomplish the transformation.* Install a system that reinforces managers for the success of their employees in improving quality. Top management's greatest contribution to quality is their recognition and reward of quality performance—and quality management.

Quality Through Consequences

The most effective way to champion a successful quality effort is to apply the principles of Performance Management. After years of frustration and failures, American managers are finally beginning to understand this. In a survey reported in *USA Today* (July 26, 1993), 91 percent of CEOs surveyed ". . . agreed that the biggest challenge in TQM involved changing human behavior, not mastering technical skills." Creating positive reinforcement for quality behaviors and results is the key to a successful quality initiative.

Obviously, word has been getting around. The following appeared in a 1992 edition of a *Continuous Improvement* newsletter*:

To Achieve Total Quality

1. Pinpoint the behaviors that will support the desired results.
2. Develop measures for those behaviors.
3. Provide performance feedback.
4. Identify specific consequences that will be seen as positive reinforcement by the performers themselves.

Is the Implementation System out of Control?   The focus of too many companies seems to be on creating a quality system rather than improving the product or service. If you do not see some improvement within 90 days of starting your quality program, your program is probably more form than substance.

Too many organizations measure their success by the number of teams trained, rather than by what is happening to quality. The focus should not be on which structures are developed, but on how people are working together and how people are using the quality process. You must correlate these behaviors to what is happening to crucial measures of quality in terms of goods and services. If quality measures aren't improving, you're not reinforcing the right behaviors. Remember, pinpoint results first and measure the change in behavior against those results. If you do that, you will be able to focus behaviors in an efficient way.

Success Equals Rate of Improvement.   The real issue for companies pursuing continuous quality improvement is not whether they can improve or whether they can continue to improve, but whether they can *accelerate the rate of improvement.* If you are improving, but your competitors are improving faster, you may find your improvement is too little too late.

As noted in previous chapters, you can get some immediate improvement with negative reinforcement. Yet the future belongs to the competitor who can accelerate the *rate of improvement,* and that can happen only with the precise and effective use of positive reinforcement.

Every quality-improvement activity, every corrective action, every problem-solving tactic requires human effort. Without the proper understanding of the laws of human behavior, you cannot ensure that this effort will occur predictably—or occur at all. Knowing how to apply Performance Management allows you to focus the human effort. Once the human effort is focused, it's only a matter of time before all the elements in any process are under control.

* Nancy A. Karabatsos, "The Quality Imperative," *Continuous Improvement,* September 1992.

16

Teams and Empowerment

You may get the impression in the first pages of this chapter that I am against teams, but that's not so. Properly used, teams can be very effective. However, teams are not the answer to all performance problems at work. In this chapter, I will explain how teams can be an effective force in the workplace.

Motherhood, Apple Pie, and Teams

The popularity and growth of teams in today's organizations have been phenomenal. Almost everyone in business talks about the "team concept." To say anything against the idea of teams is almost sacrilegious. Managers talk of the number of teams they have trained, how often they meet, and the problems they are working on. "Teams" has become such a "buzz concept" that practically no one questions whether teams are an effective way to run an organization. "Team concept" ranks right up there with motherhood and apple pie.

Could It Be . . . ? Researchers at the University of Sheffield in England, writing in the *Academy of Management Journal*, examined the long-held notion that autonomy within work groups resulted in superior performance. Autonomous work groups are those in which workers have a high degree of self-determination in the management of their day-to-day tasks. This includes control over distribution of tasks, timing and length of breaks, and even participation in the recruitment and training of new members of the group.

Despite the long-held notion that employee autonomy would increase motivation for work or performance, the researchers concluded that "no demonstrable motivational benefit derives from autonomous group working." They went on to say, ". . . it is reasonable to assume that in established organizations, autonomous work groups may result in more problems than their potential practical benefits."

Hopkins, et al. (1991) concluded in *A Digest of Some of the Literature on Self-Managed Work Groups* that this movement appears to be more driven by theory and "common sense" than by hard evidence about the effectiveness of practical methods for implementing self-managed work groups.

Although this is not an isolated case, even one report of such findings is a shock to most people who never question the effectiveness of teams over individual accomplishment. It's a myth that teams *always* come up with a better solution than one individual working alone. In fact, if only one member of the team is an expert on the subject, the team process will dilute that member's expertise.

The Team Concept: In Search of a Problem

Why, then, the fascination with teams? The most-often-used analogy of the value of teams is sports. Athletes who act only in their self-interest are not successful in sports. We've all witnessed games where team members give up the spotlight for the good of the team. Teams that work together win; teams with internal dissension don't.

Sure, working together and cooperating is better than working against one another, but many companies have confused teams with teamwork. Teamwork is *always* appropriate and desirable. A formal team structure, though, is not always necessary.

Teamwork is accomplished simply by making sure that cooperative behavior is positively reinforced. Teams, as they are typically installed, require tremendous effort on the part of the individual and the organization. Unfortunately, in many organizations *the team process has become more important than teamwork.*

Why Teams?   The first question that should be asked is, "What's the problem?" The next, "What's the best way to solve it?" If, after answering these two questions, you decide that a team is the most appropriate method to solve the problem, then the team should be formed. When approached this way, the team is doing value-added work right away. Since the problem has been clearly identified (preferably pinpointed), the team will know exactly what its job is, when the job is completed, and how well the team performed. These are the conditions under which a team can be a very reinforcing and rewarding experience.

If we insist on a team approach to everything, this productive environment won't exist. Reinforcement will be reduced and confusion and frustration increased. Few companies evaluate the effectiveness of teams against an improvement in bottom-line organizational variables.

Dr. Bill Hopkins of Auburn University conducted an extensive literature search and uncovered no record of performance improvement credited to a formal team effort. In his conclusion to the study, he wrote:

> We are interested in the empowerment movement, its history, the theory behind it, and particularly how in the world it has so effectively captured the imagination of American and West European business in the absence of almost any evidence that it yields anything in which company leaders are interested. I find it just incredible that a movement could so thoroughly capture the devotion of business with so little evidence behind it.

As mentioned earlier, some problems are better solved by people working alone than in teams. Industry spends billions of dollars each year to develop competent performers, but now, in many organizations, these same people must subject the decisions they have been trained to make to the vote of a team.

Many team advocates do not seem to understand the inherent conflict between teams and empowerment. Empowerment as I understand it is sharing decision making with all employees at every level in the organization. This means the individual makes more decisions and has more control over life at work. In a team environment, the extent to which an individual is empowered is limited by the authority of the group.

What Does All of This Mean?   What this means is that to attain the most effective and efficient workplace, a variety of skills and tools are necessary. The most effective work environment is one in which people know when to work alone and when to ask for help. When you need to work with others to develop a solution to a complex problem, teams provide a very effective vehicle.

Making Teams Work

Self-directed teams hold the promise of reducing the need for supervisors. In an era of downsizing and delayering, this is a worthy goal, but it's not easily attained. Teams also hold the promise of giving nonsupervisory staff some share in decision making. In traditionally autocratic environments this provides some potential for new ideas. But the one most important benefit of the team structure has been almost entirely overlooked. *Bringing people together* to solve problems or simply manage their daily work *dramatically increases the opportunities for receiving positive reinforcement.*

Every team member is a potential source of positive reinforcement for every other team member. Peers exert tremendous influence on the behavior of peers, for better or worse. Team members have more contact with each other than do their managers, so reinforcement can be more frequent and, since they are together while the work is occurring, reinforcement is likely to be immediate. Yet with all the team training that is being provided, little is devoted to teaching people how to positively reinforce one another for efforts made and results achieved. Without that kind of training, team members will probably use more of the common interactive practices, such as negative reinforcement and extinction. The outcome will be teams that are not very effective at teamwork.

Behavior Is the Key

The most important consideration in team effectiveness is the behavioral dimension. The requirement for the work to change is much less dramatic than the need for *people to change their behaviors and performances*. It is as simple (and as complex) as that.

Human behavior is the single greatest cause of team-implementation failure. The inability of team leaders to change the behaviors of team members and the inability of managers to change the behaviors of supervisors leads to resistance and an eventual abandonment of the process.

Let's start with the team leader. Most managers don't think in behavioral terms. When discussing the shift to work teams, they talk about "roles" changing—not behaviors. For instance, a supervisor will be told that he or she is no longer to manage employees as a boss, but as a coach. This change is usually not spelled out in behavioral terms, and with only superficial training in the new "role," the supervisor is expected to alter his or her behavior in many ways, while at the same time remaining responsible for results.

The following is a sample of the old and new behaviors that might be relevant for a supervisor who is to become a team leader or coach:

Old Behavior	New Behavior
Schedule work	Provide initial direction
Hand out assignments	Develop a positive reinforcement plan
Tell people how to do the job	Give performance feedback
Keep people on task	Provide R+ for task completion

Old Behavior	**New Behavior**
Find and punish poor performance	Mediate reinforcement between team members
Protect company information	Deliver positive reinforcement for: ■ decision making ■ creative solutions ■ cooperation ■ initiative, etc.

By now you understand that you can't just tell a supervisor or anyone else that they are to behave differently and then expect them to do it. Change requires many reinforcers for the new behaviors before new habits can be established. Yet organizations implement teams every day without any type of planned reinforcement to back up and support the many behavioral transitions that team members and team leaders require.

If there's no planned reinforcement, there's certainly a lot of unplanned punishment and extinction associated with team implementation. A study by Wilson Learning Corporation, a training and development firm, found that the use of teams and work groups isn't as effective as organizations expected. Interviews and research of 4500 teams from over 500 companies reveal that the major barriers to team success are*:

- *Rewards and compensation.* 80 percent of respondents said that their rewards and compensation systems focus on individual performance. Team performance is not usually considered. Thus team members have little incentive to work together and are compelled to pursue their own agendas.
- *Personnel and HRD systems.* Only 10 to 20 percent of respondents confirmed that team performance is included in their performance appraisals. Most respondents said that their appraisal systems do not consider team issues.
- *Organizational alignment.* Many respondents said that the organizational structures foster internal competition which limits group effectiveness.

What people are really saying is that the consequences provided by their organizations don't favor a team-oriented workplace. Remember, it's foolish to continue to do the same things and expect different results. If you have decided to implement self-directed teams, it's likely you are fundamentally changing the structure and culture of your company. This is an almost impossible task if you have no strategy for reinforcing behaviors consistent with the new work design.

If you approach implementing teams in a way that demands performers break old habits, chances are very high that you will fail. *The best way to break an old habit is to replace it with a new one . . . and reinforce it a lot.*

* *Training and Development Magazine,* February 1993.

If you can stop people from performing old behaviors, there's no guarantee that they'll begin performing in ways consistent with the team concept. Forcing or coercing people into change works only as long as you maintain very stringent controls and when you are prepared to mete out effective punishment for noncompliance. This doesn't sound much like the highly motivated workplace we all strive for, does it?

The alternative approach is to be ready to reinforce the new behaviors immediately. If you are not prepared to do the latter, get ready to do the former.

Achieving Success Through Performance Management

Most team implementation programs work on the principle of *supply-push*. That is, training programs are supplied, performers are pushed into the classrooms, supervisors are pushed into giving up control and power, and team members are pushed into sharing job responsibilities.

Instead of the supply-push model, organizations should move toward a *demand-pull* model for motivating their employees to accept and excel under the new system. Demand-pull exists when a team wants to move forward with the change, wants to receive more training, and wants to move to the next stage in the transition process. Under demand-pull, acceptance occurs faster and resistance is practically eliminated.

The demand-pull model works like this. The specific behaviors expected from team members, team leaders, and managers must be clearly spelled out. As team members and leaders begin to use these team-supportive behaviors and become more self-directed, they are given greater power and control over their work with more freedom to act, to make meaningful decisions, to gain autonomy, to solicit feedback from customers, to get access to reinforcement funds for celebration purposes, and so on.

Unfortunately, many organizations give away these reinforcers noncontingently. Worse, they unintentionally turn them into punishment by forcing or pushing these changes on team members before they are ready or capable of successfully handling the new responsibility. It would be more effective, instead, to use these potential reinforcers to stimulate demand-pull. The key is to use them contingently, making them available to team members only after they have satisfied certain performance requirements. If team members know they will be given greater opportunity and more involvement in the operation of the company when they exhibit teamwork behaviors and begin to attain certain levels of achievement, they will be more motivated to move forward.

When team members, supervisors, managers, and executives involved in the transition to self-managed teams first learn about the fundamentals of behavior management, you can almost see the lights come on in their heads. Suddenly they know why prior attempts have been unsuccessful. After learning about the importance of pinpointing, measurement, feedback, and reinforcement, these people know what to do to make the implementation effort a success.

Can You Reinforce a Team?

Rewarding outcomes or the results of team effort doesn't go far enough. As John Young, president and CEO of Hewlett-Packard, points out, "We have to look at some new methods to make sure the individual can make a difference and be recognized for it. . . . Personal recognition, that sense of being valued as an individual, is extremely important in getting people's loyalty and commitment and giving them a return for the hard work they've put in."

You cannot reinforce a team. You can only reinforce the behaviors of team members. You can reward a team, but it works best when all members are contributing equally. It's the leader's responsibility to apply consequences to team members individually in such a way that each team member is reinforced appropriately for his or her contributions to the team.

Making the Most of Reinforcement

Because each team is moving at its own pace throughout the transition process, not every team will have the same reinforcers available to team members at the same time. Slower teams will see, hear, and indirectly experience many of the reinforcers being received by the members of other, more advanced teams. They will see other teams meeting and making decisions, planning and controlling budgets and project schedules, and making personnel decisions. They will know of celebrations occurring; they will see feedback graphs reflecting improvements in performance. Chances are, the members of the less-advanced teams will also want to share in these positive consequences and will likely take the necessary actions to earn them. In this way, the positive reinforcement of the advanced teams acts as an effective antecedent for the slower teams.

Don't worry that everybody will not be reinforced and rewarded at the same time. As long as it's possible for members of every team to eventually earn the same reinforcers and rewards, there will be no problem. In fact, employees sometimes seem to understand contingencies better than their managers.

Empowerment Through Shaping

When adopting a contingent-reinforcement, team-by-team approach for organizational change, it's critical that the criteria for receiving reinforcement and rewards are clear and achievable. If the contingencies are fuzzy and uncertain, team members may think they are entitled to a reward or reinforcement when they are not. This can create an unpleasant and unhealthy air of skepticism and bitterness among team members that will quickly destroy the pride and enthusiasm that the new reinforcement system generated. If the requirements for reinforcement are unrealistic or very difficult to achieve, team members will undergo extinction and may become distrusting and cynical about the entire reinforcement system.

The best way to empower team members is gradually and systematically. You can't say to people, "Okay, after all these years of reporting to your boss, getting everything approved, and working within limited boundaries, you are now free! You're on your own! Start taking responsibility and making decisions!" While this exaggerated approach may seem ridiculous, it's been done, and it's clearly counterproductive to the empowerment endeavor.

Responsibilities for self-management and decision making should be turned over to team members on an *as-ready basis* and the *responsibilities given initially should be limited in scope*. As in all performance change initiatives, the strategy that must be used for maximum effectiveness is shaping. Reinforce small improvements—earning empowerment all the way.

You cannot give people empowerment; they have to earn it.

17
Turning Downsizing into Rightsizing

Tough Times Demand Positive Management

Since the mid-1980s, many U.S. businesses have "downsized" their work force in an attempt to run "leaner and meaner" and, of course, be more profitable. Downsizing has been the primary method used to give shareholders a higher return on their investment in a short period of time.

Especially in those businesses which are labor-intensive, the cost of salaries and benefits offers management a tempting source of quick cost reduction. The question "Has downsizing succeeded in reducing costs?" is usually answered yes. The question "Has downsizing returned profits to the company and its shareholders?" is answered quite differently. The facts speak for themselves.

One *Fortune* 500 firm (which shall remain nameless) reduced staff five times between 1985 and 1990, eliminating a total of 12,000 jobs. Using data from the Bureau of Labor Statistics and company reports, *Business Week* reported that in the 12-month period before their layoffs began, this company's return on equity was 4.5 percent. After the repeated downsizing initiatives, their return to shareholders was 2.2 percent. This type of result is not the exception—far from it. Many other companies have experienced similar or even worse results.

Westinghouse and American Express, after initiating massive layoffs, both experienced a return on equity that was 50 percent less than they were earning in the previous year. Zenith and Sears Roebuck experienced *negative* returns on equity one year following the start of their layoffs, despite the fact that each had been well into the black at the outset. Not surprisingly, one survey found that more than 1000 companies that downsized during 1992 produced the expected savings only 36 percent of the time. The American Management Association has concluded that downsizing doesn't have the desired effect on the bottom line in either the mid- or long-term.

Why do companies turn to downsizing in the first place and why does it uniformly lead to disappointment? At best, downsizing is a stopgap measure designed to "stop the bleeding" because companies are unable to solve fundamental problems like low productivity, sluggish sales, poor strategic planning, or unsound management practices. Does reducing labor cost via downsizing correct any of these problems? The answer of course is no.

Downsizing as applied by American business is akin to amputating a gangrenous leg in an attempt to save the life of a dying patient.

"Rightsizing" Is the Answer

The question that has gone unanswered in industry today is: "If downsizing doesn't work, what does work to reduce costs while increasing profitability?" The practical alternative to downsizing is "rightsizing."

Rightsizing simply means that we have the right amount of labor to get the job done in *the most effective and efficient manner.* This can never be done by simply reducing the work force. Even if an organization performs a detailed analysis of all tasks to be performed and precisely measures how many and what type of people and skills are necessary to get the job done, it will have used only the rudimentary tools of rightsizing. Cutting jobs and reorganizing is not rightsizing.

Clearly, many organizations must reduce staff size if they are to have any chance of survival. Because of past management practices or immediate economic survival concerns, the company must quickly bring costs in line with revenue. Whether to downsize or not isn't the question. The question is: "How can we get the most accomplished with the fewest resources?" In reality, the only reason a company would ever need to turn to downsizing is *people have been or are being reinforced for the wrong behaviors and/or punished or extinguished for the right behaviors.* How does reorganizing and cutting jobs change this? It doesn't.

If a manager who has been reinforced for doing the wrong things is placed in a new job, does that mean that the manager will suddenly start doing the right things? Obviously not. This is why Peter Drucker feels that turnarounds require new blood. What he really means is that new habits are needed. Doing the same old thing harder or with fewer people is not the answer.

Recessions, shrinking markets, or increased competition can cause organizations to downsize as an immediate survival tactic, but if people are being reinforced for doing the right things, there are other alternatives.

They can increase market share in recessions and, in a shrinking market, they can drive out competition.

An alternative to downsizing is urgently needed. One of the first negative aspects of downsizing is that often the people the organization can least afford to lose are the first to go. These are usually the senior people who have the option of an attractive severance package. When they consider staying and possibly being let go in a future downsizing, understandably they choose to take the severance package and leave. Believe it or not, this is negative reinforcement. They make the choice not because they want to, but because they are afraid of what will happen to them if they don't.

Their experience and talent walks out the door with them, sometimes into the employ of the competition, and the organization must now deal with a more serious problem—the people who are left.

Those who are left inevitably feel punished. From their viewpoint, the same work is now being done by fewer people. Rather than being grateful that they were spared, they feel punished and afraid that they will be the next to go. Both conditions limit future improvements.

Hence the main issue isn't which jobs to place people in or how the organizational chart will change, but how to get the survivors excited and *keep* them excited about what must be done. In almost all cases of resizing, this motivational factor has been ignored. Even in those cases when it has been considered, the final execution fails to inspire remaining employees about the new opportunities created by the downsizing.

Instead, those same employees are more likely to question the competence of management and express considerable pessimism about the organization's future.

Several recent articles on the subject of rightsizing have told us *what* must be done, but few tell us *how* to do it successfully. For example, an article in *Fortune* magazine (February 1992) offered six rules for "rightsizing your downsizing." The rules in themselves are valid, yet no instructions on how to accomplish them are included. After examining the six steps from a behavioral angle, I have interpreted them as explained in the following section.

Fortune's Six "Rules"

Fortune's Rule Number 1: Cut Unnecessary Work

Behavioral interpretation: *Change what people do.*

Ironically, in most organizations the first step is to cut people, not work. As previously stated, those who remain feel threatened and overworked. When most companies downsize they are in a survival mode and tend to manage performance through negative, rather than positive, reinforcement—further crippling incentives.

What the organization needs before downsizing are ideas for *taking work out of the system.* Of course, there must be positive consequences for doing so. Employees will not voluntarily think of ways to eliminate work if they see it as a threat to their jobs.

Several years ago, one of our clients had a program called "Step Up." The idea was to encourage people to find ways to eliminate their jobs. If they did so, they were guaranteed a higher-paying job or a bonus of 10 percent of their present annual wage and a transfer to another equal-paying job.

Shortly after the program began, several people "stepped up." Within a couple of weeks, however, people stopped coming forward. Had they exhausted the opportunities? Hardly. A closer examination revealed that when employees suggested ways to eliminate their jobs, their supervisors were then punished by their managers for not having known and reported those work-saving methods in previous cost-reduction attempts. The program was well-conceived from the perspective of the frontline employee, but not for the supervisors. Eliminating work must help everyone. If it doesn't, a lot of unnecessary work will remain categorized as necessary.

Fortune's Rule Number 2: Put Quality First

Behavioral interpretation: *Plan and deliver R+ for "quality behaviors."*

Interestingly, this rule was listed second. That fact demonstrates how we constantly say things that we don't put into action.

The *Washington Post,* in an article on quality, stated that one *cannot talk away old habits.* If different behaviors are needed to improve quality, then merely talking about quality (or providing quality training) will not produce sustained quality improvements. There must be positive, daily, and immediate consequences for the new behaviors, excluding such pie-in-the-sky and uncertain reasons as keeping one's job and staying in business.

Furthermore, if different "quality" behaviors are required, they must be specified. W. Edwards Deming and other quality gurus did a good job specifying process changes that must be made to produce quality. Yet they do a poor job specifying the behaviors necessary to make the process changes. They do an even poorer job specifying how to get people to do those behaviors when and if those behaviors are designated. Deming recognized this area of need stating, "I know it is important, but I don't have the foggiest notion how to do it." (If you've been reading carefully, by now, you do.)

Increasing quality behaviors requires positive reinforcement. If your quality system does not have a way to guarantee reinforcement as a daily occurrence, quality levels will improve only incrementally, if at all.

Fortune's Rule Number 3: Bust Your Paradigms

Behavioral interpretation: *Change what* you *do.*

A paradigm is nothing more than a pattern of behavior. It is a typical way of doing things, a habit. If we could change someone's bad habits simply by asking or even demanding they change, then no one would have any bad habits. Mark Twain said, "Habit is habit, and not to be flung out the window by any man, but coaxed downstairs a step at a time."

It's not easy to change how you do things. When we tell people they must change and they don't, it's not because they don't understand how important it is to change, or that they don't understand how to change, but because management continues to reinforce the same old habits. This is why Deming asserted that over 90 percent of all organizational problems are management problems. Management must provide consequences to promote new habits that are consistent with the organization's mission.

Fortune's Rule Number 4: Empower People

Behavioral interpretation: *Have people do more* management *things.*

Everybody has picked up the "empowerment" buzzword, but few seem to know what it means in terms of behavior change. It means that not only do we want people to do more management things, but that management must reinforce them for assuming new behaviors and responsibilities. Management doesn't accomplish empowerment solely by communicating it, or even through training.

As a guest speaker at a large corporation not long ago, I listened to several managers discussing the state of the company. The most pressing business was how to cut 15 percent from operating costs. They discussed eliminating a product line, selling a plant, and closing a warehouse, among the alternatives that would make an immediate improvement in operating expenses. When I stood to speak, I asked the group, "How many employees are represented by the managers in this room?"

Someone responded, "27,000."

Then I asked, "How many of those 27,000 are excited about cutting 15 percent out of the operation?" They all laughed nervously. "That's your problem," I said. "If 27,000 people were excited about making this company more competitive, you'd be embarrassed for setting such a low goal." One of the problems in most downsizing is that management tries to do it alone.

It is not that employees don't know that things can be done better. Studies over the years show rather consistently that people, when asked, agree they could do more on their jobs than they do. On the average, employees agree they could produce about 30 percent more, if properly motivated. In fact, a 1991 poll conducted by Teleometrics International of more than 10,000 American workers and managers indicates that employees feel they could increase personal productivity from 40 to 67 percent if they weren't laboring under what they labeled "competency-suppressing" management conditions. Competency-suppressing conditions is just another way of saying that their work is dominated by punishment, extinction, and negative reinforcement. Rightsizing offers the opportunity to take advantage of this untapped effort, but few companies do so.

How can we get everybody involved? The first requirement is for management to understand which employee behaviors are needed to be successful. The second is to know what to do when those behaviors occur. Three management behaviors are necessary to get people to become more self-managed: (1) Give positive reinforcement for assuming new responsibilities; (2) proceed slowly—reinforce small improvements; (3) don't punish errors.

Many organizations have rushed into empowerment and are facing chaos—primarily because they try to move too fast. The fastest approach to true empowerment seems to be the slowest. By setting up small successes, people will look forward to more change. When moving too fast, mistakes are more frequent, punishment is more probable, and people will inevitably resist the change. People don't naturally resist change, they resist doing things for which they get punished. If management doesn't manage that part of change, empowerment will remain just a buzzword.

Fortune's Rule Number 5: Communicate

Behavioral interpretation: *Have* management *do more management things.*

Management is responsible for communicating a vision that will rally the troops. In troubled times, few organizations give people the kind of information that will excite them about making dramatic change. The usual downsizing operation is like a retreat or entrenchment and the communique is often, "If you don't get with it, we (or you) might not be here next year." That hardly inspires one to accomplish monumental things. Effective leaders can rally troops in the face of defeat. During the Korean war, an American general commented, when asked about retreating American forces, "Retreat, hell, we're advancing in the other direction."

Proper rightsizing starts with the mission of the company. The mission should answer the question, "Why are we doing this at all?" In order to inspire, we must have a purpose greater than that which is represented by day-to-day activities. Most companies are trying to be the exemplar at something. The mission must clearly present that something.

A mission is useless if people don't know what they must do to make it a reality. When the mission has been determined and communicated, everyone must be able to translate it into personal action. Questions that must be answered once the mission has been determined are:

What results are we trying to achieve, not just in the long-term, but this month, this week, tomorrow?

What are the behaviors that are required to achieve those results?

Who is going to do them?

Vision grows out of mission. A significant part of a vision is to be able to see how the organization is going to look when it is successful. Not only should we be able to see concrete accomplishments, but we should also be able to see how people will act, and we should know how we will celebrate success. A vision that does not include a plan for celebrating success will not only fail to motivate people, but will achieve only minimal results. A vision makes people say, "I'm ready. What do we do now?" It's management's job to be ready to tell them.

Fortune's Rule Number 6: Take Care of Survivors

Behavioral interpretation: *Reinforce any and all improvement from the first day.*

Unfortunately, most of the reinforcement that occurs in the average downsizing is unplanned and coincidental with the changes in job activities. Often, when an organization downsizes, the task ahead is so great and so many dramatic changes are necessary in such a short period of time that we fail to get excited about small improvements. *Small improvements are the building blocks of monumental changes.*

In order to change downsizing to rightsizing, you must have a plan to positively reinforce the positive efforts of those who remain. Employees can't be blamed for the need to downsize. They are only doing what they have been reinforced to do. From *day one* there should be a plan to reinforce the new behaviors required to succeed. This plan should include lots of social reinforcement, and tangible rewards as well.

Rightsizing is probably the best time to implement some kind of gainsharing plan. This gives people a strong incentive to eliminate unnecessary work and implement new ideas. Also, as mentioned previously, some provision should be made to capitalize on the experience of those who are leaving. Separation packages should include reinforcement and rewards for sharing ideas, transferring skills, and imparting the special knowledge gained from years of experience to those who remain behind.

From a Performance Management perspective, the key to successful rightsizing is the reinforcement of the right behaviors, for the right people, at the right time. If initiative, risk taking, and other new and different ways of doing things are not positively reinforced, then it can only be business as usual. And business as usual leads to further downsizing.

The job of management during rightsizing is to develop a system that will ensure the delivery of the right consequences for these progressive behaviors. If this had been done consistently in the past, the need for downsizing might not exist. The organization would have continuously rightsized itself because there would have been immediate and long-range positive consequences for doing so. If we rightsize correctly, the quality and rate of performance increases an organization's ability to do more with less. And doing more with less is, after all, the essence of rightsizing.

18
Recognition, Reward, Reinforcement, and Relationships

There Are Cheaper Ways to Make People Unhappy

Few organizations are satisfied with their reward and recognition systems. Furthermore, every change in these systems results in someone else becoming unhappy. Most often, management becomes cynical, because no matter what they try, "nobody is satisfied."

Reward and recognition systems have changed little in the last 50 years. The only things that have changed about them are the size and type of reward or recognition. Companies are almost never able to prove that they get a motivational, morale, or bottom-line benefit from such systems. Yet, almost no one is willing to abandon them, because they feel that there must be a benefit somewhere.

Before proceeding further, some definitions are needed:

Recognition. Usually a symbolic way of showing appreciation for some accomplishment (including plaques, trophies, and letters of commendation). By its very nature, recognition is delayed and infrequent.

150

Reward. A tangible item, usually money or exchangeable for money, that is intended to influence behavior in a particular direction. Because most rewards are not tailored to the person receiving them, it is not surprising that they do not motivate everyone. Because most rewards are for results, without regard to the behavior used to obtain them, it should not surprise anyone that people will try to get rewards with behaviors other than those desired. The fact that people will lie, cheat, and steal to get some rewards is not the fault of the rewards but the fault of the one who designed the system that allows those behaviors to be rewarded. Because rewards are always delayed, it is possible that the behaviors that triggered the reward may not be occurring when the reward is received, which inadvertently reinforces the wrong behavior.

Incentive. Used as an inducement to perform. The term as conventionally used is synonymous with reward, but has often been used for recognition as well.

Not everyone believes that rewards are a good thing. Parents often voice concern over rewarding their children for behaviors that they should be doing already. Safety experts have concern about rewarding employees for being safe for fear that they will cover up or not report accidents or unsafe behavior. Some retail businesses advertise that they don't pay commission on sales so that customers will know that they won't be pressured by a commissioned salesperson to buy something they don't really want.

In his book, *Punished by Rewards,* Alfie Kohn,* denigrates rewards. He generally equates them with bribes, and states that they should not be used. His book was well read and his lectures well attended. Although he claimed that his book was based on research, he extrapolated considerably beyond the studies he quoted. However, the attention that he got, particularly from the business audience, is an indication of the dissatisfaction with current reward systems and the desperate attempts to find a better way. The rapid growth of the National Association for Employee Recognition (NAER) is also an indication of interest in making them more effective.

When I spoke at a recent NAER annual conference, I started my speech by saying, "Eliminate all employee reward and recognition systems." As you might imagine, considering this association's purpose, I got everybody's attention right away. However, the point I wanted to make was that the way recognition and reward systems are designed and implemented, most organizations would be better off without them.

You might ask if I am saying that rewards and recognition are bad for business and other organizations? I'm not saying that at all. When they are prop-

* Kohn, A., *Punished by Rewards,* Houghton Mifflin Company, Boston, 1993.

erly designed and implemented, they can have positive effects on the organization. When they are not, they are bad for employees and the organization.

Why is it that something that is so central to the way we do business is so problematic? In my opinion, this comes about because these systems are built from a commonsense and/or financial perspective rather than from an understanding of how behavior is affected.

Recognition and rewards systems used by most organizations have one thing in common: The recognition and reward comes long after the behavior has occurred. Any time there is a delay between the behavior and the consequence, there are potential problems. An annual recognition day where employees sit and watch a fraction of their peers get "recognition" is motivation to very few. Where large cash awards or expensive prizes are given to a limited number of individuals, the recognition program will probably demotivate more often than it will motivate.

In addition, because these awards come so long after the accomplishment, they may appear arbitrary. Many times large numbers of employees are left wondering why they weren't singled out for recognition when they worked as hard or harder than the people being recognized. Celebrating accomplishments throughout the year is a much better form of recognition and, in the last chapter of this book, I will go into detail about how to conduct an effective celebration.

For now, I'm going to describe the problems with various commonly used forms of recognition and reward systems and suggest ways to overcome them.

Ineffective Rewards, Recognition, and Incentives

Whether with rewards or recognition, the stated purpose among some executives is to have a program or system that will make positive examples of a few employees, which will cause others to work hard to achieve the same. However, most systems limit the number of employees who can get the reward or award at the same time. The words *first, most,* and *most improved* limit the number of people who actually receive the consequence. The "Top 5," "Top 10," or "Top 100" are no better. Here are a number of commonly used and ineffective recognition and reward procedures and programs.

Employee of the Month

People often ask me what I think of Employee of the Month (EOM) programs. My advice to companies who have the standard EOM program is to eliminate it as quickly and as painlessly as possible.

Employee of the Month is the most popular form of recognition in the country. Unfortunately, this form of recognition violates practically every known principle of effective recognition and positive reinforcement.

These programs do not specify precisely what must be done to get the award; they do not recognize performance immediately or frequently; they assume that the same form of recognition is desired by all; and, most troublesome, they allow for only one or at most a few winners.

EOM programs represent a very simplistic approach to the significant problem of employee motivation and human performance. While the goal of these programs is to recognize outstanding performance so that employees will feel better about their jobs, themselves, and the company, more often than not they accomplish the opposite. It is assumed that EOM will improve employee performance daily, but there is nothing in the program that delivers consequences daily.

Pinpointing Error. Employees generally do not understand what the EOM program is really about. The next time you see a plaque in a hotel or restaurant, ask an employee to explain it. At best they will tell you something vague about hard work and good attitude. At last count I had asked 77 people at various establishments, "What do you have to do to earn that?" Not one was able to tell me the criteria. The most common answer by far was, "I don't really know." One said, "Make more friends, I guess."

The answer that probably got closest to the truth came from a woman who worked at a rental car agency. She said, after a couple of minutes of reciting the company line, "I guess be nice to your manager."

Delay Error. The fact that most of the EOM plaques you see are often months out of date certainly says a lot about how important management thinks these programs are. Why an organization would publicly advertise its lack of importance is beyond me. You would think they would at least take down the plaque until it was brought up to date. But even the most up-to-date program is way too late. An award given once a month, even if all other elements were done well, would still not affect performance.

Just imagine that you have chosen your employee of the month because of some very important and appropriate action he or she took during the first week of the month. You have the employee's name inscribed on the plaque and wait until presentation time at your end-of-month staff meeting. The day arrives and as you step out of your office you see your recipient in a violent argument with a customer. The customer storms out of your building vowing never to return. Your award ceremony will be very interesting indeed.

Even without this nightmare scenario, recognition given 12 times a year is far from sufficient to motivate performance.

Competition Error.   The most detrimental part of the EOM approach to recognition is the competitive nature of the system. There is only one winner and many losers. I saw a very dramatic example of the competition error at a sales banquet where I was the speaker. Before I got up to speak, they had the presentation of their salesperson-of-the-year awards.

They were into this "big time." They gave away automobiles to the winner in each of several divisions. In one division, the sales manager talked for at least five minutes explaining how difficult it had been to choose the winner from the top two finalists. The winner got a new mid-size Chevrolet. The man who came in second received a working model of a Rolls Royce, valued at over $100.

Even though it was a classy model—the doors opened, the lights worked, the company had even thoughtfully provided the batteries—can you imagine how employee number 2 felt? I seriously doubt that this employee rejoiced in the success of the winner.

Some companies have tried to solve the competition problem by having several "winners," possibly the top 10. However, having a few more winners is not better, it's worse. It's one thing to shrug off the fact that you are not the best performer, but when you are not even in the top ten, it could be humiliating.

Any recognition system where one person's success limits another's is a bad system. Whether you have 1, 10, or 100 winners, there is a problem if even one person can't win because of competitive rules.

When every company in the country is preaching teamwork, it doesn't make sense to use a recognition technique like this.

Contingency Error.   Another problem with EOM is its distribution. Long ago, organizations realized if they gave the award to the "best" performer, the same person would win every time. In order to solve that problem some companies made a rule that a person could not win the EOM award more than once a year. This of course means that any trace of a contingency between performance and the award is eliminated. At this point the award becomes a "pass-around" award. In other words, what is created is another noncontingent employee benefit. If you stay employed long enough, eventually you get your turn.

Perception Error.   A brokerage firm advertised in a popular business magazine that it sent its top 10 brokers for the year on an all-expense-paid trip for two to someplace warm during the winter months. They showed a picture of Maury, one of the 10 winners. They were certain that it was a thrill for Maury to have his picture in the magazine.

It might have been a thrill, but not necessarily. Maury may have been embarrassed by the recognition and harassed by his coworkers for having been the chosen one. I can imagine that potential clients who responded to the ad would insist on speaking only to Maury to make sure that they got the "top performer."

Create a Bigger Winners' Circle

The goal of every organization is to have *all* winners. How can we achieve that if our recognition systems *force* us to create losers. The goal for every organization is to make our employees better than the competition, not better than each other. We certainly don't want our employees slugging it out with each other in order to win.

Anytime you reward the first, most, best, highest, or even most improved, you have destructive potential. The alternative is to develop *criterion* systems. When you have people working to accomplish a specific outcome, success is determined by whether the person or team reached that level, target, or goal independent of what others did. In this kind of system you discover that people will not have secrets, but will share the techniques and procedures that led to their success (sounds like something akin to teamwork).

Mary Kay Ashe, founder of Mary Kay Cosmetics, has a criterion system. Each year she gives every sales associate who reaches a predetermined dollar volume of sales the use of a pink Cadillac for a year. In 1988 she awarded over 500 cars, and by 1999 that number had increased to 9000! I'm quite sure that from her standpoint, this is still not enough. Every time she puts someone in a pink Cadillac, a pink Gran Prix, or a red Grand Am, Mary Kay Ashe gets a little bit richer.

An effective recognition system meets several important criteria: (1) It allows for an unlimited number of winners; (2) the performers know what must be accomplished to earn recognition and reward; and (3) the manager's success is tied to employees' success.

We fail employees when we have losers because there is not enough room in the winners' circle. If the difference between the best performer and second place is measured in tenths or hundredths of a point, you can be sure that the difference is only numerical. There is no way that such a difference would be significant enough to merit different levels of recognition. Yet I have seen situations where two decimal places were necessary to determine a winner.

The goal is to have your employees perform better than the competition. If you want competition, benchmark your company against your best competitor and rally everyone to close the gap between you and them if you are behind, or widen the gap if you are ahead.

Contests

I love a contest, whether at work, at home, or at play. Golf would not be as much fun if it were not for the $2 Nassau. So why would contests be a problem at work? Primarily because of the large tangibles associated with them. When trips, television sets, and other valuable items are given to the winner or winners, some people will lie, cheat, and sabotage others in order to win.

A number of years ago we did an assessment of a national sales promotion sponsored by a major U.S. corporation where the top 2500 winners of the contest won trips to the Superbowl. From the organization's perspective it was highly successful. However, on a closer look at the data, it was discovered that less than 20 percent of the sales force had earned significant points toward the trip. During an interview one nonwinner was asked how many points he had earned. He answered, "Did I get any points? If I did it was a coincidence. The day they announced the contest, I knew who would win from this office. They always do."

The contest was credited with generating $18 million in additional sales on an investment of $10 million, but just think what would have happened if the contest had been structured in a way that got the other 80 percent of the sales force participating.

This is the problem with most contests that involve money or its equivalent as prizes. They are highly motivating to the winners and a turnoff to the losers. Remember, those "losers" also work for the company.

Contests That Motivate.   To run an effective contest, there are a few rules to follow:

1. Use small tangible items as prizes and focus on bragging rights as the main reward.

2. Next, make the contest short, usually not longer than a quarter. Year-long contests put all the consequences too far from the behavior, and even the highest performers will tend to get weary by the end of the year.

3. Most of all, make the contest fun! When there are only a few large, tangible prizes, it takes out the fun for most people.

4. Finally, make sure everyone can win. Set criteria to be reached. Do not set a limit on the number of winners, and you will discover that you have more winners than you ever dreamed.

Embarrassment Awards

When I say make recognition fun that does not include the kind of contest where the winners eat steak and the losers eat beans. I have seen a wide variety of embarrassment awards such as the "pigpen" award for poor house-keeping and the "8-ball" award for the poorest performer or group of performers. These kinds of activities are very risky.

Public humiliation is at the top of most peoples' list of fears. Some people will lie, cheat, and steal to avoid embarrassment. Others will approach the workplace with cynicism and depression.

Poor performers need positive reinforcement for improvement, not punishment for trying to improve, which is what these programs do. There are better ways to have fun at work.

Suggestion Systems

One of the most common sources for recognition and reward used by business today is suggestion systems, but they too have their pitfalls.

A staff member of a well-known company said to me recently, "We are getting too many ideas." "You are?" I questioned. "Yes," he replied, "It costs us about $125 to process an idea and most of them are not worth that much. Next year we are not going to accept an idea that is not worth at least $125." "That will work," I said. "I am absolutely certain that strategy will not only reduce the number of little ideas, but most of the big ones as well." This man, and apparently the company, had no idea of what it takes to reward and motivate creativity.

They did not have the benefit of a study just published by the Employee Involvement Association (EIA), formerly the National Association of Suggestion Systems. Their study showed that the net savings per idea in the United States in 1990 was $7102 compared with $129 in Japan.

However when you factor the level of participation into the figure, on a per employee basis, the figure is $3612 in Japan and $398 in the United States. These figures are based on the fact that in Japan the average employee submits 32 ideas per year and in this country the average is only 0.17 per employee, down from 0.20 in 1980.

That's a ratio of 188:1! What is worse is that of the few ideas that we generate, only 33 percent are actually aadopted. In Japan the rate of adoption is 87 percent.

Finding Joy and Gladness at Work

I visited a Fuji Electric plant just outside of Tokyo as a part of a study group. Before our meeting with them, I looked through their annual report. I saw some numbers that looked like suggestion-system data, but they were so large that I was sure I was not reading them correctly. As the meeting started, I asked the plant manager to explain the numbers. It was suggestion-system data. This plant of about 1500 employees had over 193,330 ideas submitted. An engineer from a highly respected U.S. computer manufacturer leaned over to me and said, "I'll bet some of them weren't worth a dime!" I'm sure he was right. Some of these suggestions weren't worth anything, but the process that encourages the generation of many suggestions is worth millions. Unfortunately, this is not a common opinion in U.S. business. We too often believe "if it ain't big, we're not interested."

In this Japanese company, the average return per suggestion over a 17-year period was in excess of $50 per suggestion. Small potatoes? Well, multiplied by the hundreds of thousands of suggestions received, these "small potatoes" accounted for almost $10 million in profit in a single year. That should be big enough to get even an American manager's attention. It is clear that they are doing something different than we are doing when it comes to recognition for creativity and participation.

About now you may be thinking that you are tired of hearing about Japanese management methods, but rather than being defensive about their success, we should examine how we can profit from what they have learned.

A manager said to me when I told him of the Japanese rates, "Yes, but you know in Japan, if a team comes up with an idea, they credit everybody on the team with the idea. That one idea would count as eight in their system." My response was to divide the total number of suggestions by eight, the average size of a Japanese work team. That would bring their superiority down to a rate that is still 24 times as high as ours. And I reminded the manager that the all-for-one behavior that sharing the credit created would go a long way toward developing teamwork and minimizing intrateam competition.

Another element of the Fuji Electric suggestion system which I particularly liked was their theme: "Finding joy and gladness at work." This single program provided 193,330 occasions for finding joy and gladness at that plant in 1979. Do we have *anything* that compares with that? The Japanese seem to have an innate understanding of shaping. Remember that old Oriental saying, "Many raindrops make an ocean."

The Japanese are much more likely to celebrate small improvements than we are. They know that somebody submitting an idea that "ain't worth a dime" today may, if reinforced, submit one worth a million dollars tomorrow.

Handled correctly, suggestion systems should not be competitive. However, they can be and have been, especially those that violate one or more of the principles of recognition presented earlier in this chapter.

Let's say you have the germ of an idea that could save your company millions of dollars. Lets also say that you could earn a cash award of $50,000 if the idea is accepted. Would you bring the idea to work and ask the help of your coworkers and supervisor to iron out the details, or would you go home, get in your basement, close the blinds, and work on "your idea" in your spare time?

Not long ago, after making a speech on a related subject, a man told me, "I've got an idea that will save this company $250,000 this year, guaranteed! And I ain't telling nobody." He went on to tell me about some politics and rules in their system that would possibly keep him from getting the award. His solution was to sit on the idea until "the time was right."

Large cash awards to individuals often generate hard feelings among coworkers. I discourage it. It's much better to use either a small tangible or a symbolic reward rather than large cash awards. Ideas have value only when they are implemented successfully. It usually takes many people and much effort to integrate ideas into the normal routine. The behaviors of making those ideas work need to be reinforced and rewarded.

Think also what it would be like to work in a place where there were hundreds of attempts being made and reinforced every day to make your business work better. It would indeed be a place of joy and gladness.

Group Incentives

The research has been equivocal on the effect of group pay on performance and satisfaction. It seems to be clear that group incentives improve the performance of hourly paid employees. However, as researchers isolate variables that affect performance under these plans, new findings are emerging. It seems that while there may be some benefit to the organization in improved performance on the variable that is rewarded, the gain may be more than offset by the negative effect that it has on the organization's best performers.

For example, Honeywell, Dickinson, and Poling (1997) found that when given a choice, high performers chose the individual incentive system, and low performers chose the group incentive system.[†] London and Oldham (1977) found that low performers performed the same when paid group-based incentives and individual incentives.[‡] However, higher performers performed an average of 17 percent lower when paid group-based incentives.

You see, therefore, that although group incentives do improve performance of hourly paid employees, they have a negative effect on the most

---

[†] Honeywell, J. A., Dickinson, A. M., and Poling, A., "Individual Performance as a Function of Individual and Group Pay Contingencies," *Psychological Record*, vol. 47, 1997, pp. 261–274.

[‡] London, M., and Oldham, G. R., "A Comparison of Group and Individual Incentive Plans," *Academy of Management Journal*, vol. 20, 1977, pp. 34–41.

productive performers. Average performers seem to be split in preference for group incentives. Therefore, when satisfaction scores are taken across high, average, and low performers, the numbers tend to show satisfaction with the plan, although the high performers you most want to reward are the ones who wind up being the most dissatisfied.

Annual Bonus Plans

From what we know about reinforcement, the typical end-of-the-year bonus has limited effect on performance. The fact that people will choose small immediate rewards over larger delayed ones has been substantiated by many researchers, including Herrnstein (1990),[§] Ainslie (1975),[‖] Davison and McCarthy (1988),[#] and Green and Myerson (1998).[**] Although it is possible to have a reward so large that it will be preferred over a small one, the amount required is impractical in most situations at work. State lotteries are a current example where people will play even though the probability of winning is very, very small. The reason is that the rewards are huge—usually millions of dollars.

I have concluded from the available research that: (1) if a bonus is uncertain (meaning that there may not be funds to pay it), it has minimal effect on day-to-day performance; (2) if a bonus is certain (meaning the money will be paid if performance merits it), it has to be quite large to have substantial effect on performance; (3) when the bonus is delayed and uncertain, the bonus is no more effective than any form of delayed compensation.

Does this mean that bonuses should be eliminated? Not necessarily, but to make them effective, you need to have a way to measure bonus-eligible achievement on a continuous basis and have feedback on progress on a frequent basis. Combining social reinforcement for progress with a delayed and uncertain bonus can overcome some of the drawbacks associated with this form of organizational reward.

[§] Herrnstein, R. J. "Rational Choice Theory," *American Psychologist*, March 1990, pp. 356–367.

[‖] Ainslie, G. "Specious Reward: A Behavioral Theory of Impulsiveness and Impulse Control," *Psychological Bulletin*, vol. 82, pp. 463–496.

[#] Davison, M., and McCarthy, D., *The Matching Law: A Research Review*. Earlbaum, Hillsdale, NJ, 1988.

[**] Green, L., and Myerson, J., and Ostaszewski, P., "Amount of Reward Has Opposite Effects on the Discounting of Delayed and Probabilistic Outcomes," *Journal of Experimental Psychology*. (In press.)

Gainsharing

Although there are many forms of gainsharing, practically all have problems with delay, uncertainty, and control. In most of the plans, there is a formula to determine the amount to be shared and a formula to determine the distribution to employees. The gainsharing pool is usually determined by a formula that calculates the gains as a function of cost reduction or productivity improvements. The distribution to employees is typically based on pay, length of service, or some other nonperformance variable.

The concept of gainsharing is good. The methods of determining the amount of money to be distributed are fiscally sound. The problem is with the way the individuals earn their share. If the money is given without regard to an individual's contribution to the organizational result, you would not expect a poor or even average performer to become more productive or efficient as a result of receiving gainsharing.

For gainsharing to be effective over the long run, the system must have the capability of measuring and rewarding individual contribution. That is, the gains should be divided based on individual contribution, not by team or larger group.

Too Little, Too Few, Too Late

By this point in the chapter, you should understand the relevant characteristics of positive reinforcement that are critical to the effectiveness of any organizational system that is designed to affect performance. (That is, of course, all organizational systems!) Let me summarize.

The requirements of positive reinforcement are that the consequence must be (1) valued by the person receiving it, (2) contingent on performance, (3) delivered immediately, and (4) delivered frequently. When you understand that for recognition and rewards to have an effect on behavior they must meet the above criteria, you can begin to understand why there are so many problems with these systems. They lack almost all the critical characteristics. They are almost always delayed. Because they are delayed, the link between the behavior and the reward or recognition is weak. Because reward and recognition cost money, they certainly are not given frequently. Finally, noncash recognition is limited to a few items or privileges and, as such, may appeal to only a few people. If the reward is cash, the amount available is not usually meaningful to most employees.

Making Rewards and
Recognition Effective

1. *Positive reinforcement has to be a daily affair.*   No matter how much money or time you spend on rewards and recognition, you will not get the results you want, or could have, if the organization gets things done with negative reinforcement day to day. Think about it. How much money would it take to make you happy if, hour by hour, you were being threatened, embarrassed, confronted, and pressured? This does not generate excitement about work and accomplishments. As Tom Odom of Shell Oil says, "Its hard to celebrate when you've been beat up on the way to the party."

2. *The reward and recognition must be earned.*   There must be a direct relationship between individual performance and the reward and recognition. One of the real problems with team recognition and rewards is that everyone gets them whether they contribute equally or not. This is not usually a problem for the poor performers, but it causes considerable heartburn for the top performers over a period of time.

3. *The recognition must have personal value.*   The dollar value of the recognition is unimportant as long as the items are meaningful to the performers. If it creates a positive memory of some accomplishment, the amount of money spent on recognition is irrelevant. The T-shirt, coffee mug, or key chain will be valuable only if it is combined with, or reminds the person of, an accomplishment that makes the performer proud. Telling people they should be proud does not make them proud.

4. *The delay between the behavior and the reward and recognition must be bridged.*   Because reinforcement is immediate, some event that has reinforcing value must occur in proximity to the valued behavior or performance. Points that are related to an incentive are one way to bridge the gap. The points must be paired frequently with social reinforcement to create their motivational value.

5. *The presentation of the incentive should be preceded by a celebration.*   A celebration in this context is an opportunity for the performers to relive the accomplishment. The participants, not the bosses, should be allowed to recount the things they did to meet the goal. Done this way, the incentive anchors a memory of an accomplishment and, as such, is more valuable.

6. *Money is not the best incentive.*   Although money can be used occasionally, it should not be the main incentive. Even though most people, in most circumstances, like money, it provides limited reinforcement for the cost. Money is soon spent and the memory of it soon fades, whereas

other tangible incentives are kept longer and act as a constant reminder of some accomplishment. If celebrated appropriately, the behaviors involved in producing the results will be remembered long after the memory of the cash has faded away.

Relationships Make It Happen

I was talking to a senior manager in her office one day when the topic turned to recognition. She said derisively, "I got recognized once with a 'black onyx pen-and-pencil set.' " She was pointing to a pen-and-pencil set on her desk. She continued, "My boss didn't even have the decency to present it to me in person. It just appeared on my desk one day."

As she talked it became clear that she didn't have much respect for the boss. The conversation was not really about the pen-and-pencil set; it was really about her relationship with her boss. Her boss was like many others I have known. He thought that he was a positively reinforcing person; however, he was the only one who thought so.

There are a great many managers in organizations today who think because they give people pay raises, promotions, and various rewards and recognition, they are effective managers who are perceived positively by the people who work for them. They are usually shocked when they find out through a morale survey, or in some other way, that they are not.

If people don't like you, practically nothing you do will be received well. You can brag on them, give them money and merchandise, and it will do little to change their opinion. To make reinforcement, reward, and recognition effective, you must first develop good relationships with people. Although companies used to be able to get by with onerous supervisors and managers, that day has passed. It is risky business today for companies to promote supervisors and managers on the basis of technical and professional skills while minimizing or excusing weaknesses in social skills.

Years ago, we constructed a morale survey to measure the extent that managers were using positive reinforcement as a management practice. The question that accounted for the most variance was, "Do you like your supervisor?" If they didn't like their supervisors, nothing the supervisor did in a formal way had the intended or desired effect. If they liked the supervisor, the employees would overlook some of his or her shortcomings.

How do you establish good relationships? Most people don't need to be told how to do this. As Dale Carnegie said, "Liking someone is the other side of having them like you." By this point in the book, I don't need to go into detail about how you can accomplish this, but I will say that the first order of business is to establish yourself as a positive reinforcer by pairing your presence with positive comments. Ask the other person questions about their life—their interests, hobbies, and other things that are likely to elicit a positive response. Compliment them; listen to them. Try to establish your presence as an antecedent for good things, not that you will ignore poor performance, or even poor habits, but that the predominant interactions are positive.

Remember that just being positive will not make you a good manager, because if you are positive at the wrong time, in the wrong way, or at the wrong frequency, you will surely be ineffective in your relationships. On the other hand, you surely can't be the most effective manager if you are not a positively reinforcing person.

Relationships are the foundation on which effective rewards and recognition are built. When you have that foundation, rewards and recognition enhance other forms of reinforcement. If you don't have it, you will waste your money and your time trying to buy discretionary performance.

19

Compensation and Performance Appraisal

Compensation and performance appraisal are two of the most talked-about aspects of corporate life. Unfortunately, most of the talk is negative. Neither compensation nor appraisal, as they are usually administered, brings out the best in people.

Entire books have been written about both subjects, a number of prominent firms specialize in compensation consulting, and myriad training programs have been developed to train managers to design and conduct effective performance appraisals. So, in this one chapter, I can't even begin to describe specific prescriptions for curing the ills so many good intentions have created in these two important areas.

What I will try to do is make you aware of specific problems with traditional appraisal and compensation systems. The principles in this book and the ideas explained in this chapter should provide you with guidance to help you increase the effectiveness of these two systems in your company.

Compensation As Reward

The hope of receiving a reward is a motivating factor for getting a response, but as has been said many times in this book, it is not sufficient to maximize performance. Rewards that are Positive-Future-Certain (PFC) don't exert much influence on daily behavior. Therefore, regular compensation can't maximize performance, but it can help or hinder.

Money is important. Very few people can afford to work without being paid but, contrary to popular belief, money is not the most important consideration for people at work. The way people are treated at work is much more important for determining performance than the money they receive. When we work we expect to be paid fairly and competitively for what we do. However, some compensation plans actually work against day-to-day motivation; therefore, it's important to know when that is occurring and make adjustments.

Frederick Herzburg in his book *The Motivation to Work* (1959) said that pay is a "dissatisfier" which will not make workers happy at work but can be, and often is, a source of considerable dissatisfaction. The source of the dissatisfaction ultimately lies in the design of the compensation plan. Although the design of the plan is determined by things such as philosophy of pay, company resources, competitiveness, or profit margins, in the end, for the employee, it all comes down to, "How do I get paid?"

Following are some of the problems with usual compensation designs as seen from the Performance Management perspective.

Compensation Is a PFU

The time lag between the behavior and the receipt of compensation poses an obvious performance problem. When employees are performing with an eye toward a regular biweekly or monthly paycheck, other more *immediate consequences* can pull them off track. To minimize these distractions, we recommend moving reinforcement as close to the performance as possible. Whenever we've been able to put consequences, particularly positive reinforcement, closer to behavior, we have never failed to increase performance even with people paid by piecework or commission. When performance increased, the performers' compensation also increased. It was made possible by positive, immediate consequences.

Regular paydays don't influence daily behavior, but even less effective are the usual attempts companies make to motivate performance improvement using money.

Annual bonuses, a typical attempt at associating improved performance with increased compensation, are almost always PFUs, (Positive-Future-Uncertain). As such, they have little daily motivational value. These plans usually turn out to be an increased expense to the company rather than an investment that pays performance dividends.

The same can be said for the typical *profit-sharing* plan. Profit-sharing plans provide as uncertain a consequence as you can find. The reason that profit-sharing plans can't improve performance is that profits are out of the average performer's control.

An employee can work as hard as he or she can, and there may be no profit. The IRS, accountants, the exchange rate of the dollar can all have much more bearing on profit than the performer's work. Remember from previous chapters that people should not be rewarded or punished for results that are out of their control. When profits are available and are shared, employees like it; when profits are too small to share, employees are disappointed. In either case, the reward is too far removed from employee behavior to influence performers to do anything different.

Pay and Contingency

The most serious problem in the typical compensation plan is the lack of performance contingencies. As you know, every performer has choices about how well to perform the tasks that make up a job.

With the usual salary and wage systems, whether you work hard today or whether you don't will make no difference in your next paycheck. Whether you take a little extra time, collect a little more data before making a decision, or do the first thing that comes to mind, you will still get your paycheck, and it will be for the same amount. Traditional compensation plans have very little impact on behavioral contingencies that affect daily performance.

Pay As a Form of Competition

Most pay raises are competitive. Since there is a finite amount of money to be divided among employees, if one person gets more than the average raise, someone will get less than the average. In other words, one person's financial gain is another person's financial loss.

Since most organizations have not developed an accurate method for appraising performance, the decisions about average versus above average are frequently debated and can tear a department or company apart. The way most companies minimize competition for compensation is to give everyone an across-the-board increase. Of course this exacerbates the problem of *equal treatment of unequals,* and we've already discussed how demotivating that practice can be.

Noncontingent Benefits

Other than attracting good people, all the average company gets from the typical company benefit plan is a higher cost of doing business. It is rare that there is any performance contingency tied to increases in benefits.

Unfortunately, in some companies executives expect increases in motivation and performance as a result of improvements in benefits. They shouldn't count on it.

While attractive benefits help companies recruit good people, a good benefit plan will not increase motivation and performance unless there are performance contingencies associated with the plan.

Even the popular "cafeteria" plans don't impact employee performance. People do like them, but again, the poor performers get to choose just as freely as the outstanding performers.

Performance Appraisal

Over the years, our consultants and I have seen the performance appraisal programs of hundreds of companies. And I have finally come to this conclusion:

> *Apart from documentation for legal purposes, the annual performance appraisal is a waste of time.*

The managers who do the appraisals don't like them, nor do the performers receiving them. It is a masochistic and sadistic ritual of business. The way we appraise performance must change.

Performance is usually appraised on some form of rating scale. Three-point, five-point, seven-point, sometimes ten-point scales are commonly used (and no one has ever been able to clearly explain why one scale is better than the others). In any case, *the highest number on the scale usually represents outstanding performance and the lowest number on the scale,* 1 or 0, *represents poor performance.* Each employee must fall somewhere on the scale.

A number of techniques may be used to come up with this final rating. One that is particularly bad, and very popular, is to rate a number of performance factors on the same scale, add all the numbers, and divide by the number of factors considered.

This usually gives you a whole number and a fraction (3.17, for example), which you then round off to the nearest whole number. That number is the employee's rating.

In a typical measurement system, there is no way that the differences between the scores represent real differences in performance. We treat them as real, however, because the ratings carry real consequences with them.

If you give mediocre performance ratings to a high performer, you will make that person a mediocre performer. If you give high performance ratings to a mediocre performer, you will continue to have a mediocre performer.

Some organizations have tried to make performance appraisals more effective by rating performance more often. They now do semiannual or quarterly ratings. These companies keep people stirred up constantly. I have somewhat facetiously told managers how to double the effectiveness of their performance appraisal system: *Do it half as often.* If the system is flawed, doing it more often is not better, it is worse!

Some human relations experts have suggested that the problem with the appraisal process is that financial consequences and the appraisal are closely associated, so they separate the two discussions. This just creates more paperwork for managers and supervisors and adds to the frustration of the employee. I have not met anyone in business who thinks that there is no connection between their appraisal rating and their pay. The reason they are separated is to try to make a bad system better. It doesn't.

Forced Ranking—As Bad As It Gets. As bad as this may sound, it gets worse, because almost every organization places limits on the number of employees who can fall into each rating group. This is known as a *forced ranking or forced distribution system.*

Many managers think that they don't have this system when, in reality, they do. The acid test of whether you have a forced-ranking system is this: Can every performer get the highest ranking at the same time? If they can't, then you have the system.

For example, let's say you are responsible for the appraisals of 20 people. Let's also say that your rating system uses a five-point scale where a rating of 1 is "poor"; a 5 is "outstanding."

After you have completed rating all 20 employees, go to your boss and say, "Boss, you're gonna love this. All 20 of my staff got 5s." If your boss says anything other than "Great!" you have a forced-ranking system.

The system that most companies use forces performance into a distribution which is some variation of the "normal curve." Figure 19-1 illustrates a typical distribution.

Using this curve, you are "forcing" 70 percent of the performers to be average or below. What organization can survive in today's economy with only 30 percent of its employees above average? In reality, most organizations have a distribution that is skewed to the right allowing more employees to be rated "above average." This is not a true picture of performance, but an attempt to minimize complaints and maintain morale. See Figure 19-2.

A forced distribution of any kind creates unhealthy competition among employees. One employee's high rating "forces" someone else to get a lower rating since there can be only a limited number in the top group. Employees who continue to try to get the top rating and end up in the next-to-the-highest group eventually quit trying (extinction).

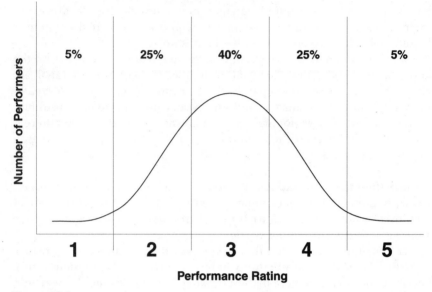

Figure 19-1

Proponents of this system say that if you measure people on almost any variable, you will get a normal distribution. In other words, performance is probably normally distributed, so forced ranking should be fair. The problem with that logic is that organizations don't hire on the basis of a normal distribution.

Every organization I know hires as many people as they can who are in the 90th percentile of whatever selection indicators are used. However, after they've gone to the trouble of hiring the best people available, they force them into the normal appraisal distribution and label them "Average."

That reminds me of the story of the highly recruited Harvard MBA who, while crossing a busy street on his way to a job interview, was struck by a bus and killed. He arrived at the Pearly Gates where a distinguished-looking individual informed him that he had his choice between heaven or hell. Amazed, the Harvard man asked if he could review his options before deciding and was shown to a nearby elevator. "Push Up to preview heaven and Down to preview hell" was the direction he received.

The young man pushed Up first and, when the elevator doors opened, the view of heaven was exactly as he had imagined: choirs of

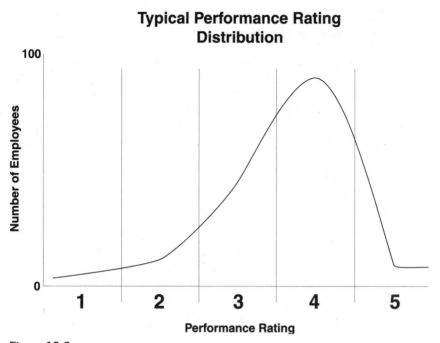

Figure 19-2

angels, harps, peace and quiet, everyone smiling serenely. He then pushed the Down button and was extremely surprised by what greeted him this time.

Hell was a beach! A beautiful beach with beautiful people sunning, wind-sailing, playing volleyball, drinking piña coladas. He returned to the main floor where he advised his distinguished host that he had made his choice. "As much as I always thought I wanted to go to heaven, I believe that hell is the more appropriate venue for my talents," he announced.

With that the MBA returned to the elevator, and once again pushed the Down button. The doors opened, but this time he was greeted by a terrifying sea of flames. He heard screaming and smelled burning flesh. Before he could close the doors he was grabbed by a huge demon who threw him bodily into the inferno. Horrified by this turn of events, he cried out, "What happened to the beach?" The demon gleefully shouted back, "You were a prospect then; you're an employee now!"

I believe the forced-distribution appraisal system came about as a way to distribute raises and bonuses. Such a system allows management to control costs better and administer the system easier. To pretend that it truly evaluates worker performance is a sham.

Pinpointing Results:
The Performance Matrix

The first thing to do to improve the effectiveness of compensation and appraisal systems is to pinpoint the results and behaviors needed from every job. While this seems like a formidable task, it pays dividends. If you recall, this is also the first step in Performance Management.

The best job you will ever have is one where you know how you did at the end of every day. The ideal performance appraisal is one that is done every day. It is certainly not practical for management to measure performance every day, even if measures are available. However, if performance can be monitored by the performer, it is possible to get the benefits of daily measurement without the high cost of management time.

An ideal format for this is the *performance matrix*. The performance matrix allows us to measure every job, from the boardroom to the shop floor.

The matrix is ideal because it is totally flexible. As business or job responsibilities change, the matrix can change to reflect them. If someone is on a production job one month and is changed to a creative job the next month, performance can be exemplary in both jobs. The performance matrix lets you measure how well the performer is doing against expectations.

Figure 19-3 is an example of a completed performance matrix. A score of 5 is the baseline performance. A score of 10 indicates goal performance. Scores from 11 to 13 are overachievement. Scores on the various performances can be anchored by counts, checklists, or BARS.

Anchors and their values can be changed as often as conditions change, but I recommend that you not change more often than monthly. If a new process is introduced on the job, you can very easily change the scores and their corresponding anchors to reflect this.

As priorities change the weighting of the various items on the matrix can also be changed. The weighting represents the percent of time that a person should spend on any particular performance or behavior. Although weighting is rather difficult to do in the beginning, it is of considerable value to the performer and the boss. Practice and adjustments during early attempts will improve your skills in determining weighting.

From an organizational perspective, the ability to shift weighting allows the company to rapidly shift the focus of performance to meet the changing needs of internal and external customers as well as changes in the work unit itself. An item that may have had a 10-point value one month may have a 30-point value the next month because of a customer emergency. Because of a shift to a new process, production may be minimized while yield may be emphasized. These shifts can be easily accommodated on the matrix by changing the weighting of those items.

PERFORMANCE MATRIX

Name: A. Daniels Position: ___ Manager: ___ Date 11/1/99

BEHAVIORS/RESULTS — PINPOINTS	4	5	6	7	8	9	10	11	12	13	x WEIGHT	POINTS
Employee Contacts (Non-office)	<2	2	4	6	8	10	12	15	20	(25+)	15	195
Improve PM Seminar (Documented Changes)	<2	2	4		(6)		10	To Tracy 11/11	By 11/7	By 11/4	10	80
Complete EOM Article		Review Billie's input		Add research		Revised draft	Final draft	Before Thanks-giving			15	165
Review Direct Reports' Matrices	<2		2	3	4	5	6	50% in person	75%	100%	20	220
Commitments Met (Percent on time)	<75%	Record		90%	(95%)		100%	Early			15	120
Customer Contact (from Checklist)	<3				4	6	8	12	(16)	20	15	180
Administrative (See Checklist)	<6	6	7	8	9	10	(11)	+3	+6	+10	10	100

SCORE 1060

Next Review Date 12/1/99

REINFORCEMENT PLAN

Points	R+	Comments	Plans
1000	Golf	No score below 8	Friday afternoon
1200	Golf	No score below 10	Friday A.M. golf

Figure 19-3

With this type of system you have a foundation for appraisal and compensation systems. This matrix system allows you to accurately tie future pay and other recognition and rewards to day-to-day performance.

Appraisals and Contingent Compensation.   With the preceding performance matrix, you can predetermine performance targets and their consequences, financial and social. Consistent scores above 1000 might result in a certain assignment, a bonus, or a raise in pay.

Under this system an organization would want all performers to get the maximum rating since high ratings would result in high value to the organization. The matrix connects employee success to organizational success.

The manager who has developed a good performance matrix is ensuring that both the performer and the organization are getting their money's worth.

The matrix method eliminates peer competition because every performer is competing against his or her own targets and goals. It permits a supervisor to tailor each person's performance and development plan to the needs of the performer and the organization without regard to what others are doing.

Compensation and the Matrix.   Once you have the matrix in place, you can have a true pay-for-performance system. Dollars can be tied to matrix scores, which are tied to value-added behaviors and results.

In setting up the matrix, all aspects of effective reinforcement and reward can be taken into account. Obviously, items on the matrix must be within the control of the performer, but when they are, contingency is built into the process (i.e., you earn a score, you get the consequences stated).

The reinforcement plan associated with the matrix allows you to tailor the plan to the individual. Since the supervisor, coach, or team leader knows the results that performers are accountable for and the behaviors and accomplishments that are associated with them, he or she will be able to reinforce immediately and frequently. Since the performers are also aware of these expectations, they are potentially able to provide self-reinforcement as well. Every time the performers engage in the desired behaviors or make progress toward the final goal, they can see their progress and reinforce themselves immediately and frequently.

Increasing Bonus and Gainsharing Plan Effectiveness.   The effectiveness of bonus and gainsharing programs can be increased considerably by the matrix.

Take a typical gainsharing program. Let's say there are 50 employees in the plan. Let's also say that there is $50,000 in the pool and that it will be shared equally. That means that each employee would get $1000. This method of distribution rewards poor performers and good performers equally. You know by now that this is a problem.

Using a matrix, a better distribution system could be developed. Under this system each person would have the *opportunity* to earn an equal share *depending on performance.* Using the preceding example, if one of our 50 people scored 800 on the matrix, he or she might get $800 of the $1000 available. If another scored 1000 points, that person would get the full $1000. Those who achieved over 1000 may be eligible for additional recognition and rewards—usually noncash.

If the performance of the group as a whole does not merit distribution of the total pool, the remainder should not be given out. This would send the wrong message about contingencies. Also, redistributing the excess among the best performers allows them to benefit from the poor performance of their peers, and could introduce unhealthy competition again.

How About Equity? Equity in rewards is the responsibility of the supervisor and should be an item on the supervisor's matrix. The supervisor and his or her boss should discuss what is involved in the tasks that are on the matrix so that there is *perceived* as well as *real* equity. Believe it or not, if performers feel they are being treated fairly you will have few complaints.

If you get complaints about equity, you should check them out. However, if you reinforce complaining you will get more of it. For example, if you ask someone to do something and they ask, "What am I going to get for it?" you know that you have been reinforcing the wrong behavior. If someone complains about what another is getting and you reinforce it, you are teaching people to be jealous.

When one employee complains about what another is getting, the first response should be, "Do you want what they are getting?" It might surprise you that many times the person does not want what the other has but just wants to complain about it. If you reinforce this kind of behavior you will create petty jealousies among performers.

On the other hand, if the employee says "Yes, I want what they've got," then say, "Good. Let's talk about how you can earn it." In many cases, when the behaviors and performance are pinpointed for them, they decide that they don't want the reward after all. If they still want it, you have an additional way to reinforce and reward improved performance.

Taking Action. I recognize that most managers reading this book will not have sufficient flexibility where pay and benefits are concerned to implement a fully contingent compensation plan. In fact, the bulk of this book is dedicated to bringing out the best in people *in spite of traditional compensation and appraisal systems.*

However, if you can affect the way your organization handles these two vital systems, I urge you to consider how you can apply these basic performance management techniques. Compensation and performance appraisal systems are for the most part well intended but, as my mama used to say, "Good intentions pave the road to hell!

PART 5

Revitalizing the Workplace

20
Performance Management: The Executive Function

If you think this is easy, you are doing it wrong.

Edward Gibbon, an English historian, said, "The winds and waves are always on the side of the ablest navigator." I interpret this to mean that the sailor who thoroughly understands the winds and the ocean currents will have few problems sailing a ship in the desired direction. Changing conditions don't present insurmountable obstacles for expert sailors, just additional opportunities for them to exercise their skill. If the winds shift or the tide changes, the expert sailor simply modifies the sails and moves the rudder to adapt to changing conditions.

To the executive who understands human behavior, changing business conditions don't present problems, just additional opportunities to exercise his or her skill. *By now, the CEO who doesn't know the science of human behavior and how to apply it to leadership will have great difficulty surviving and will put his or her company at financial risk.* I'm convinced that as executives understand and implement the principles set forth in this book, they'll make dramatic gains in the performance and profitability of their companies.

The Executive Role
in Performance Management

Executives should learn and apply every Performance Management technique described in this book, but because of their positions in the organization they have some additional responsibilities.

Results/Behavior Selection.   It's the responsibility of a company's executives to determine the desired organizational results. Once this is determined, the executive should define, within limits, which behaviors will be reinforced as a means of obtaining those results.

This task is value-driven. It answers the question, *"What are acceptable and unacceptable ways to get results here?* Is it results at any cost? If not, what are the limits? How are they determined? *What are our guiding principles and values?"*

Although values are not usually stated in pinpointed terms, doing so is the only way you can ensure that your organization lives by them. Concepts such as honesty, teamwork, innovativeness, concern for people, customer service, commitment to quality, and so on can be defined in behavioral terms. In fact, if you can't define your organization's values in terms of specific behaviors, they will be practically useless in helping you accomplish your mission.

The ultimate purpose of developing a mission statement is to determine which results to reward and which behaviors to reinforce. (Listing the behaviors and results that will *not* be reinforced and rewarded is an equally useful exercise when a significant shift in behaviors and results is being attempted.)

A vice president of one of our largest clients recently asked me, "How do you think we're doing with our Quality Management program?"

I said, "Some are doing well and some are not doing so well."

"Who's not doing well?" he then asked. "I'm not going to tell you," I replied. Looking puzzled, he asked, "Why not?"

"Because," I continued, *"one of the managers who isn't doing anything to support Quality Management just got promoted."*

I refused to single out this manager because it was obvious that he had done everything that *really* mattered. The organization *said* Quality Management was important, but actually valued other behaviors more. Until the executives in this company decide which behaviors are important and which are not, they will continue to have spotty success implementing any new technology.

After determining organizational results, the task of determining organizational values and their associated behaviors is the highest priority of executive management. This task should come before all other executive responsibilities, including those that directly affect profit. The executive cannot exercise true financial responsibility if profit is attained by behaviors that are self-serving, wasteful, or repressive—not to mention illegal, unethical, or immoral.

Systems and Structures

Executives have the responsibility for designing the organization's systems and structures. These elements affect behavior in general ways. For example, if a vice president of sales establishes revenue goals, the sales staff will try to meet those goals. If, in addition, he asks for a certain number of new accounts, the sales staff will spend time prospecting for new accounts in addition to simply trying to maximize revenues from a few good customers. These rules or structures affect what the sales staff does from day to day.

However, if that same sales exec provides bonuses only for revenues, independent of whether they come from an old or a new account, the message of what is really important will be determined by the reward. No matter how clearly the goal is communicated or how important it is said to be, performance will be determined more by what is rewarded than by what is said. First and foremost, executives must be sure that all systems and structures link reinforcement to all the behaviors they want and only the behaviors they want.

One of our recent customers worked very hard to deploy our behavior-based safety system. Protecting employees from injury and even death was very important to them because they were engaged in dangerous work involving heavy, moving equipment. They diligently trained a large number of employees as observers and reinforcers. They set up an accurate measuring system to track the increase in safe behavior on the job. They celebrated the improvements—less accidents, less lost time, and fewer injuries. In other words, they established meaningful structures that set the stage for and reinforced safe behavior. They were successful, but they did not achieve the highest levels of safety until they also involved first-line supervisors in the process. What the supervisors were trained to do was to comment on and actively support the observers for observing safe behavior on the job. When supervisors were reinforced for reinforcing observers, the number of safe behaviors increased dramatically and safe behaviors have become the norm.

In an organization of any significant size, senior executives can never personally deliver enough reinforcement to affect front-line employee behavior. Therefore, they must make sure that the systems and structures facilitate and positively reinforce the behavior of supervisors, team leaders, and peers. They must be reinforced for knowing what to reinforce, who to reinforce, and how to reinforce effectively. Ensuring that formal organizational systems and structures support day-to-day reinforcement is the most important role an executive can play in maximizing performance in the organization.

Reinforcer/Reward Selection. Reinforcer and reward selection are ultimately determined by the performers in the company. However, executives should define the limits of the reinforcers and rewards available for managers and supervisors to use. Is time off allowed as a reward? If so, how much? Extra breaks? How many? Can money be used? If so, how much? What about celebrations? What are the limits on how big, how extravagant, and where they will be held?

Although the boundaries should be broadly defined, it's helpful for people throughout the organization to know the limits. If executives spend some time on these issues they will minimize troublesome surprises that may otherwise come up later.

Reinforcer/Reward Distribution. The prime consideration in reinforcer/reward distribution is to make sure your system is noncompetitive. All systems affecting human performance should be monitored to identify and eliminate contingencies that create internal competition. *Reinforcement should multiply opportunities for more reinforcement, not reduce them.* That is, one person's reinforcement and reward should increase the chances that others will be reinforced. If one performer finds a better way to do something, would that individual automatically share his or her discovery with all the others who do the same thing? Where there is competition for reinforcement, performers are reluctant to share discoveries that might give them a performance advantage.

As explained in Chapter 18, the second consideration is that there be a direct linkage between the behaviors and the reward. Reward systems such as bonuses, profit sharing, and gainsharing should be tied to individual performance, not to some mathematical formula. There should be measurement of what each person actually does to add value to the company.

Reinforcer/Reward Effectiveness. Executives have the overall responsibility for ensuring that performance is managed effectively. This encompasses all corporate performance, including initiatives such as TQM, continuous improvement, behavior-based safety, reengineering, and so on.

It's important for executives to understand techniques of evaluating performance such as multiple-baseline, ABA, and other research designs to make sure they get their money's worth from their investments. Internal performance management personnel should have the responsibility to evaluate and report on the investment status and make recommendations to the executives about continuing any initiatives, increasing their use, or pulling the plug. All such decisions should be data-based. The final evaluation should be based on results data, not just on behaviors or counts of behaviors.

Herrnstein's Hyperbola

To completely understand the executive role in Performance Management it's necessary to know about Herrnstein's hyperbola. Dr. Richard Herrnstein, professor of psychology at Harvard, has done extensive research on what is called the *matching law.*

In general terms, the matching law states that *the amount of reinforcement a person receives for a particular behavior is matched by the time spent engaged in that behavior.*

In other words, if a person is in a position to choose whether to do behavior A or behavior B, and 90 percent of the reinforcement is available for behavior A and only 10 percent available for behavior B, the person will spend 90 percent of his or her time doing A and 10 percent doing B.

If we wanted the person to do more of B, we would move reinforcement from A to B. This would mean that B would occur more often and A would occur less often.

Herrnstein's research discovered that the matching law applies to all behavior, not just simple choice situations. He notes that all behavior is choice behavior. We choose to do one thing at a time over all the other things available to us at that time. For example, we choose to finish talking to someone in our office before we answer the telephone; we choose to watch one television program rather than another; we choose to look out the window rather than work on the papers on our desk.

What Dr. Herrnstein's work means for the executive is that every time you introduce a new corporate initiative, you potentially dilute effort on existing initiatives. In other words, when someone spends more time and effort doing something new, that person will have less to spend on some previous behavior. On the other hand, if a new initiative is introduced with no reinforcement, little time will be spent with it since reinforcement will continue to occur for the old ways of doing things.

The formula for Herrnstein's hyperbola is as follows:

$$R = k \, \frac{r}{r + r_e}$$

Where R = Rate of approach of the target behavior to the asymptote
        k = Asymptote (highest level for the target behavior)
        r = Reinforcement for the target behavior R
        r_e = Reinforcement for all other behaviors

For more detailed information on the matching law see *The Matching Law,* a research review by Michael Davison and Dianne McCarthy (1988).

Simply stated, Dr. Herrnstein's research tells us the following:

1. Noncontingent reinforcement typically dilutes job focus and accomplishment.

2. When there's little reinforcement for doing a job, it takes only a little extraneous reinforcement (r_e) to pull someone off the task.

3. When there's an increase in non-job-related reinforcement, it takes an *increase* in job-related positive reinforcement *to maintain the same level* of job-related effort.

4. If you introduce any new program or system without concentrated, planned reinforcement, you will get only minimum participation in that program or system because of the large amount of reinforcement still existing for prior behaviors.

Executive Behaviors

MBWA Through the Chain of Command

MBWA (Management by Wandering Around) has been a much discussed management technique for executives. The problem with MBWA is that it's a good thing to do only if you understand *why* it's a good thing to do. Tom Peters encouraged executives to get out into the work area because he saw this being done in the best companies.

Dr. Judy Komaki would make the same suggestion, but for a different reason. Her research has shown that the best managers spend more time in the work area *because it makes for the most effective delivery of positive reinforcement.*

Peters told executives to get out and see what's going on. What they did while they were out there was left to chance. A plant manager once told me, "I wish I could get my hands on that Peters guy. I'd pinch his head off. Ever since my boss read that book, he's in the plant all the time! You can tell where he's been by the smoke. He starts fires wherever he goes."

One thing we don't need these days is more executives wandering around reinforcing the wrong behaviors or inadvertently delivering punishment.

The potential problem with MBWA is that most executives and upper-level managers don't know what they're looking at when they do go out and wander around on the plant or office floor. I sometimes call this form of MBWA "Management by *Wondering* Around," as in: "I wonder why this person is doing that"; "I wonder why that person is not working"; "I wonder why that machine isn't running." Because their sampling of behavior is limited to a minute or so on a very infrequent basis, executives can't possibly have enough facts about a performer to know what to reinforce and what to ignore.

Rich Malloy, an exemplar in the use of Performance Management at Kodak, was talking to some students about MBWA in a Performance Management class. He perplexed them when he told them that as a department manager he would never reinforce an operator. He explained that he had been away from frontline supervision so long that if he were to go on the floor and reinforce an operator for doing something exactly like he had wanted it done when he was a supervisor, he could easily get himself into hot water. Because of changes in procedures of which he may not be aware, he might inadvertently reinforce some behavior that the current supervisor was trying to change.

I've asked many supervisors, "Has somebody from 'upstairs' ever come out and 'bragged on' an employee and created a problem for you?" Practically everyone answers with an emphatic, "Yes!"

A colleague, Tom Connellan, tells about an automobile plant where the supervisor gave the performers an unscheduled break after they more than doubled their productivity. An exec, who just happened to be in the plant, saw the group on an "unauthorized" break and chewed them out. Performance almost immediately fell to previous levels.

If you're an upper-level manager and you want MBWA in the plant or in the office, *at least* wander around with someone who knows what's happening there. Then, *ask that person to point out the best performers to you.*

And, when you're on the floor, pay attention to the best performers *first*. Only after you've spent time with employees who are doing good things should you visit the problem area or look at that new piece of equipment. Stop to recognize the good things first, even if you are on your way to see a specific problem. Then do the same thing on the way back through the plant.

The best place to do MBWA is where you *know* that the performers are doing what they're supposed to do, usually the people who report directly to you. The further you get away from your direct reports, the more likely you are to create problems with your aimless wondering/wandering. Do your homework first.

One more word on MBWA. An executive's first responsibility regarding reinforcement is to provide it for the people he or she sees everyday.

Mr. Toy Reed, retired president of Eastman Chemical Company, asked me, "How much time should I spend attending team celebrations?"

I responded, "I don't know how you find the time to do as much as you do." Even though he had an organization of over 10,000 employees, Reed rarely missed an opportunity to visit a team celebration.

I further suggested that he spend most of the time he had available for reinforcement with his management team and their direct reports. Not that he should never attend a frontline team celebration, but his primary MBWA should be at a different level.

Remember, reinforcement multiplies as it goes through the chain of command. Those who are reinforced tend to reinforce more. If people at the top are getting reinforced, they are much more likely to reinforce those who work for them, and so on through the organization. Don't bypass your direct reports!

Tough Times Demand Positive Reinforcement—An Example

The vice president of Research and Development at a southwestern telecommunications company was in trouble. His department had just missed several important product release dates. This crisis had been caused by faulty releases prior to his appointment. No matter. This company had recently been acquired by a larger company with similar capabilities, and the president threatened to eliminate the department and turn their work over to the new parent company if they missed another release date.

Fortunately, this executive understood that negative reinforcement resulted in only incremental improvements, and incremental improvement would not save the department. He assembled all of his managers and supervisors and said, "We've lost the luxury of managing by negative reinforcement and punishment. As of Monday morning, I want a plan from each of you detailing how you will use positive reinforcement to get us out of this predicament."

Prior to this time, managers in this department had no mandate to use positive reinforcement. Although they had all been trained in Performance Management techniques, and many were beginning to use them, some were not. With this new directive, all the managers began to put Performance Management to work.

Not only did the department not miss any more release dates, but the quality of the releases reached an all-time high. The department went on to become three times more efficient than the research department in the larger company.

While it's true that the VP's directive had an implied threat, he used it as an antecedent to get behavior that could be positively reinforced. As his subordinate managers began to implement their plans for using positive reinforcement, he provided them with lots of reinforcement, recognition, and celebrations.

Usually, tough times cause managers to get tough, meaning they crumble under pressure and use more punishment and negative reinforcement. It's a rare manager who has the understanding of behavioral concepts and the courage and foresight to use positive methods in the midst of a crisis. For the sake of American business, I hope that leaders like this VP become more and more the rule and less the exception.

A Current Exemplar: Blue Cross and Blue Shield of Alabama*

In 1980 the executives at Blue Cross and Blue Shield (BCBS) of Alabama finally looked one another in the eye and agreed they had come to an impasse. With plummeting morale and dwindling productivity, complaints and stress were the only things the company collected in surplus. Bill Mandy, then president of the organization, thought the management team had tried everything, but on recommendation of a colleague he decided to implement a behavioral management process called Performance Management (PM).

In 1981, 12 officers and 150 managers completed training and began using PM. By 1982, Blue Cross and Blue Shield of Alabama enjoyed its best year in history. Net productions rose more than 1500 percent over the first half of 1981, which had also been a record year following the implementation of PM. Dick Jones, then vice president of sales for BCBS, observed that before Performance Management, sales representatives spent most of their time explaining the company's poor service and defending its critics. In a 1983 article entitled "Alabama 'Blues' Don't Sing the Blues Anymore" (*Performance Management Magazine*, Vol. 1, No. 2) Jones stated, "The best thing that ever happened [to the company] was putting in Performance Management."

"I still feel the same way today. We wouldn't be here if it weren't for PM," Jones confirmed in a recent interview—only now he speaks as the president and COO of BCBS and successor to Gene Thrasher, CEO, who retires in June 1998. The "here" to which Jones refers is BCBS of Alabama's current standing as a premiere local employer, a winner of several national excellence awards and a company that has grown and excelled every quarter for the past 10 years.

Thrasher and Jones each share the experience of two decades with BCBS as well as a solid vision of the organization's future. However, that solid vision didn't always exist. Thrasher, who has nurtured the growth of PM since its introduction to the company, explained the factors that contributed to BCBS's state of affairs in 1979. "We were in pretty desperate straits when we started PM almost 20 years ago," he said. We had a series of things that were working against us in terms of employee morale and support. First of all, we didn't have a clear vision of our future. Second, we didn't have an understanding about appropriate interface between managers and employees. Third, we had very limited facilities. Our space was crammed and our electronic systems were not up to date and automated. We were trying to put in a systems change at

---

* Gail Snyder, "Into the millennium," *Performance Management Magazine*, vol. 16, no. 1, Winter 1998.

the same time we were overwhelmed with work. On top of this, our managers were under such stress to get the work in that they forgot about the individual—the need to acknowledge, recognize and appreciate the individual.

"When our work increased dramatically with the increase of Medicare in 1965, with tremendous increases in the cost of health care and the natural responses to the rising costs which required change which causes anxiety, we emphasized quantity over quality. We thought that machines would get us out of this and we tended to begin to think of our associates as machines."

Such top management forthrightness and honest self-appraisal coupled with support for the process is what Gwen Vines, training manager, sees as the simple key to BCBS's success. Vines, a BCBS of Alabama employee for 26 years, said, "What keeps PM going is the fact that the president, the CEO and the COO of the company never address a group of managers without saying, 'Performance Management is the reason we're here.' " Vines quickly adds that talk of support must be followed with action.

According to Jones, management mouthpieces to a process that isn't truly practiced is the first sign of a company on its way to failure. "We have learned to measure or quantify what everyone does and we have reinforced them to do it. Only if we reinforce that continual behavior will we continue to improve. If we stopped today, we'd plateau, then we would not stay where we are; we'd go backward. You can tread water but for just a few minutes. Then you're drowned," he commented.

Jones' advice serves as a heads-up to all executives but even more importantly, BCBS of Alabama's actions serve as example.

A Marketing Corporation

Because both Thrasher and Jones rose from the sales and marketing ranks of BCBS, they easily made a conceptual leap that appears difficult for some executives. They realized the value of incentivizing the sales and marketing forces long before PM made its debut at the organization. PM brought along the concept that since measuring, giving feedback and positively reinforcing the sales and marketing employees improves their productivity, those methods just might work for everyone else as well. "For years before we came to PM, we did incentivize the marketing force, but it was very difficult because the rest of the company didn't share the same enthusiasm," said Jones.

One might make the conjecture, from a behavioral perspective, that many executives are blindsided to their own reinforcement contingencies. Perhaps the immediacy of sales figures and the incoming revenues they represent provide quick reinforcement to executives who know they will share in the gains. But the gains can't be optimized without the participation of every person in the organization. "First, you get to the point with the PM process that you can measure and evaluate what everyone does that could impact getting and retaining a customer, and you reinforce them for that. All of a sudden they realize they can help get business and keep it. We have worked at causing people from every discipline of the company to develop relationships with the customers. It isn't just the marketing person that calls and has a rapport. It's someone in claims or accounting or the managed care nurses. The whole organization is a marketing effort!" said Jones.

Equitable Gainsharing

All personnel at BCBS of Alabama receive compensation according to a pay-for-performance formula. "Everyone has the opportunity to put some pay at risk and earn extra money based on how, individually, they contribute," Vines explained. Depending on one's position in the corporation, the percentage of pay at risk is based solely on elements of performance over which he or she has complete control, with the remaining percentage based on the performance of the company as a whole. It follows that as one progresses up the corporate ladder, with increasing responsibility and thus control, the percentage of earnings at risk escalates. For example, overall company performance determines 100 percent of Thrasher's gainsharing. "The percentages of performance-based pay are set by degrees. If people have positions that don't allow them to have as direct an impact on overall company earnings, they're not punished for that," said Vines.

In fact, many employees track their own performance-based pay with tick marks on the calendar. Imagine the incentive and sense of control for people when upon reaching a predetermined performance standard, they know the rest of their weekly efforts will be rewarded with bonus pay.

Strategic Planning

An individualized matrix for officers, managers and other professionals allows salaried employees to know if they are on target with their own sometimes difficult to quantify performance. The first step to creating the matrices was for BCBS to align its strategic plan with corporate goals. Then the company developed an operational plan and its accompanying budget. Finally, gainsharing goals, or pay-for-performance goals, were determined, basing individual goals on behaviors that impacted three distinct corporate objectives.

"Each operational plan goes through a matrix that supports three corporate goals and each salaried employee's individual goals are tied into the corporate goals," said Thrasher. "We try to spend a lot of time telling all associates what's going to happen to our company if we attain these things in their area, department or section. I think we have people who see that we do have a plan, that we do have values and they also understand how their work contributes to success."

Management and Employee Development

Jones and Thrasher sing the praises of Gwen Vines, who is almost invariably the first person to introduce new employees to PM. A veteran trainer, Vines explained that the organization has, by design, not created the position of PM coordinator. All training for Performance

Management and employee and management development resides in the human resources training department to ensure a common foundation. Vines said: "Besides Performance Management, we're responsible for teaching many other skills such as how to interview, how to discipline and the legal issues encompassed by EEO and so on. By not separating the two training functions, we can integrate PM into everything else that we are required to do. JoAnn McKee, our management development instructor and also a 26-year employee with BCBS, is integral to ensuring such consistency in all of our training."

Such an emphasis has placed the company in the limelight as a premiere local employer. In fact, Vines notes that some local industries have expressed curiosity as to why their employees are defecting in droves to work for BCBS of Alabama. "We hired one or two people who interviewed here and they said that this is like going to heaven," Vines said with a laugh. "They then called and told their peers and now we have nine or 10 managers who came over from the same company. They said they heard we were using something called Performance Management and that employees actually had an opportunity to talk about what they wanted, could take part in setting their own goals and received positive reinforcement for achieving the goals."

BCBS immediately trains all new hires, including management candidates in PM methods. "While they're in the program, one of the things we access about the new managers or those who are manager candidates is how well do they do PM," Vines noted.

"I'm not going to fool you. Some people here do PM better than others," she added. "But we always try to address it and cause it to happen." Every few months, Vines leads Thrasher and Jones on a PM tour of every division in the facility. The tour appears to operate as a reciprocal reinforcer. "Gwen Vines knows it reinforces us to see people using Performance Management and seeing the results. That reinforces us so we turn around and reinforce them," said Jones.

Tangible and Social

The means of recognition and reinforcement has evolved at BCBS of Alabama as the people there learn more and more about the intricacies of tangible and social rewards. One valuable lesson they point out is that tangible rewards are of less value without some accompanying social recognition, but that a mix of both types is valued by everyone.

Is money a performance motivator? "I know it is!" states Jones. "People who say money isn't a motivator must have all the money they need. You pay peanuts, you get monkeys. However, the key is that you have to do more than money and contingency is the kicker." At BCBS "more than money" includes notes and words of thanks, plaques, trophies and celebrations. "It blows people away when you do things to show your appreciation for their actions. And that's Performance Management," Jones remarked.

The thing to remember, according to Vines, is that tangible reinforcement only carries maximum impact when social recognition is also forthcoming. "Early in the 1980s we discovered that we could tangibly reward people and never see them or have any contact with them," she said. "When performance leveled off, we wondered what had happened. We were not initially cognizant of the fact that we were not even speaking to the employees. Now we've learned much more about the value of social reinforcement. I would make the point to any company that social reinforcement makes such a difference in what we do every day."

Every day BCBS does what it takes to keep performance at a high-and-steady rate. Their sustained emphasis on measurement, feedback, recognition and reinforcement has resulted in sustained success and continual improvement. As the organization's leadership makes plans for the use of Performance Management into the millennium, they can also take pride in the way they conducted business in the past. Bill Mandy, former president of the organization, consistently closed his presentations of PM diplomas to managers with the following words:

"Before I present to you the diploma you have earned, I want to extract a promise from you, one that I ask of all managers. . . . That promise is that, long after I am retired and you and your fellow managers are managing Blue Cross and Blue Shield of Alabama, you will continue to use this people-oriented Performance Management philosophy in carrying out the day-to-day activities of your company."

They kept the promise.

21
Accelerated Learning

Teaching More with Less

*If you think things are changing fast today,
wait till tomorrow.*

*Organizations learn only through
individuals who learn.*   PETER SENGE
The Fifth Discipline

The Need

As modern business is experiencing ever-increasing rates of change, there is
an imperative to find ways to teach employees new skills more efficiently and
to have them perform at high rates in shorter and shorter periods of time. It
is common in many businesses that before employees become fully profi-
cient in the current processes, procedures, or technology, new ones come
along to replace them. This means that businesses rarely experience the
return on investment from the old technology before the new one is introduced. It also means that because of the short life span of any given procedure, method, or technology, human performance is rarely maximized and
often only rises to mediocre levels before the next change occurs. Indeed, if
it were not for the increase in efficiency of the new technologies themselves,
we would actually be losing ground because of slow learning rates.

Every organization is experiencing the problems associated with poor
performance on new equipment and processes. How many of us have
waited patiently in a department store because the clerk had not yet devel-

oped the skill to use the latest computer upgrade. Often, when the computer is down, even simple tasks can't be performed because the performer hasn't been taught an alternative way to complete the job.

The modern technology that organizations really need is the one that will enable people to learn quickly (in a fraction of "normal" learning times), perform at high rates, and retain what they learn for long periods of time. Peter Senge, in *The Fifth Discipline* (1990),* has made a case for the *learning* organization. He suggests that in the future, the most successful organizations will not be the ones with the most innovative products or the best marketing campaigns. Rather, *the most successful companies will be the ones that can most efficiently train their work force to assimilate and use vast amounts of ever-changing information.* This means that modern organizations must develop a culture where people look forward to change—one where people want to, and can, learn new things.

Hopefully, by this point in the book, you have some ideas about how you would create such an organization. The problem still remains that even if employees want to learn more, they may not be able to learn at a rate that will keep the organization ahead of the competition. Traditional educational methods certainly have little to offer to solve this dilemma.

What Is Wrong with Traditional Education?

Probably nowhere in modern society are there more opportunities for improved efficiency and effectiveness than in American education. Noted behavioral psychologist, B. F. Skinner, wrote an article in 1984, titled "The Shame of American Education," in which he stated that we had the technology at that time to double rates of learning. In the 15 years since he wrote this, not only have the gains not occurred, but in some ways students are achieving less now than in 1984.

There is no point to reciting all the problems of modern education in America. The poor showing of U.S. education in comparison with the other major economies of the world is well known. It has been documented too frequently, and still nothing seems to change.[†,‡] Even though by many measures of our economy and standard of living, we outperform almost all countries, continuing to lag behind educationally can only have negative effects on both.

---

* Senge, Peter M., *The Fifth Discipline: The Art and Practice of the Learning Organization,* Doubleday & Company, Inc., N.Y., 1990.

† Miller, A. D., and Heward, W. L., "Do Your Students Really Know Their Math Facts?" *Intervention in School and Clinic,* 28, 98–104.

‡ Wingert, P., "The Sum of Mediocrity," *Newsweek,* December 6, 1996, p. 96.

The promise of computers in improving education at work and at school has yet to be realized. In my opinion, this is not because computers can't increase learning rates substantially, but because those who design educational software and those who use them to teach often don't really understand what learning is all about. So-called computer-assisted instruction (CAI) often turns out to be nothing more than a fancy page-turner with beautiful graphics for the students, adding little that they couldn't get from reading an "old-fashioned" book, and less than they could get from an "old-fashioned" lecture. At least in the old-fashioned lecture, the students could ask questions! Even though the word "interactive" is appearing more and more with computer programs, they still fall short of maximizing the learning potential of the tool.

There are still too many educators who believe that the solution to student learning lies in more hours in the school day, more days in the school year, and smaller classes. Unfortunately, this kind of thinking does not encourage looking at new ways of increasing the efficiency and effectiveness of teaching methods. In fact, there has been a consistent reluctance on the part of the education community to examine teaching methods. Skinner noted it in 1984, and it hasn't changed much since then.

Sigfried Engelmann, professor at the University of Oregon, wrote *War Against the Schools' Academic Child Abuse,* a book that should be of interest to anyone who cares about education.[§] He defines *academic child abuse* as "the use of practices that cause unnecessary failure . . ." Engelmann cites two studies that deserve to be repeated. Coles (1978)[‖] reviewed approximately 1000 research studies on "learning disabilities." Not *one* considered the relationship between instruction or other school factors and the learning disability! Similarly, Alessi (1988)[#] discovered that of about 5000 children referred by school psychologists for remedial education, not one case was considered to be the fault of the curriculum, the teaching practices, or the school administration.

Consider these findings against the following quote by Engelmann (1992): "During the years that I've worked with kids and teachers, I have never seen a kid with an IQ of over 80 that could not be taught to read in a timely manner (one school year), and I've worked directly or indirectly (as a trainer) with thousands of them. I've never seen a kid that could not be taught arithmetic and language skills. During these years, however, I've

---

[§] Engelmann, Siegfried, *War Against the Schools' Academic Child Abuse,* Halcyon House, Portland, OR, 1992.

[‖] Coles, G., "The Learning Disabilities Test Battery: Empirical and Social Issues," *Harvard Educational Review,* vol. 48, 1978, pp. 313–340.

[#] Alessi, G., "Diagnosis Diagnosed: A Systemic Reaction," *Professional School Psychology,* vol. 3, no. 2, 1988, pp. 145–151.

become increasingly intolerant of reforms formulated by naïve spectators who don't really understand what school failure is and how it can be reversed."

Watkins (1997)** summarizes the problem by saying, "Suggestions about how to address the problems of education have included changing the content of instruction, raising educational standards, increasing the amount of instructional time, increasing pay for teachers, and a long list of other 'solutions' that would change just about every structural and functional aspect of education except *how children are taught.*"

· The traditional method of teaching has been around for centuries and is usually as follows:

1. The teacher or instructor presents material to the class as a group.

2. The teacher or instructor asks a few questions, which only a few students get a chance to answer.

3. The opportunity is there, usually, to do a couple of problems in class, or work through an example.

4. The homework or study assignments are given, where some practice sometimes occurs.

5. The students are eventually tested and if they score a passing grade, usually about 70 percent, they are considered to have learned the material.

Business has basically adopted this same model. The only difference is that the homework is on-the-job training (OJT). Typical of training in business settings is the training that I received on Windows 95. Even though we were all on the computer, the teaching model required that we all stay together in learning. This was most inefficient as some in the room had considerable experience with computers and some had none. This procedure is reminiscent of a quote from Skinner in *Walden Two,*†† which discusses the use of grade levels in schools: "The grade is an administrative device which does violence to the nature of the developmental process."

The instructor would show us her computer screen using an LCD projector, and walk us through each step. She would then check each person's computer to see if he or she had done it correctly. Once everyone had satisfactorily completed the assignment, she went on to show us another feature. Sitting in the room I had a clear understanding of how to do things. However, by the time I got back to my office the next day, I could not do most of what she covered in

---

** Watkins, Cathy L., *Project Follow Through: A Case Study of Contingencies Influencing Instructional Practices of the Educational Establishment,* Cambridge Center for Behavioral Studies, Cambridge, MA, 1997.

†† Skinner, B. F., *Walden Two.*

the class without referring to the manual. With so little practice, retention of the material for an extended time was impossible.

Many people would respond to my situation by saying, "Of course. Isn't that the way it is supposed to be done? She taught you, now the rest is up to you." I remember my college history professor telling his freshman class, "Going to college is like going to the drug store and ordering a soda. The soda jerk can fix you the very best soda he knows how, but whether you drink it is up to you." He then proceeded to read from the same old musty yellow notes that he had written back in 1902.

This model of teaching is inefficient in both business and academic settings. To be sure, students learn, but the problem is, *How many learn, how much do they learn, and at what rate do they learn?* To put the problem in some perspective, lets look at Morningside Academy, a private school in Seattle, Washington.

The Morningside Model

Dr. Kent Johnson, founder of Morningside Academy, estimates that core academic content from kindergarten through 12th grade could be taught easily in six years. In his school, which is composed primarily of problem learners, students achieve at a rate 4 to 6 times the national average.

Dr. Johnson began Morningside Academy in 1980. He has maintained meticulous records of actual learning since that time. He has to do so because he gives parents a written, money-back guarantee that their child will advance the equivalent of two grade levels per subject per year. Since 1980, no parent has requested their money back because the average achievement at Morningside is 2.4 grade levels per year. Gains have been increasing since 1980, and it is now common for the school average on some subjects to increase over three grades per year as measured by the California Achievement Test. Contrast those figures with the national average of less than one grade level per year!

However, if that doesn't impress you, maybe this will: *All of Morningside students have been referred to the school because they have been unable to learn in regular school classes. They all have a formal diagnosis of some learning disorder*—ADD (attentional deficit disorder), dyslexia, and retardation, among others. Snyder (1992)[‡‡] states that at Morningside, "Children diagnosed as learning disabled, who have never gained more than a half a year in any one academic year, typically gain between two and three years in each academic skill per year."

[‡‡] Snyder, G., "Morningside Academy: A Learning Guarantee," *Performance Management Magazine*, vol. 10, 1992, pp. 29–35.

Their results are equally impressive with adults. Adults, who tested between second and eighth grade level in reading upon entering Morningside training, gained at the rate of 1.7 grades per 20 hours of instruction. The U.S. standard is one grade per 100 hours of instruction. How do they do it?

Fluency

In 1967, the U.S. Government funded a program, *Project Follow Through*, to compare a wide range of teaching methods to find effective methods for educating disadvantaged children. The results showed that the methods, called *direct instruction* and *behavior analysis*, came in first and second among 22 different approaches tried. The traditional classroom method came in dead last. As incredible as it might seem, the outcome of this research was that funds were provided to improve the traditional method rather than adopt any of the methods that demonstrated academic superiority!

At Morningside, Dr. Johnson combined direct instruction and behavior analysis to form a teaching method that he calls the *Morningside Model of Generative Instruction.*[§§] Dr. Engelmann, mentioned previously, developed the direct instruction (DI) technique.[‖] Direct instruction is carefully scripted both in the order of presentation of the academic material and what the teacher says. Through systematic analysis, Engelmann has been able to determine the most effective presentation of the material as well as the most effective sequencing of it.

The behavior analysis approach added measurement, feedback, and positive reinforcement to Engelmann's material. In addition, Dr. Johnson used a technique developed by Dr. Ogden Lindsley of the University of Kansas. Dr. Lindsley named this method "fluency." The usual connotations of the word *fluency* come close to describing its academic definition. If we say someone is fluent in several languages, we know that they can switch from one language to another the instant they hear the other language being spoken or see it written. They don't have to think about what the equivalent words are in the other language. They respond, automatically and unhesitatingly.

Fluency, then, is automatic, nonhesitant responding. If people are fluent in a particular subject, they do not have to think about what they are doing, and they can respond accurately after long periods of no instruction. They are also able to respond for extended periods with less fatigue and can generalize from what they have learned and apply it to new or novel situations.

[§§] Johnson, K. R., and Layng, T. V. J., "Breaking the Structuralist Barrier: Literacy and Numeracy with Fluency," *American Psychologist*, 47, 1475–1490.

[‖] Engelmann, S., and Carnine, D. W., *Theory of Instruction*. Irvington, New York, 1982.

To attain fluency, responding at high rates is required. Because the method deals with measurable, observable behavior, the rates necessary to attain fluency can be determined for any academic subject. For example, certain basic math concepts such as addition, subtraction, multiplication, and division may require a student to be able to do as many as 80 math facts a minute with no errors. Some students can do up to 120 a minute. Although Morningside concentrates on basic skills, they also teach such subjects as problem solving and fluent thinking skills.

Because practice is the hallmark of fluency training, a Morningside classroom hour is divided as follows: 10 minutes of instruction, 40 minutes of practice, and 10 minutes of break. By the way, students have no homework. The average teacher may not be able to relate to this model of classroom instruction because it is so different from the way traditional classroom teaching is done. This model seeks to determine the minimum amount of information that needs to be given to allow the maximum time for active involvement of the student with the material.

Dr. Johnson's methods have also been applied in regular schools with impressive results. He has developed a model of individualized instruction that is manageable and effective for public education. However, the move to adopt it by the traditional educational community is slow.

The work of Johnson and others has made one thing very clear: To learn efficiently, learners must have the opportunity for high rates of interaction with the material to be learned or the skill to be mastered. We know this is true because a high frequency of learner response dramatically increases the amount of positive reinforcement the learner can receive for her or his efforts—and *positive reinforcement will accelerate learning.*

Sources of Reinforcement

Where does all this reinforcement come from? Clearly, no teacher or instructor can provide positive reinforcement for every learner behavior. In fact, the reinforcement comes from the students seeing, or knowing, they got the correct answer. In most of our learning histories, external reinforcers have been paired with correct answers to the point that getting an answer correct is reinforcing to almost everyone. Therefore, students given many opportunities to answer questions correctly will have an opportunity for high rates of reinforcement quite independent of the social reinforcement that they might get from the teacher, parents, or other students. A big part of the fluency model depends on high rates of correct responding. Nothing is more reinforcing than doing well, and students of all ages who get the opportunity to perform successfully at high frequency will be highly reinforced. This high level of positive reinforcement will accelerate learning.

One of the criticisms of fluency techniques that has come from traditional educators is that it smacks of "rote learning," and as I have been told many times by school staff, "Rote learning went out 20 years ago." My response to them is that maybe it is not coincidental that learning rates in schools have been going down for the last 20 years, also! Of course, in my day, rote learning was accomplished by drill, and the drill was accomplished by negative reinforcement. Under such conditions, students would not be excited about doing it. When drill and other rote learning methods are done with positive reinforcement, students beg to do them.

A number of years ago, one of our industrial clients asked me if I would share what they were learning with a local school. Of course, I said that I would. They selected six teachers to pilot positive reinforcement methods in their classes. To give the method a fair test, we chose teachers who varied in their enthusiasm to try these techniques. At a review I conducted after several weeks, one of the older teachers was still a little skeptical about this new approach. As I was talking to the group, I said, "You will really have it made when your students beg you to test them." Toward the end of school that year she sent me a card. It read simply, "Dr. Daniels, I've really got it made!"

None of the criticisms of this approach that I have seen advanced by traditional educators has been supported by credible research. However, research support for fluency as an effective method of learning is coming from several unrelated sources.

Motor Performance Research

Richard A. Schmidt (1991), in *Motor Learning and Performance*,[##] says that in most motor learning, about 300 repetitions under the most favorable conditions are required to produce automaticity. He says, "Automatic responding can develop with several hundred trials of practice under the most favorable conditions, but it appears that many more trials than this are needed in less optimal real-world settings."

Schmidt notes advantages to "automaticity" similar to those discovered quite separately from researchers working on fluency. He says that, "This capability to produce skills automatically means component parts (e.g., dribbling and running in basketball) do not require much attention, which then frees attention capacity for other important elements in a game (where to pass) or for style or form in dance. Also, automatic processes are faster than controlled processes, allowing the performer to respond more quickly and certainly."

[##] Schmidt, Richard A., *Motor Learning and Performance: From Principles to Practice*, Human Kinetics, Windsor, Ontario, Canada, 1991.

Walter Schneider (1985)*** made similar discoveries. In training air controllers, he found that in training them to rapidly visualize flight patterns, "we compress simulated time by a factor of 100; for example, making a judgment of where an aircraft should turn (a maneuver that normally takes about 5 minutes) would take about 0.5 second. By compressing time in this way, we can provide the trainee with more trials at executing this particular component in a single day of training than he or she could get in a year of training with conventional methods." He says further, "Active participation is enhanced if subjects need to respond every few seconds."

Expertise Research

Dr. Anders Ericsson[†††] at Florida State University has done extensive research on the acquisition of expertise. Over the last 15 years he has investigated expertise in every field in which there are objective ways to separate experts from others. His list of fields includes chess, music, sports, medicine, engineering, and ballet dancing.

There is an amazing consistency to what he has discovered about what it takes to become an expert in any field of endeavor. He has discovered that it takes a minimum of 10 years of deliberate practice to become an expert at anything. Ericsson's investigations have revealed that anyone who has attained expert status has engaged in at least 10,000 hours of deliberate practice. This amounts to an average of 20 hours of practice for 50 weeks a year over the course of 10 years.

One of his findings that flies in the face of popular notions about high performers is that at least 96 percent of the variance in performance is accounted for by deliberate practice alone. Another way of saying this is that less than 4 percent of their performance is due to all other factors, including something often referred to as "natural talent." This is a very important finding for anyone who wants to become an expert at anything. What it means is that almost anyone who wants to excel at something needs to engage in deliberate practice for 10,000 hours. Ericsson points out that this must be deliberate practice—that is, a concerted effort to improve one's skill. (Unfortunately, four hours on the golf course doesn't count as deliberate practice.)

It becomes clear from the research in all these areas that the number of reinforced repetitions is a very important element in teaching and learn-

---

*** Schneider, Walter, "Training High-Performance Skills: Fallacies and Guidelines," *Human Factors*, vol. 27, no. 3, 1985, pp. 285–300.

[†††] Ericsson, K. Anders, and Charness, Neil, "Expert Performance: Its Structure and Acquisition," *American Psychologist*, August 1994, pp. 725–747.

ing. Although the relationship between speed and number of trials is not fully understood, the fact is clear that more repetitions lead to more reinforcement, which leads to faster learning, greater retention, the ability to generalize to novel situations, and the ability to perform under stressful and distracting circumstances. What manager in any organization would not want that?

As noted above, the research of Ericsson, Engelmann, and Johnson and Layng suggests that most failures in learning are actually failures in teaching methods, not the result of student motivation and/or ability. This finding has tremendous implications for business, industry, and government. It means that most performance problems are not because the performer is incapable of performing at a high level, but because of either poor training or lack of a reinforcing environment, or both.

What we see in most organizations is that there are many performance problems that can be addressed successfully and economically by employing teaching methods that involve high rates of responding and frequent reinforcement. Some of it is being done already.

As an example of what fluency techniques can accomplish in business, let me tell you about an application at a Delta Faucet plant in Tennessee. Delta started a new plant and it was important for them to train a large number of people in a short period of time to assemble faucets quickly and correctly. By developing a computer training program based on the fluency technology, they were able to reduce learning time from 24 hours plus extensive OJT to less than 10 hours plus only 1 hour of OJT. The first assembly teams went to the line having never seen a faucet part except on the computer training system and successfully built their first faucets in 42 minutes! Bill Hampton, human resource manager said that each one-half hour spent in fluency training was the equivalent of three to four hours of hands-on training on the assembly line.

Blue Cross of Georgia used fluency-building techniques to teach clerks medical terminology. Previous classroom training was three days with no control over what students knew. Deficiencies in training were discovered and eliminated in the workplace. With the computer programmed for fluency training, all of the students performed to criteria in less than five hours. These results are typical, not extraordinary.

Recently, a large health care provider used an accelerated learning program we developed and reduced total training time for billing clerks from six months to three months. Also, the new clerks achieved fluency in their tasks during the training, which allowed them to generate correct billing statements the first day on the job. The customer expects this training will result in a savings of 4.5 million dollars.

Accelerated learning is not a thing of the future. It is available now. Organizations faced with the need to train more people more often should avail themselves of this powerful educational method. The educational community, having less pressure to teach more in a shorter period of time will be, unfortunately, slower to adopt these methods. In the meantime, businesses will have to continue to do the educators' jobs for them. Because of the demonstrated effectiveness and efficiency of these techniques, business and government should not only use them—they should encourage local schools to do likewise.

22

Increasing Creativity and Managing Change

Nature has never been content with the merely successful.
New ways to grow will always be found.

GEORGE LAND, *Grow or Die**

Creativity Is Behavior

The most important thing you will read in this chapter is that creativity is behavior, and as such is subject to the laws of behavior that you have learned in this book. Creativity is not a brain thing. It is a behavior thing. It is not mysterious. It can be explained.

Some common notions about creativity are that only a small part of the population is creative, that only really smart people are creative, that to be creative you have to be a little bit weird, that creativity is largely genetic. I am happy to tell you that none of these are true. These notions are not only incorrect, they inhibit creativity and innovation in most organizations every day.

Years ago, I was visiting a manufacturing plant in Florida. As I was talking to the plant manager I asked, "What do you make here?" "I don't know," he

---

* Land, G., *Grow or Die: The Unifying Principle of Transformation*, Dell Publishing, New York, 1973.

203

replied, "I've only worked here a year and a half, and it takes us two years to make one." He was only being halfway facetious. The plant made the first guidance systems for satellites, and unreliability and failure to meet production schedules were serious problems.

As we walked through the plant, I saw rows and rows of desks where engineers worked. To illustrate some of the problems of managing such an operation, the plant manager stopped and pointed down one of the rows. "See that man?" he asked. He was pointing to an engineer who was racked back in his chair blowing smoke rings at the ceiling. "How much do you want to bet that if I go up and ask him what he's doing, he will say, 'I'm thinking.' And how much do you want to bet that just as soon as we go into production, he will be the one running down the hall waving a change order. And if he does, I'm going to fire him."

He was venting his frustration at managing the creative process. Like many people, he thought creativity was a "mind thing," not a "behavior thing." Of course, he was stymied because you cannot manage someone else's thinking. That the engineer was not thinking about work-related issues concerned the manager, but he had no idea how to confirm or refute this concern. One thing he could have done was to ask the engineer to make a list of what he was thinking about that day, how the items on the list related to the problem or project at hand, and a list of next steps to take to complete the task. If he had done that, the manager would have had some behavior to work with.

Too many managers hesitate to interrupt the solitude of "thought workers," like engineers, because they are afraid they might interrupt the creative process. To them creativity is a fragile and mysterious process. Many managers, even those in charge of research laboratories, have told me that you can't manage creativity! Indeed, you can't manage creativity until you define it behaviorally, but once you do that, you can apply positive reinforcement to accelerate the behaviors that enhance creativity every day.

All Behavior Is Creative

You never do something exactly the same way twice. As many times as you have signed your name, there are minor variations in each signature. Although this fact may seem insignificant, it is the primary source of creativity. The fact that behavior is variable means that some things are selected by reinforcement to be repeated and some are not. Variability in behavior that is strengthened will lead to new behaviors that, in turn, produce new results, innovative products, or unique services. Conversely, when new ways of behaving are punished, they will stop.

Of course, not all variability in behavior is appropriate. Behavior that is creative in one setting may be obnoxious in another. Everyone has been in meetings where a person has a funny response to about everything that is said. Whereas that may be annoying in a corporate setting because it detracts from getting something accomplished, in Hollywood that same behavior may earn a screenwriter a substantial living.

Because creativity is related to new forms of behavior, products, or services, variability in behavior is grist for the mill of creativity. There are some situations in organizations where variability is not valued and others where it is prized. In delivering a service or manufacturing a product, we usually don't want variability. We want consistent quality. It is, therefore, important for managers to identify when variability is valued and when it is not. It is also important to know how to manage variability.

Creativity and the ABC Model

Antecedents. Antecedents can be useful in the creative process. When we put people in situations where they have no experience, they will typically try a wide range of things to find reinforcement. *Candid Camera* was famous for putting people in situations where they had no experience. They, *predictably*, did some strange and often funny things. The reaction after they saw themselves on the screen was, "I can't believe I did that." Therefore, by varying the environment in which people do what they do, you can increase the probability that they will do new things. The use of cross-functional teams is a common business practice designed to put people in unusual situations to help develop creative solutions. Marketing personnel in meetings with design engineers frequently ask questions and make suggestions that the engineers would never think of. Because they are in unfamiliar settings, they have to behave differently. Innovation is their only behavioral choice.

Consequences. As with other behavior, each of the behavioral consequences has a predictable effect on the creative process. Let's take each in turn.

Positive Reinforcement

As you have already learned, positive reinforcement can be used to get people to do things again and again. When learning a new skill, positive reinforcement narrows the variability of behavior to the point that you can do the same thing over and over again with a minimum of variability. This is a naturally occurring learning process. How then can positive reinforcement be used to generate creativity?

When novelty or variability is positively reinforced you will get more novel and variable responses. What you must realize ahead of time is that for creativity, you are not interested in decreasing, but rather in increasing, the variability of behavior. Positive reinforcement is so powerful, you have to use it precisely. If you don't, you may end up inadvertently increasing behaviors that not only do not increase creativity, but also interfere with current efficiencies.

For example, one of the problems in developing any skill is that an extraneous behavior often gets accidentally reinforced when a desired result is produced. You need only to watch a basketball player shoot a free throw, a golfer swing a club, or a baseball player as he anticipates a pitch. You will see a very wide range of behaviors that the athletes think is essential to high performance, but in reality adds nothing to the probability of their success.

Some basketball players bounce the ball several times before shooting a free throw; others don't bounce it at all. Karl Malone recites his mantra before every free throw. Some golfers take a practice swing before every shot. Others take none. Some batters in baseball waggle the bat before the pitch. Others hold it very still. Many of the behaviors they perform contribute nothing to their success, and in some cases, they are successful in spite of them.

This same phenomenon occurs in businesses where work processes evolve over time. Many of the behaviors in the process do not contribute to the outcome and some, in fact, limit results. The reason is that in most processes, behavior can vary in many ways and not substantially affect the outcome. When this happens, those variations are accidentally reinforced and will be added to the process. For example, we have a soft drink machine in our training room break area. Drinks are free, but you need to push the coin return lever before making your selection. For some reason, there is a delay of a couple of seconds before the drink can falls into the receptacle. I happened to hear Phil Hurst, one of our instructors, tell a new class how to operate the machine. He told them that you had to push the coin return three times to get a drink. I can understand how he came to believe this. When he operates other machines the drink usually falls out immediately. On our machine, when he pushed the coin return once and it appeared that nothing was happening, he pushed it quickly two more times and that's when the drink happened to fall out. From that time on, he pushed the coin return three times, and the drink fell out immediately—after the third push. Even though what he learned was neither correct nor efficient, it worked. This is precisely how processes come to be inefficient in both time and money. Organizations would do well to check all processes and systems periodically to detect such behavioral drift. Remember that positive reinforcement will increase the behavior that is occurring at the time reinforcement is delivered, so you must use it deliberately and precisely.

Because some kinds of variability are more desirable than others, you must identify which ones are likely to produce the outcomes you want and which are not. Then, you must use reinforcement precisely to increase the kind you want. For example, if you are not precise, you might end up reinforcing arguing or complaining when you intended to reinforce listing ideas for solving a problem. This variability is most often counterproductive to the creative process. When you positively reinforce the right variable behavior (i.e., new or novel behaviors), you will get more of them. This kind of variability is at the heart of creativity.

Negative Reinforcement

Negative reinforcement has limited value in managing creativity and innovation. As discussed earlier, it is one of the reasons people "resist change" at work. However, negative reinforcement can be used to increase creativity, but remember that people will give you only as much as they have to, in order to avoid the negative reinforcer. In many situations, people have come up with new ideas because they have been told something like, "If you don't find a way to do it, I will find someone who can." Solutions can be found under those conditions, but at a very high cost to the organization. Under those conditions, people will certainly give you no more creativity than you demand.

Punishment and Penalty

Obviously, punishment and penalty have no value in promoting creativity and innovation. Most managers understand that fact. As it relates to creativity and innovation, the problem in most organizations is not deliberate punishment, but unintended punishment. Systems, processes, and procedures often punish and penalize behaviors related to introducing new ideas. Budgets, accounting practices, job descriptions, compensation, and management systems are but a few of the factors that create obstacles for introducing innovative change in an organization. When we introduced a professional sales force into our company, the sales manager intentionally avoided installing common sales management systems. He did not arbitrarily develop sales goals, territories, or industry targets for the account executives (AEs). Instead, he encouraged a great deal of variability in the approaches used by the AEs. What we found was that sales success came quickly and from some unexpected sources. Our approach to sales is now becoming more consistent, which allows us to teach what we have learned to new people more quickly. In the early days, however, variability was very desirable as a means of finding methods that worked.

The Impact of Extinction on Creativity

At first glance, extinction, the result of no reinforcement, would not seem to have much of a role in creativity because it is described as decreasing behavior. However, if you understand what happens to behavior during extinction, you can see that it plays a very important part in change and creativity at work.

Whereas positive reinforcement decreases variability, extinction increases variability. Remember that variability is grist for the creative mill. It could be said that *most creativity is extinction induced.* When a behavior, process, or procedure fails to produce satisfactory results, the behaviors involved undergo extinction. We will gradually abandon the old ways as more satisfactory ones can be found.

If "necessity is the mother of invention," then *extinction is certainly the father of creativity.* For example, if you go to a store several times and fail to get good service, you will find another store. If every time you go to your bank, you have to wait in a long line for service, you will probably find a new bank or do your banking on-line or by ATM. Most golfers I know have bought many different drivers. The primary reason is that when they were having trouble hitting their first driver far enough or straight enough, they began to look for one that would do better.

How does extinction foster creativity? Let me review the typical extinction responses:

1. *Extinction burst.* A common reaction to the loss of reinforcement is to actually repeat the old behavior—the one under extinction—more often. We repeatedly look for lost objects in the same place. A child who is ignored will cry louder and longer. When the elevator does not arrive in what we consider to be a timely manner, we push the button again and again.

2. *Emotional behavior.* If repeating the behavior still does not get reinforcement, we often resort to emotional behavior. We blame our spouse or children for moving a lost object. The child lacking attention or the desired response from the parent, may hit the parent, a sibling, or the family pet. Someone waiting for the elevator may kick the door or curse hotel management. An employee may question management's ability to run the organization when they abandon the old process that worked very well from the employee's perspective.

3. *Resurgence.* Sometimes, after new behavior patterns have been established, an older behavior will often reemerge (i.e., people revert to old behavior patterns for no apparent reason). This results from the lack of adequate reinforcement for the new behavior. Mysteriously, children

revert to old behavior just when we're sure we had them trained. (Remember potty training?) A manager, who has apparently developed some new positively reinforcing management techniques, suddenly reverts to negative, punishing behavior. When asked about this turnaround, I tell our clients that the boss changed her behavior because she did not get enough reinforcement for the new or innovative management behavior she had been attempting.

4. *Habit breakup.* After people try everything and nothing works, their behavior may become erratic. You've experienced this if you've ever found an error in your account when balancing your checkbook, and after going over the statement systematically from the first check to the last, you find yourself looking at checks in no particular order. Your attention may wander to nearby papers or activities. It is usually at this time that you find your error.

When habit breakup begins to occur, this is often the point that people "get an insight" into the problem that they are facing and solve it. They say things like, "It just hit me," or "Suddenly I just saw the solution." At this point the old behavior has disappeared, and new ones can emerge to take its place. As Kupferberg said, "New worlds can appear only when old worlds disappear."

We have been told often that we need to change "our paradigms," as though we can will ourselves to do so. People do not forsake old paradigms when they are working, even if they are told to do so. Extinction has to occur if the old is to be replaced with the new.

Is Chaos a Necessary Part of Change?

Tom Peters wrote a book, *Thriving on Chaos,* in which he described an emerging world where change was the norm.[†] The book was intended to help managers deal with the resulting problems. Does change always produce problems? The common notion is that it does. Most people accept uncritically the notion that people resist change. By now, you know that this is not so. However, we have all witnessed problems with changing organizational systems, processes, and procedures. Is there any way we can predict when change will be resisted, and is there anything that can be done to make change easier? For those who understand behavior analysis there is.

[†] Peters, T., *Thriving on Chaos: Handbook for a Management Revolution,* HarperCollins Publishers, New York, 1988.

For those who don't, the future will produce more of the same—that is, a period of chaos and a cost of change that is much more expensive than it need be, both financially and emotionally.

Change and Creativity

Change and creativity are similar in that they require some old behaviors to be replaced by new ones. However, the intentional processes you can use to accelerate them are different. Following are a number of steps for you to consider, first for accelerating change and then a second set for increasing creativity.

How to Make Change Easy and Efficient

1. *Plan R+ for the new behavior involved in the new system, process, or procedure.* Although enough has probably been said on this subject already, I don't think it can be overemphasized. In this case, you must plan the R+ before you make the change. The day you announce the new changes, you must have the R+ contingencies in place. People need to experience benefits of the change on the first day, not six months or a year later. The reason most organizations have difficulty with reengineering, resizing, or changing products and processes is that there is almost never a plan for positive reinforcement for the behaviors that will make the change work. Many plans do include rewards, but these do not work any better than most organizational rewards. If there are no immediate positive reinforcers in the plan, rewards will be given too late to be effective and motivational.

2. *Eliminate all R+ for the behaviors associated with the old methods.* You must make sure that the old methods no longer work and that managers and supervisors will not find themselves in a situation where they say, "O.K., I'm going to let you get by this time, but from now on you must do it the new way." You know if this happens, the person will be reinforced for coming up with more reasons why he needs to do it the old way, one more time.

3. *Positively reinforce the new behavior more than you think you should.* This is just another way of saying that positive reinforcement must occur immediately upon making the change and that it must be delivered frequently. The first few days and weeks are critical in determining whether the change will be easy or difficult. Frequent social reinforcement should be a priority for all supervisors, managers, and team leaders. Because change may be difficult, any attempts to implement it should be positively reinforced.

4. *Expect an extinction burst.* Don't be caught off guard by the fact that there is reluctance to change. Remember that an extinction burst means that change is taking place. If people are trying the old way harder as a means of aborting the change process or slowing it down, that should indicate that they are getting less reinforcement for the old way, which is what you want. Stay the course, and do not reinforce the burst.

5. *Expect emotional behavior.* When someone comes to you and questions the motivation or intelligence of the person behind the new process, don't take it personally. Remember that emotional behavior is a natural response to the loss of positive reinforcement. It is unfortunate that managers who don't understand extinction get caught up in questioning employee loyalty and punishing the emotional responses. This causes the chaos that Peters writes about. Listen and ask for ideas about how to make the change work better. Do not reinforce complaining and faultfinding.

6. *Both the extinction burst and the emotional behavior can be attenuated by adequate reinforcement of the new behavior.* Because all change is not resisted, what is different about change that is resisted and change that is not? It boils down to the amount of reinforcement received for the change. When reinforcement immediately follows attempts to change, and when it is frequent, there will be much less of the extinction burst or emotional behavior. Remember to plan and deliver more positive reinforcement than you think you need to do.

7. *Resurgence indicates a failure to reinforce new behavior sufficiently.* If things seem to be going along reasonably well and one day, out of the blue, there is a return to the old way of doing things, this means that you did not reinforce the new behavior enough. This happens frequently to managers who try to be more participative, less directive, or less hands-on. When they don't get the results they were expecting and they also get no reinforcement for the change in their behavior, you can expect them to return to a more autocratic and negatively reinforcing style of management. If resurgence occurs, you must make sure that it doesn't get reinforcement, because it will make future changes extremely difficult.

Ten Strategies for Increasing Creativity

1. *Reinforce all ideas.* Any behavior that indicates a person is thinking about how to do a job better or how to find a new or improved product or service should be reinforced. Nothing should be so trivial or outrageous as to be ignored or punished. An idea that is trivial or outrageous has the potential to give birth to a more efficient process, a new piece of equip-

ment, or a new product or service. If the silly or the trivial is punished or ignored, the company will be deprived of that possibility.

Most executives would think it to be an ideal company where every employee would spend some time after work thinking or talking with others about how a job could be done better or how to add value to the company in some way. If they do, that activity is worthy of positive reinforcement.

2. *Remove obstacles and other contingencies that are punishing or penalizing creativity.* It is certainly not unusual that people who have ideas are inadvertently punished by others or by systems and procedures. If you make the procedure for submitting ideas burdensome, you can count on low participation. It is a well-established fact that the length of time between the submission of an idea in a traditional suggestion system and the acknowledgment of the submission influences the number of suggestions made—the longer the time, the fewer suggestions. If you can shorten the time that it takes for someone to acknowledge the submission of the idea, you will increase participation.

The very act of asking some people to write a complete description of an idea for submission is enough to punish the idea-generating behavior. Remember that the easier you make it to get an idea into the system, the higher the number of suggestions you will get.

3. *Look to unlikely people as a source of ideas.* It is a fact that many great ideas came from people who had no expertise in the field where the idea finally came to fruition. Prejudging people because of education, job title, and even appearance can be a serious mistake. The person doing the job doesn't always have the best ideas, but they may have some good ones that can be turned into great ones.

4. *Form unlikely teams.* We tend to form teams that are natural work groups and, to a lesser extent, cross-functional ones. When trying to come up with better ways of doing something, you may find that the more diverse the composition of the team by experience, job, education, gender, and national origin, the more effective they are at discovering new ways to solve problems.

5. *Catch and record.* Make it easy for employees to record ideas. Some companies have idea pads and boards conveniently located where employees can write them down. Sharing ideas can be stimulating to others to build on the idea or be an antecedent for a different idea. Obviously, this will only work in an environment of positive reinforcement.

6. *Multiple antecedents.* By varying people's surroundings you can stimulate new associations. Get those engineers away from their computers. A New York–based client of ours designs coverings for office walls and fur-

niture. In an effort to change their image and their products from standard and dependable to unique, stylish, and dependable, they have begun exposing their designers and buyers to any number of atypical experiences. They took their entire team to the new Getty Museum in California for a tour and series of lectures, and then they held brainstorming sessions to develop innovative products. They were very happy with the increase in the number of different and "creative" ideas that resulted.

7. *Stretch goals.* You didn't have to read much of this book to learn that I am not in favor of the practice of stretch goals as a management technique. However, there is a place for them in increasing creativity. Why they work in the creativity arena is exactly why they shouldn't be used in normal operations. They work in creativity to extinguish current ways of performing. In normal operations this could result in unwanted variability in process, quality, and productivity.

Stretch goals can be used effectively only if the performers are working under conditions of positive reinforcement. If they are, then they will try for a longer time before they give up on finding a solution. Second, there must be a solution. Although it may not be known, there must be a possible solution. If you have doubts about whether the problem can be solved, stretch goals would not be the technique of choice.

The reason stretch goals work in creativity is that the goals are so far from the acceptable results that typical behaviors will not work. That means that the old ways will undergo extinction.

8. *Multiple repertoires.* Hire people with diverse backgrounds and experience. For example, make it a practice not to hire all your people from the same university. Hybrid vigor comes from combining diverse repertoires. If everybody has the same training, skills, or experience, they tend to see situations similarly. Diversity really does pay in the creativity arena.

9. *Train performers to fluency.* When you are fluent at more than one thing, you are able to recombine these fluent repertoires in new and novel ways. Contrary to the popular notion that repetition makes one less creative, under the right circumstances, fluency makes creativity possible. Think of an expert tennis player practicing for hours every day to master the standard shots of the game. During a match, however, unexpected situations always arise. It's at these times that spectators are often amazed at the "creativity" of the tennis star. "How did he do that?" is the frequent reaction of the fan. How "he did that" one-of-a-kind shot is a result of the fluency developed in those standard shots through years of practice. Because he doesn't have to spend time and energy thinking about how to do the standard shots, he is free to combine two or more behavioral repertoires into one that is novel.

10. *Serendipity.* Don't discount chance. Chance favors those who are prepared for it. It is certainly true that the harder you work the luckier you get. When you create an environment using techniques that favor creativity and innovation, you will find that, increasingly, things just happen to come along at just the right time.

A behavioral understanding of creativity and change demystifies the processes and makes them manageable. The intense global competition between providers of goods and services in today's marketplace demands that a creative approach to discovery, invention, and innovation is needed. The behavioral approach is just that.

23

Managing the Nintendo Generation and Beyond

This generation is the first in history to know more than their parents about something central to society.

DON TAPSCOTT
"Growing up Digital"*

The "Force" Is with Us

I have been asked many times by older supervisors and managers, "Why do we have to do all this reinforcement stuff today? We didn't used to have to do it, and we got along OK." The answer to that question is that the world has changed. Management methods that worked for the past 30 to 40 years worked because of the political, social, and economic circumstances of the day. You don't have to be much of a historian to know of the significant changes that have occurred, are occurring, and will continue to occur since that time.

---

* Tapscott, Don, *Growing Up Digital: The Rise of the Net Generation*, McGraw-Hill, New York, 1999.

No one would argue that computers have fundamentally changed our society, but has anyone noticed what they have done to reinforcement? Computers have increased reinforcement rates available to people today to a degree undreamed of just a few years ago.

Every generation complains that they don't understand the younger generation. They talk differently, dress differently, act differently, and show little interest in established values and culture. In other words, their behavior is different. By now you should have some appreciation of why. They are, of course, no different than we were, or our parents were, because they respond to the consequences of their behavior in behaviorally lawful ways— just as we did.

In his book, *What Remains to Be Discovered,* John Maddox[†] points out that toward the end of every century, as people look back on what has been discovered, every generation tends to think there is not much left to be discovered because of the rapid change in that century. Yet, even more is accomplished in the next one. As much change as we have seen in this century, as the saying goes, "You ain't seen nuthin' yet!" I'm amazed that researchers have been able to get brain cells to grow into computer implants in the brain allowing stroke victims to communicate by computer. We can only wonder what will be discovered next. History has taught us one thing that we can count on: What will be thought of next cannot even be dreamed of now.

Even though positive reinforcement works in a lawful and predictable way to strengthen behavior, the world is so complex that the behaviors of the future that will be selected by the environment for reinforcement cannot be known with certainty. One thing we do know with certainty is that the pace of change will only accelerate. How change is affecting behavior is most visible today in the younger generation.

The Nintendo Generation

When George Orwell wrote his classic book, *1984,* in which he predicted a rather grim world, he could not foresee an event that was to occur that year that has changed the world forever. *That was the first year Nintendo was widely available for sale.* Why would a computer game change the world? How could it have such far-reaching consequences?

In reality, the game has not changed the world, but the technology that made it possible has changed the world and continues to do so at an amazing rate. By now, you understand that positive reinforcement accelerates

---

[†] Maddox, John, *What Remains To Be Discovered: Mapping the Secrets of the Universe, the Origins of Life, and the Future of the Human Race,* The Free Press, New York, 1998.

the rate of change. Guess how many positive reinforcers a person playing Nintendo gets per minute? I recently did a pilot study for research on this subject and found that an average player gets, conservatively, between 65 and 85 reinforcers per minute of play.

Think of it. Children born since the late 1970s have, for all intents and purposes, not known a world without Nintendo. These are cyberkids that have literally grown up at the center of the high-tech revolution. They have never known a world without high-speed computers, the Internet, and the instant gratification available in video games. They have never known a world without fast food, speed dial, automated cash machines, MTV, and one-hour photo stores.

Hal Lancaster, writing in *The Wall Street Journal* on October 6, 1998, quotes Marc Prensky, a vice president of Banker's Trust, as saying that the younger generation works at "twitch speed." He uses this phrase to describe how fast the younger generation absorbs information. They work on several tasks at once. While they are waiting for a search to be completed on "slow" computers, they open other windows to work on other tasks. They prefer graphics to text and are most comfortable in a sound bite world. They are impatient, in a hurry for everything, and resent anything that slows them down.

Patience, A Lost Virtue

It is easy to see that the younger generation is impatient, but you may not have noticed that you are becoming more impatient as well. Although you may have attributed it to getting older, that is not the cause. Usually patience comes with old age. The reason you are getting impatient is that the rate of reinforcement in your world is increasing also. We all are exposed to the high-speed world where we have come to expect that we shouldn't have to wait. It is amazing that we complain that computers are too slow when, within seconds on the Internet, we can find a million references to some search that we have initiated. Computer printers that print several pages in color in a minute seem to be too slow. Fast food is not fast enough and drive-in lines seem to "take forever." We even complain that the ATM is too slow because we have time to drum our fingers between commands.

Management and NinGen

Organizations are already experiencing problems managing the Nintendo crowd. They want continuous challenges and more money, and when they don't get what they want, they quit and seek it elsewhere. Bill Peard, a manager with Arthur Andersen, LLP, said, "Kids come in and say, 'I want this and this and this, and I want balance in my life, fast promotions, and lots of money." There is a new acronym that describes the Nintendo crowd that is prevalent in many talent-short, high-tech fields: It is MT-BOO, or "mean time between other offers."

The NinGens are confident in their skills and abilities, and if their present job doesn't give them what they need to meet their ideals, they will quickly seek it elsewhere.

An ADD Epidemic

Can you see a problem with children brought up in a Nintendo world in which they get reinforcers at the rate of 60 to 100 a minute, when they go to the average classroom? No wonder they are hyperactive. The rate of reinforcement available to these students is woefully inadequate to maintain their attention for any period of time. Producers of TV shows and commercials know this. How many times do you think a commercial changes scenes per minute when it is aimed at the under-30 crowd? *It is about once a second!* Rather than advise parents to limit TV and the Internet, teachers should focus on how to provide similar frequencies of reinforcement in their classes. It is interesting to note that many children diagnosed as ADD by school officials can play computer games for hours at home. When they are engaged in the game, they are almost impossible to distract.

I teach a session in a continuing education class at MIT called "The Birthing of Giants." To get in this class you have to be under 40 years of age and own your own business. The business must have sales of over $1 million a year and be growing. The class is limited to 60 students a year. The demand for the class is such that more classes are currently being added. Over the several years that I have been teaching this class, I have noticed that the average age is getting younger each year. This year it is in the low 30s, and next year will probably be in the high 20s.

It is the most frustrating, and at the same time, the most exciting class that I teach. When I start talking about positive reinforcement, 60 hands go up. I never finish my planned lecture because there is a constant flow of questions. They don't have to be convinced, as many older managers do, that positive reinforcement is the way to manage. They impatiently want to know how to do it. Then I ask them, "What organizational model did you use to design your company's management system?" This question usually causes a gasp from the group, because at that moment they realize that they organized and now manage their company just like the one that they hated and left. As Bill Abernathy, the author of *The Sin of Wages*,[‡] says, "An entrepreneur is someone who starts a company in which he/she would never work and if they did, would promptly be fired."

After this question, you can see "the lights come on," and the rest of the class is like a piranha feeding frenzy. There are nonstop questions, and I have a crowd around me at break and a group following me to my car as I leave. They want to make changes immediately in the way they manage, because they realize the importance of positive reinforcement in their lives, and they recognize that they have too little of it in their management structure.

Not More Variety—More Reinforcement

In my opinion, many organizations are already making serious organizational mistakes in their approach to solving the problems of the Nintendo Generation. First and foremost, more money is not the solution. In a recent poll of college students, conducted by Ernst & Young, ". . . enjoyment of everyday work is the number one factor for a rewarding and successful career." This was followed by work/life balance. Third on the list was money. In that same poll, 71 percent of the students thought they would become millionaires. Obviously, they assume the money will come, so their concerns are for personal and social reinforcement.[§]

If what the NinGen is after is high rates of reinforcement, money will not provide it for reasons that have been outlined earlier. It is possible to pay them enough to keep them longer than they otherwise would stay, but if the rate of reinforcement in the work is the problem, money will not keep them when a more reinforcing opportunity appears. Remember MT-BOO.

Because they become bored with a job quickly, some companies have resorted to job rotation. Moving people from job to job to prevent boredom is a short-term solution. The problem with this is that, even in large organizations, there is a limited number of jobs to which people can rotate. What do you do when they have rotated through them all? Because supervisors and managers are getting younger and younger, the promotional opportunities are fewer and fewer, so promotions are infrequent and do not do much to provide additional reinforcement for the younger generation.

[‡] Abernathy, Wm. B., *The Sin of Wages: Where the Conventional Pay System Has Led Us & How to Find a Way Out*, Abernathy & Associates, Memphis, TN, 1996.

[§] Peters, C., *Intern Leadership Conference*, Disney World, Ernst & Young, August 1999.

It is important to note that what bores the Nintendo Generation is not repetition. It is not doing the same job for a long period of time. Think how many times they will play the same computer game. Think of how many hours the Internet can absorb them. The problem for them is no different from the rest of us. Repetitive jobs are not the enemy. It is the lack of reinforcement for repetition that is the enemy. *For the NinGen, it is the frequency of reinforcement that is the critical issue.* Those of us who have grown up on lower rates of reinforcement complain that things are moving too fast. NinGens complain that things aren't moving fast enough.

Are They Worth the Trouble?

Don't get the idea that the NinGens are not worth the trouble. As Tapscott points out, they are the authority on the big revolution that is changing business, entertainment, learning, and government. Even better, though, they are a good bunch of kids. As he says, "They have a strong sense of responsibility; they care about the environment; they are the least discriminatory generation ever; they care about poverty and AIDS." His research is validated by a Northwestern Mutual Life study, "Generation 2001: A Survey of the First Graduating Class of the New Millennium." Some of the study's findings are that (1) honesty and integrity are the most admired attributes of a person, and (2) having idealistic and committed coworkers and doing work that helps others is the top requirement of a job. They believe that doing some form of volunteer work is important, that fixing education is a top concern, and they all believe they will get where they want to be in life.

What Is the Answer?—Quickly!

The answer lies in finding ways to increase the rate of reinforcement in today's jobs by a factor of 10 or more. How can you do that? I use Nintendo as a model. Let's examine Nintendo from the perspective of the five-step problem-solving model presented earlier.

1. *Pinpoint.* It is clear in all computer games what behaviors get reinforced. Most of these games require little or no instruction for the performer to begin to get R+. Business will have to do a much better job of defining both the results and the behaviors that add value for every occupation.

2. *Measurement.* All computer games are measured. All jobs in the future must be measured because, without measurement, reinforcement is limited. Remember, what gets measured *can* be fun.

3. *Feedback.* Most computer games provide continuous feedback. There is real-time performance tracking. A readout is available on the screen at all times. Computers give business the tool to provide the same form of feedback for all jobs.

4. *Positive reinforcement.* As has been stated, high R+ rates are possible because measurement and continuous feedback allow performers to see progress toward some goal. Positive reinforcement is built into the game in the form of sounds, music, and action on the screen. All of these become conditioned reinforcers because they are usually associated with some form of social reinforcement from peers or others, and of course from the results of the game. Because progress is visible, others can see what the player is doing, how successful he or she is, and can provide social reinforcement to him or her. Continuous improvement eventually becomes a value because it is frequently paired with social reinforcement from other players.

Organizations in the future will need to put a priority on managers and supervisors who are skilled at delivering social reinforcement, designing reinforcement into jobs, and training teams in peer reinforcement.

5. *Rewards.* Most computer games have many levels of accomplishment. Measurement allows the differentiation of performers by accomplishment. Organizations of the future will need to rethink reward structures and develop rewards for all contributions at all levels of the organization.

In Sum

Workplace reinforcement has changed little in the last 50 years. However, reinforcement in everyday life has increased dramatically and will continue to do so. To work effectively with the younger generations, a must for management will be an in-depth understanding of reinforcement and its effects. Indeed, even now, reinforcement skills are at least as important as technical job knowledge in capturing the discretionary effort of the NinGen and beyond. The ability to design high rates of reinforcement into the workplace will be the key to high and sustained performance for the workforce of tomorrow.

24
Thank God It's Monday— Celebrating Work

Reinforce behavior; celebrate results.

People think there are some jobs that can never be made positive. In fact, a job is just a series of behaviors. By adding positive reinforcement to these behaviors, you improve performance while making people feel better about their work. Meaning cannot be put into a job by changing what one does. Meaning comes from the consequences of what one does.

> *Meaning does not reside in behavior; reinforcement does not reside in an object.*

Sports are fun because games were designed to get people to *want* to do them. Everything you've read about improving performance plays a part in all team sports. What performers *do* in most sports is not what makes those sports fun. Rather, it is the reinforcement they receive from coaches, teammates, and fans for doing something well, for improving their skills, for setting new records that encourages them to continue and to do even more.

Think of placing an ad in the newspaper for an offensive lineman in the National Football League. Who would apply for that job if you only listed the behaviors required?

WANTED: Large individual, preferably male, to block for running backs. Position requires squatting down many times a day. Candidates are expected to push and punch other large individuals and can expect to be knocked down frequently. All equipment will be provided. Benefits include Mondays off to get treated for injuries. Candidates must be prepared to participate in all kinds of weather and may be involved in one or more fights a week. Injuries are likely and could be life-threatening. Knee injuries are common and may limit ability to walk in later life.

(Did it ever occur to anyone that OSHA would shut down football if it were a regular business?)

You get the idea. If a person didn't know about all the positive reinforcement involved in the game, there would be no applicants for this job. People would say "You can't pay me enough to do that!" Yet we all know many people who play football for no pay, and look forward to it.

Now, contrast sports with work. Jobs originated because we needed people to do them. They weren't designed to cause people to want to do them as sports were. Jobs originated because we *had* to get certain things done. If you added to work what you have learned in this book, jobs could be as exciting as sports.

It amuses me to watch businesspeople participate in sports. They encourage team members, positively reinforce often ("Good shot!" "Great catch!"), hug each other, give high fives and low fives, and otherwise display unusual positive emotion. But put these same people in the workplace and they usually do none of these things. No wonder we feel differently about work than we do about sports! So why have we taken the fun out of work?

Making Work Fun

Many managers think fun is "out of place" at work. That's because they're accustomed to seeing people having fun by participating in dangerous horseplay, annoying practical jokes, by congregating around the break area, throwing birthday parties, and so on. Often these events are seen as opportunities to avoid work, or to take a break from the monotony of work. But, when fun comes as a result of accomplishments at work, it's quite another story. When celebrations happen as a result of some best-ever performance, what manager wouldn't want to have lots of them?

When most people think about celebrations, they think about elaborate functions, with speeches by management, a catered meal, and gifts for all. A celebration, as I define it, *is an occasion to relive an accomplishment.* It's an occasion to get together and share all the things that were done to meet or exceed some goal. Reliving the tough times or the good times, remembering the laughs and the frustrations of an accomplishment, can happen in a large group or with only two people. It can happen in an auditorium, a meeting room, or by the vending machines.

Participants, Not Recipients

The key to deriving bottom-line benefits from a company, division, plant, department, or shift celebration is to make it a special time to share what people did to meet or exceed goals. Employees should be active participants in the process, not just recipients of the company's benevolence.

In a typical celebration, management tells employees what they have done and the impact of the accomplishment on the organization's future. These boilerplate comments may be mildly appreciated at the moment, but their effect lasts about as long as the bubbles in the champagne used to toast the achievement. Management's role in a celebration is to listen and encourage the performers to relive their accomplishments—not tell the performers what they did.

People should tell their own stories. Frequently they're the only ones who know the details of what caused the success that is being celebrated. A manager can emphasize the importance of an accomplishment but will not necessarily know the finer points of how it was achieved. Unless you are sure of your facts, you should avoid making remarks such as, "You all pitched in," and "The results show what can be done when you work together as a team." It is very possible the results were accomplished in spite of a lack of teamwork. Such misstatements about how results were attained can damage a manager's credibility and dampen the impact of an otherwise successful celebration.

You Had to Be There.   Everyone has probably tried to tell about a funny happening only to discover that it doesn't "tell" as funny as it happened. You may have ended by saying, "I guess you had to be there. It was really funny."

Have you ever worked very hard on a yard project and when you were done the results just didn't show how much energy and hard work went into it? This is a problem with trying to celebrate based on just looking at a result. You need to give people a chance to tell you how hard it was, how long it took, how long it would have taken if they had not come up with a great idea, how they would have never been able to complete it without the help of Sue in engineering or Sam in accounting.

In a successful celebration, management asks employees to share what they've done. The manager can ask questions such as, How did you do that? What did you do? How did you figure it out? Who helped you? How hard was it? Asking questions gives employees an acceptable opportunity to brag, and an opportunity to publicly thank those who helped them. An added advantage to this format is when other participants hear about what was done and how it was done, it's usually an effective antecedent for them to try similar things in their own work areas.

Tangible Rewards Should Create Memories

The purpose of a tangible reward is to anchor a memory. Unfortunately, in most celebrations tangibles are the focus of the occasion rather than an aid to the celebration.

When tangibles are presented at a celebration, they should always be given *after* the accomplishment has been relived, near the end of the celebration. An effective lead-in to presenting a tangible reward is, "To help you remember what you have accomplished, I have something for you." If done correctly, the cost of the tangible item given is irrelevant.

When the focus is on creating a memory, small items work well, particularly if they have been selected on the basis of how well they would symbolize the accomplishment or some aspect of it: a knife for being on the "cutting edge"; biscuits and gravy for "being in the gravy" on sales; a pair of scissors for "cutting costs."

When not done correctly, the cost of the item becomes an issue. In other words, if the focus is on the tangible, it better be expensive. I have been to celebrations where managers have talked about savings from a project that ranged in the hundreds of thousands of dollars. They then made the mistake of saying something like, "As a token of our appreciation, I have a baseball cap with the company logo on it for everybody." The reaction from many people is, "We save the company a quarter of a million dollars and they give us a lousy cap?"

The pairing here is money saved–cap received, and it doesn't match. Done differently, the pairing is relive accomplishment–cap received. This way, the focus is on the accomplishment. Celebrations don't have to be large, expensive, or lengthy. They can occur whenever and wherever accomplishments occur.

Results are the occasion for celebration; efforts should be reinforced daily.

Take a Celebration Walk

If you are a manager and you want to see what's going on in the operation, take a celebration walk. Ask someone to point out people who are doing things or have obtained results that can be celebrated. Spend some time on a celebration walk on every visit to the plant or office. It's that important.

You'll be surprised at what you learn and the impact your attention will have on the organization.

A question that is practically always positively reinforcing on the walk is, "How did you do that?" Let the employees teach you something about what they do.

But don't use this visit to do correcting. A division vice president was visiting a plant where they were having a problem getting expected yields out of a new piece of extruding equipment. The team was making great progress, and actually getting yields above what was expected. The plant manager thought it would be reinforcing if the division vice president would go to see what they were doing. Unfortunately, the plant manager forgot to warn the VP that they had been neglecting housekeeping to some extent in order to focus effort on getting the new machine up and running.

Before he saw the graph showing their improvement and spoke to the operators and engineers about the good work they had done, he began to rant and rave about the poor housekeeping. By the time he got around to seeing the positives, his visit was anything but reinforcing. Yields dropped, and it took over two weeks to get them back to their previous highs. The VP should have talked to the plant manager about his housekeeping concerns after the tour.

Use Customers, Vendors, and Visitors

It's usually reinforcing for employees to tell customers, vendors, and other visitors how they do things. The more visitors you have in your facility, the more opportunities you have to celebrate work. If you want to show a customer how you manufacture the product, find a good performer and let that person tell about how he or she works. But don't just choose anyone who's handy.

Use every opportunity to show, through your actions and attention, that high performance pays off.

TGIM

Since five-sevenths of the week is spent at work, it's important for people to approach work with the notion, "Thank God It's Monday (TGIM)." This can only be realized when everybody understands and applies the principles of performance management to each other.

In a company of 1000 people, there are potentially 1000 sources of positive reinforcement: 999 others and yourself. If you walk through a company of 100 or more people and can't find evidence of a recent celebration for some accomplishment, you know that company is not bringing out the best in people and is sitting on a performance gold mine.

Imagine having a job where you wake up every morning excited about going to work. Now imagine everybody else in the company is as excited as you are. Just consider the possibilities. In an organization like this, all things would be possible. But can a company like this really exist? You bet it can. The technology is here. All that is required is for you to begin to use it.

I hope you will try the ideas you've found in this book. The laws of human behavior presented here are immutable. Your understanding and application of these laws is both necessary and sufficient to bring out the best in people, and the rewards possible for you and your business are beyond your imagination.

Epilogue

PM and the Question of Values

Science is said to be amoral. Science can be used to invent instruments of healing or weapons of destruction. Lasers can be used in healing and in killing. Likewise, the laws of behavior can be used to make someone a thief or a humanitarian, a confident leader or a hostile recluse. Reinforcement can be used to get people to do immoral, unethical, and illegal things. What, then, does this say about its propagation?

Immoral, unethical, and illegal behaviors have been occurring since the beginning of time. It is only now that we have the knowledge to arrange our environment to be able to affect these behaviors in a constructive and meaningful way. Could someone use this knowledge for harm or to increase ill-gotten gain? Yes. Is its potential harm reason to restrict its systematic use? To paraphrase B. F. Skinner, the best defense against tyranny is the education of everybody in the (behavioral) technology so that the power of reinforcement will not be in the hands of a few.

The Performance Management approach is value-laden. Values come from behavior. They are statements about desirable behavior patterns which a group seeks to promote. To the extent that values can be pinpointed, they are much more achievable in any group, whether at home, at work, or in society in general. Let's examine some basic values and see how they relate to the concepts in this book.

Honesty. Honesty means that everything is aboveboard. There are no hidden agendas. The stated purpose of asking for a certain behavior or performance is clear to everyone.

In Performance Management there are no secrets. There is nothing in this book that you would not want everybody in your organization to know and use with each other and with you. The techniques in this book are not some secret method of getting people to work harder and not know it. Attempts at deception are shortsighted and do not bring out the best in people.

Some people think that if the performers know that you are using reinforcement, the reinforcement will not work. This is wrong. If what you are doing is reinforcing, it will work whether people know what you are doing or not.

If someone thanks me for doing a good job or laughs at my jokes, I may recognize that they are trying to influence my future behavior. To the extent that they use the reinforcers effectively, I will respond like everybody else. I will do a good job again, tell more jokes.

Integrity. Performance Management teaches that a manager should carefully follow up to make sure that the consequences match the antecedents. This is the basis for trust. The follow-up is to make sure that what the company *says* will happen after a certain behavior or performance *does* happen. This might be a positive consequence following good performance, or it might be a negative consequence following a poor performance. Either way, the credibility and integrity of the company are on the line. This is how the value of *integrity* is promoted by PM.

Obviously, if a company has announced that bonuses will be paid for a certain goal attainment, and then *doesn't* do it, it is teaching its employees not to trust it. Such a company need not be surprised when people are slow to give discretionary effort in the future.

Employees will be thinking, "Why put extra effort into the job? They don't mean what they say anyway! Remember when they promised us those bonuses? They didn't do what they promised. Why should we think this time is any different?" For their employees, this company will have demonstrated that it has no integrity and can't be trusted.

This issue most often surfaces in less obvious ways. Often a company will announce: "We are committed to quality. Please tell us when there is a quality problem in your job because we want to make it right." Then, when someone points out a quality problem that necessitates stopping a production line or reworking a deficient product, that employee is told, "Oh, let that go. It will be okay. We are behind in our production today."

This type of integrity problem can devastate a company and create a work force for whom integrity holds no meaning.

Equality and Respect. The Performance Management approach implies a certain equality and respect in the way we approach another human being. The basic assumption in the approach is that most behavior is learned from consequences in the environment. Therefore, we conclude that there are logical reasons for the behavior of others: they act the way they do because they have *learned* to act that way.

Looking at behavior from this perspective, we are less likely to be judgmental in our estimation of others. Furthermore, we can begin to see that in many cases, *we* are part of the environment that *taught* the other person how to act that way! So, if we want to change the way *they* act, we must change the way *we* act.

Recognizing the universality of the laws of behavior also helps us to realize *we* are as much a product of our environment as *they* are. We can understand the true meaning of the old saying, "There, but for the grace of God, go I."

We realize that if we had been punished for telling the truth, we might have become compulsive liars. If our work experience had come in a company where cheating the customer was common, we might be distrustful of others.

If the consequences and events we had experienced in our family life had been different, we would be different also. This knowledge tends to make us a little more humble and a little more willing to take people as they are, without judging and condemning them.

This is not to say that we are *satisfied* to accept people as they are, only that we accept them as they are as a starting point, without trying to make them feel guilty about it. We learn to say, "Okay, this is where you are. Let's see what we can do to help you get better."

Whether we are addressing a poor performer or a good performer we say, "Let's see how we can help you get better." The only presumption we make is that anyone, no matter where they are now, *can be better.* Including you and me.

Beyond the realization of equality is respect for what the other person brings to the party. Everybody has a unique perspective on life. It is unlike any other. It remains for us to capture it and capitalize on its value.

Justice.   In a larger sense, the value of *justice* is also implied and promoted by Performance Management. Justice means that each person gets what he or she deserves. This is certainly what justice means in the courtroom sense. In Performance Management, this is what we say about managing people: *Those who perform well should get more reinforcement and rewards than those who perform poorly.*

In case after case in business and industry, low performers receive exactly the same compensation and recognition as high performers. The question higher performers ask, then, is a question of justice. "If we high performers are treated exactly the same as low performers, where is the fairness (justice) in that?" And, of course, after a while they will stop performing at high levels (extinction). Thus, the employer also ultimately gets what he or she deserves—low performance. Justice is served.

Further, giving poor performers the same reinforcement and rewards as better performers is not fair to the poor performer. Undeserved reinforcement and rewards maintain the poor performance. When management provides equal consequences for unequal performance, it actually robs the poor performers of the opportunity to improve.

When you give people something for nothing, you make them good-for-nothing.

Self-esteem and Personal Growth.   Reinforcement and rewards that are earned lead to higher self-esteem and personal growth. Earned recognition and rewards increases performers' feelings of confidence and competence. These performers have visible evidence that they add value to the organization. Confidence leads to an increase in initiative and a willingness to try new ideas. What organization can't profit from that?

Peace of Mind (Personal Security).   By pinpointing for people exactly which behaviors are wanted and the nature of the consequences for those behaviors, you encourage calm, well-thought-out decisions, and stress is reduced. When the relationship between behaviors and consequences is not clear, when people do not know how to earn positive consequences or how to avoid negative consequences, mental confusion and stress is the result.

Extensive studies have shown how noncontingent, random use of reward and punishment produces "psychoses." The inconsistent, inexplicable application of consequences "drives people crazy." They never know which behaviors will be reinforced and which will be punished.

A client of mine described her boss's style as "jungle-fighter." "You don't know exactly what he wants," she said, "and you never know when he is going to drop from the trees and surprise you." This is not good management, and it produces physical and mental stress.

When we are secure in knowing that right is rewarded and wrong is punished, and we know which behaviors define each, we feel secure, calm, and confident because we are *in control of our own consequences!* Rewards come because we earn them, not through chance. Rather than wiggling helplessly in the clutch of fate, we can do something to help ourselves.

You can reduce the stress in your work environment simply by increasing positive reinforcement. You can increase security simply by letting people know through word and deed what will be reinforced and punished. The organizational benefits of a low-stress, secure workplace are well documented.

The Golden Rule.   When positive reinforcement becomes a way of life in the organization, with reinforcement going from boss to subordinate, peer to peer, and peer to boss, adversarial relationships begin to disappear. People begin to treat each other as they would like to be treated.

When management believes that the way to get results is to threaten and punish, the counterresponse from employees is to threaten and punish in return—often through unionization, sabotage, or reduced effort. Thus, the classic "theory X" adversarial relationship is created. In contrast, when management demonstrates that the way to get the best results is to reinforce and reward top performance and to punish only in order to help poor performers improve, the counterresponse from employees is to perform better and ask how more reinforcement may be earned. In this way, a mutually reliant partnership is formed.

In this atmosphere, people learn that they can earn bigger rewards by working together than by resisting each other. This is what the various conflict-resolution and negotiation books call a win/win situation. When people are not operating out of the suspicion and fear generated by punishment and negative reinforcement, then they are better able to realize the benefits of working together. Remember what Sherman Roberts said: "The best way to run an organization is also the best way to treat people."

Performance Management in a Nutshell

Performance Management focuses on the here and now. It is not an abstract, convoluted management principle with limited applications. *It is a precise scientific approach that works.*

There are no tricks or gimmicks. Unlike motivational theories, you don't need to delve into your workers' deep-seated feelings, anxieties, or motives. Performance Management requires no psychoanalysis or role-playing. You don't need to find out what kinds of childhoods your performers had, what their birth orders were, or how they were raised. Since everyone operates under the same laws of behavior, applying these universal laws in a positive, effective way will bring about the behavior changes you are seeking in employees—whether you manage 2 people or 20,000.

References

Abernathy, Wm. B., *The Sin of Wages: Where the Conventional Pay System Has Led Us & How to Find a Way Out,* Abernathy & Associates, Memphis, TN, 1996.

Ainslie, G., "Specious Reward: A Behavioral Theory of Impulsiveness and Impulse Control," *Psychological Bulletin,* vol. 82, pp. 463–496.

Alessi, G., "Diagnosis Diagnosed: A Systemic Reaction," *Professional School Psychology,* vol. 3, no. 2, 1988, pp. 145–151.

American Journalism Review, March 1993.

American Quality Foundation, *International Quality Study* (IQS), 1992.

Bailey, J., "The Rise, Decline and Fall of Educational Panaceas," research, University of Texas, Austin, Texas, 1971, quoted by Ronald Zemke, "Bluffer's Guide to TQM," *Training* magazine, April 1993, p. 48.

Berquam, E., "STRAT Analysis: Using Stratified Celeration Stacks to Summarize Charted Data, *Journal of Precision Teaching,* vol. 2, no. 1, April 1981, pp. 13–17.

Binder, C., "Fluency Building," PT/MS, Inc., Nonantum, MA, 1987.

Coles, G., "The Learning Disabilities Test Battery: Empirical and Social Issues," *Harvard Educational Review,* vol. 48, 1978, pp. 313–340.

Crosby, P., *Quality Is Free. The Art of Making Quality Certain.* New American Library, New York, 1979.

Daniels, A. C., *Performance Management. Improving Quality Productivity through Positive Reinforcement.* Performance Management Publications, Tucker, GA, 1989.

Davison, M., and McCarthy, D., "The Matching Law," research review, cited by *REAPS DataSharing Newsletter,* Behavior Prosthesis Laboratory, Waltham, MA, March 1981.

Deming, W. E., *Out of the Crisis,* MIT Press, Cambridge, MA, 1986

Employee Involvement Association (EIA), 1990 study.

Engelmann, Siegfried, *War Against the Schools' Academic Child Abuse,* Halcyon House, Portland, OR, 1992.

Engelmann, S., and Carnine, D. W., *Theory of Instruction.* Irvington, New York, 1982.

Ericsson, K. Anders, and Charness, Neil, "Expert Performance: Its Structure and Acquisition," *American Psychologist,* August 1994, pp. 725–747.

Ernst & Young Study, cited by *The Wall Street Journal.*

Gilbert, T., *Human Competence: Engineering Worthy Performance,* McGraw-Hill, Inc., New York, 1978.

Green, L., Myerson, J., and Ostaszewski, P., "Amount of Reward Has Opposite Effects on the Discounting of Delayed and Probabilistic Outcomes," *Journal of Experimental Psychology.* (In press.)

Hart, B., and Risley, T. R., *Meaningful Differences in the Everyday Experience of Young American Children,* Paul H. Brookes Pub Co., Baltimore, MD, 1995.

Haughton, E., *REAPS DataSharing Newsletter.* Behavior Prosthesis Laboratory, Waltham, MA, March, 1981.

Henkoff, R., "Cost-Cutting: How to Do It Right," *Fortune,* April 9, 1991, pp. 40–49.

Herrnstein, R. J. "Rational Choice Theory," *American Psychologist,* March 1990, pp. 356–367.

Herrnstein, R., "The Relative and Absolute Strength of Response As a Function of Frequency of Reinforcement," *Journal of Experimental Analysis of Behavior,* vol. 4, 1961, pp. 267–272.

Herzburg, F., Mauser, B., and Snyderman, B., *The Motivation to Work,* John Wiley & Son, Inc., New York, 1959.

Honeywell, J. A., Dickinson, A. M., and Poling, A., "Individual Performance as a Function of Individual and Group Pay Contingencies," *Psychological Record,* vol. 47, 1997, pp. 261–274.

Hopkins, B., et al., "A Digest of Some of the Literature on Self-Managed Work Groups," a study done at Auburn University.

Ivarie, J., "Effects of Proficiency Rates on Later Performance of a Recall and Writing Behavior," *RASE,* vol. 7, issue 5, September/October 1986, pp. 25–30.

Johnson, K. R., and Layng, T. V. J., "Breaking the Structuralist Barrier. Literacy and Numeracy with Fluency," *American Psychologist,* vol. 47, no. 11, November 1992, pp. 1475–1490.

Kohn, A., *Punished by Rewards,* Houghton Mifflin Company, Boston, 1993.

Komaki, J., "Toward Effective Supervision: An Operant Analysis and Comparison of Managers at Work," *Journal of Applied Psychology,* vol. 71, no. 2, American Psychological Association, Washington, D.C., 1986, pp. 270–279.

Land, G., *Grow or Die. The Unifying Principles of Transformation,* Dell Publishing Company, New York, 1973.

Latham, G., "The Application of Behaviorological Principles in School Settings at Home and Abroad: The Worst of the Best at Best," *Behaviorological Commentaries,* summer 1992, pp. 3–10.

Levering, R., and Moskowitz, M., *The 100 Best Companies to Work for in America,* Currency/Doubleday, New York, 1993.

Lindsley, O., "B. F. Skinner—Nmemonic for His Contributions to Precision Teaching," *Journal of Precision Teaching,* vol. 3, fall 1991, pp. 2–7.

Lindsley, O. R., "Dangers of Percent and How to Avoid Them," Unpublished paper, Behavior Research Co., Lawrence, KS, 1994.

Lindsley O., "What We Know That Ain't So," invited address, third convention, Midwestern Association for Behavior Analysis, Chicago, IL, 1977.

London, M., and Oldham, G. R., "A Comparison of Group and Individual Incentive Plans," *Academy of Management Journal,* vol. 20, 1977, pp. 34–41.

Maddox, John, *What Remains To Be Discovered: Mapping the Secrets of the Universe, the Origins of Life, and the Future of the Human Race,* The Free Press, New York, 1998.

Madsen, C. H., Jr., and Madsen, C. R., *Teaching and Discipline: Behavior Principles Toward a Positive Approach,* Allyn & Bacon, Boston, 1974.

Mayer, R. R., and Pipe, P., *Analyzing Performance Problems, or "You Really-Oughta-Wanna,"* Fearon-Pittman Publishers, Inc., Belmont, CA, 1970.

Miller, A. D., and Heward, W. L., "Do Your Students Really Know Their Math Facts?" *Intervention in School and Clinic,* 28, 98–104.

Peters, C., *Intern Leadership Conference,* Disney World, Ernst & Young, August 1999.

Peters, T., *Thriving on Chaos: Handbook for a Management Revolution,* HarperCollins Publishers, New York, 1988.

Peters, T. J., and Waterman, R. H., *In Search of Excellence,* Harper & Row, New York, 1982.

Premack, D., "Toward Empirical Behavior Laws: I. Positive Reinforcement," *Psychological Review,* vol. 66, 1959, pp. 219–233.

Schmidt, Richard A., *Motor Learning and Performance: From Principles to Practice,* Human Kinetics, Windsor, Ontario, Canada, 1991.

Schneider, Walter, "Training High-Performance Skills: Fallacies and Guidelines," *Human Factors,* vol. 27, no. 3, 1985, pp. 285–300.

Senge, P., *The Fifth Discipline. The Art and Practice of the Learning Organization,* Doubleday/Currency, New York, 1990.

Skinner, B. F., *The Technology of Teaching,* Prentice-Hall, Englewood Cliffs, NJ, 1969.

Skinner, B. F., *Walden Two.*

Snyder, G., "Morningside Academy: A Learning Guarantee," *Performance Management Magazine,* vol. 10, 1992, pp. 29–35.

Stuart, R. B., "Assessment and Change of the Communication Patterns of Juvenile Delinquents and Their Parents," from *Advances of Behavior Therapy,* Academic Press, New York, 1971.

Tapscott, Don, *Growing Up Digital: The Rise of the Net Generation,* McGraw-Hill, New York, 1999.

Thomas, D. R., Becker, W. C., and Armstrong, M., "Production and Elimination of Disruptive Classroom Behavior by Systematically Varying Teacher's Behavior," *Journal of Applied Behavior Analysis,* vol. 1, no. 1, 1968, pp. 35–45.

Training Magazine Annual Report, October 1992.

University of Sheffield, research report by John I. Cordery, Walter S. Mueller, and Leigh M. Smith, "Attitudinal and Behavioral Effects of Autonomous Group Working: A Longitudinal Study," *Academy of Management Journal,* vol. 34, no. 2, 1991, pp. 464–475.

Watkins, Cathy L., *Project Follow Through: A Case Study of Contingencies Influencing Instructional Practices of the Educational Establishment,* Cambridge Center for Behavioral Studies, Cambridge, MA, 1997.

White, M. A., "Natural Rates of Teacher Approval and Disapproval in the Classroom," *Journal of Applied Behavior Analysis,* vol. 8, no. 4, 1975, pp. 367–372.

"Wilson Learning Corporation Study," published in *Training and Development Journal,* February 1993.

Wingert, P., "The Sum of Mediocrity," *Newsweek,* December 6, 1996, p. 96.

Index